Dressed Up for a Riot

Dressed Up for a Riot

Michael Idov

Misadventures in Putin's Moscow

FARRAR, STRAUS AND GIROUX   NEW YORK

Farrar, Straus and Giroux
175 Varick Street, New York 10014

Printed in the United States of America
Published in 2017 by Farrar, Straus and Giroux
First paperback edition, 2018

Lyrics from "Bigger Than Ben" courtesy of Oxxxymiron.
Lyrics from "Punk Prayer" courtesy of Pussy Riot.

The Library of Congress has cataloged the hardcover edition as
    follows:
Names: Idov, Michael, 1976– author.
Title: Dressed up for a riot : misadventures in Putin's Moscow /
    Michael Idov.
Description: First edition. | New York : Farrar, Straus and Giroux,
    2018 | Includes index.
Identifiers: LCCN 2017038311 | ISBN 9780374223151 (cloth) |
    ISBN 9780374715922 (ebook)
Subjects: LCSH: Idov, Michael, 1976– | Periodical editors—
    United States—Biography. | Americans—Russia (Federation)
Classification: LCC PN4874.I36 A3 2018 | DDC 070.92 [B]—dc23
LC record available at https://lccn.loc.gov/2017038311

Paperback ISBN: 978-0-374-53816-3

Designed by Richard Oriolo

Our books may be purchased in bulk for promotional,
educational, or business use. Please contact your local
bookseller or the Macmillan Corporate and Premium Sales
Department at 1-800-221-7945, extension 5442, or by e-mail at
MacmillanSpecialMarkets@macmillan.com.

www.fsgbooks.com
www.twitter.com/fsgbooks • www.facebook.com/fsgbooks

P1

For Garros

In the end, of course, we'll botch it like always.
But we'll botch it beautifully.

—Alexei Lapshin, campaign manager for an unnamed
    opposition candidate, in Roman Volobuev's *Tomorrow*

2012. Russia. The year's main event, also
known as "the furry furor," "the pussy riot,"
and "the bush league revolution," was the
glamorous unrest in which society ladies
stopped grooming their *mons pubis* as a
protest against barbarism and tyranny, and
their oligarch lovers were forced to rise up
against the despot. The unrest died down
when the full bush went out of fashion again.

—Viktor Pelevin, *Batman Apollo*

Authority smiling sexily
Waxed skin hiding weaponry
Use one gadget and you're an accessory

—Oxxxymiron, "Bigger Than Ben"

Contents

Dressed Up for a Riot

Chapter One

A Rootless Cosmopolitan

M y parents, Mark and Yelena Zilberman, who live in the suburbs of Detroit, keep a little portrait of Lenin inside their fridge. It's made of tiny beads sewn onto a napkin-size cloth and resides in an old Ziploc, in the covered dairy bin next to the eggs. Through these two layers of murky plastic, the leader of the proletariat is meant to observe the plenty that the Zilbermans are enjoying here in the United States, and presumably bawl his beady eyes out.

This, in short, is the crux of my family's identity: less American than no longer Russian. Their escape from Russia's orbit in 1992 was the bravest and most radical act of their lives, and it defines them still. Like every other immigrant child, I grew up quite aware that this sacrifice—of home, language, career, context—was performed in large part for my benefit. I owed them America.

So here I was twenty years later, in my Manhattan home on New Year's Eve, about to dial them up as 2011 flipped over to 2012 to tell them that I was moving to Moscow.

I ran through my reasons again. For one thing, I wanted my infant daughter, Vera (When should I mention that I'd be taking my kid there, too?), to have native fluency in Russian—something my wife, Lily, and I, who speak a sort of macaronic Nabokovian jumble when no one else is within earshot, might not have enough discipline to provide. For another, the job was a huge promotion—from a staff writer directly to editor in chief of a major magazine. And I would still be working for a U.S. company: specifically, Condé Nast, one of whose flagship Russian properties—*GQ*—I had, in a bewildering turn of events, been invited to run.

There was another factor, too. I wasn't sure if I should include it in the list. Russia, I felt, was on the verge of something fascinating. Just a month earlier, Moscow had seen its first middle-class protests against the Putin regime, protests gaining in volume and size with each passing week—seven thousand people in the streets, sixty thousand, one hundred thousand. A wave of global unrest was toppling regimes around the world; Moscow's Bolotnaya Square could be the new Tahrir. What's more, the people organizing and leading these protests were media folk like me—editors, columnists, bloggers—quite a few of whom I counted as personal friends. Some had stayed in my apartment, played with Vera, professed inevitable awe of New York. Well, it was my turn to be awed. I was writing dry municipal-interest stories for *New York* magazine; they were rewriting history. A part of me already wondered what job I could wangle if they got to run the country—or what book I could write if they didn't. Moscow was the place to be. And it just handed me a reason to be there.

Sure, the previous American to move to Moscow to edit a magazine, *Forbes*'s Paul Klebnikov, was shot dead there in 2004. (Best if that didn't come up in the conversation.) But, in post-Soviet Russia's wildly sped-up timeline, 2004 was already the distant past. That, in fact, was the most exhilarating thing about Moscow: it seemed to always barrel ahead, making up for lost time by repackaging itself half-blindly after whatever coolness it espied in other cities. It wanted to be London, Paris, and Rome at the same time— but, above anything, it wanted to be New York. Boy, did Moscow in 2011 ever want to be New York—and for a New Yorker like me, this made it into a veritable playground of wish fulfillment. The starving-hysterical-naked 1990s, when a pimply student's flash of the U.S. passport at a club's *feis kontrol* instantly gathered a harem, were gone, and certainly for the best; but American work experience still bestowed upon the bearer a kind of magic authority. To anyone whose ambition outpaced their patience, Russia was thus a space-time shortcut, a wormhole to success. Wildcat start-ups found funding, third-rate musicians became adored household names, things got *done*—badly, more often than not, but done. In return, as wormholes are theorized to do, it changed you on the atomic level. The "you" emerging on the other side might just be a little different.

█

I had never lived in Russia proper. My family came to the United States from Riga, Latvia, a Baltic republic affixed to the western-most edge of the U.S.S.R. in 1940 as part of the Hitler-Stalin pact.

Thanks to its tiny size—and perhaps to a similarly sounding "Lat-veria" in the Marvel Comics universe—Latvia is a kind of go-to place for sitcom jokes when one needs to quickly connote Eastern European obscurity; in reality, Riga is rather more Germanic than Slavic—a city of prim boulevards and frothy Jugendstil architecture, presided over by a trio of rooster-topped Gothic spires. Throughout the rest of the Soviet era, it managed to preserve a self-image as an occupied entity (provincial tourists were sometimes unsure if their rubles would be good here). My grandparents settled in Riga as schoolteachers after the war, which would technically make them part of the occupation. By the time my mother was born, however, Latvian Russians had already developed a kind of in-between identity. When the U.S.S.R. broke apart, remarkably few of them would take Russia up on its limited-time offer of citizenship.

Then there was the matter of our Jewishness, which the Soviets treated as a strictly ethnic affiliation. Being Jewish meant zip in the way of religion; it meant a funny last name (Zilberman—check), a funnier nose and/or hair (check and check), and the stigma of "rootless cosmopolitanism," a sticky Stalin-era formulation guaranteeing that no Jew would ever be considered fully Russian. For a college admissions board, an employer's HR department, or even a Communist Party membership committee, the word *evrei* on the notorious "ethnicity" line of the internal passport might as well read *flight risk*. (The essence of state anti-Semitism is to accuse Jews of wanting to leave until they want to leave.)*

My childhood thus may not have been a typical Russian one, but it was certainly Soviet enough. Most of it took place in the same

---

*The obverse of that libel was our fabled desirability as marriage material for those dreaming of emigration: "A Jew is not an ethnicity," a popular joke went, "but a means of transport."

dreary communal apartment at 6 Karl Marx Street where my mother had lived since *she* was a kid, watching the neighbors' boy go from a listless fifth grader to a frequently jailed alcoholic whose preferred mode of operation after a day of drinking was to launch tentative ax attacks on his own father. His prone bulk, still and huge like a felled tree, sprawled along the hallway next to shelved skis and shrouded bikes, forms one of my earliest visual memories. Another neighbor, an elderly madman, had long ago convinced himself that the other denizens of the apartment were out to poison him. So he would hover in the communal kitchen waiting for other cooks to leave, then thrust his hands into their boiling soups, fish out piping-hot gobs of meat, devour them bent over the pot—the logic being that the neighbors wouldn't poison their own food—and toss the bones back in. My mother and grandmother would find their cooking violated so many times that they started putting out decoy soups.

Here's where I wish I could write that I found escape, salvation, and a sense of belonging in the great works of Russian literature. But that would be a complete lie. In truth, the Soviet schools force-fed kids the classics far too early, and through the rusty funnel of collectivist ideology at that ("Eugene Onegin as a 'superfluous man,'" etc.)—so those books just felt like a distilled essence of boredom, at one with the chalky walls around and the strobing fluorescent lights overhead; the only place to which a Russian adult escapes by picking up *Anna Karenina* is the Soviet classroom. I didn't learn to love Tolstoy until much later, and I detest Dostoyevsky to this day. Instead, my first real connection to the Russian culture ran through its glorious, inept, heroic rock music.

When Russian rock 'n' roll first got going in the 1960s, it was a straight-up copy of the real thing, or its daintier aspects anyway—the Beatles were everything, the Rolling Stones meant little. (Incidentally, Latvia led the charge: a Riga rockabilly purveyor named

Pete Anderson was by consensus the first Soviet rock performer.) The 1980s, however, brought an explosion of a radically new kind of music, mostly coming out of Leningrad. This was "Russian rock," as it became known: New Wave–y instrumentation, minor-key melodies, and ambitious lyrics that shied away from the themes of love and sex in favor of abstract poetry. Imagine a culture where Joy Division somehow usurped the place of Wham!, and you have 1987's U.S.S.R.

The Soviet rockers' preferred pronoun was *we*, not *I*: song after song, album after album, wrestled with the identity of the country itself, imagined as a train on fire, an abandoned temple, and even "an ancient reptile dying / with a new virus in its cells." The chorus to the latter song, by the band Nautilus Pompilius, deceptively titled "Striptease," exhorted its female subject to disrobe—but as an act of protest performance art, not titillation:

Undress
Go out into the street naked
And I will stifle my jealousy
If our mission requires it
Undress!
Be insultingly sober
They love 'em drunk and crazy
They deserve to be pitied

It took twenty-five more years until a new kind of rock band— Pussy Riot—puzzled out an actual strategy from this premise. For the time being, I and my two best friends—Alexander Garros and Alexei Evdokimov, who after my departure would form a writing duo and pen several Russian bestsellers together—devoured all of it. We dubbed tapes for one another, memorized and recited lyrics, and, after August 15, 1990, scratched *Tsoi Lives* into our school desks: on that date, the twenty-seven-year-old lead singer of the megapopular Kino died in a car crash, oddly while vacationing near Riga.

Between March and May of that year, the three Baltic states— Lithuania, Estonia, and Latvia—one by one declared their independence from the Soviet Union. The fall of the Berlin Wall the prior November, which the United States still tends to treat as the official V-Day in the Cold War, had in fact flashed by us as a largely local German matter: the Soviet state was too busy fracturing to notice the renovations in the neighbors' yard. In a paroxysm of half-justified vengeance, the newly free Latvia immediately turned on the "occupants"—anyone who had arrived after 1940, their children, and grandchildren. Russians were stripped of citizenship, denied education in their language, and barred from holding public-sector jobs in a purge that included firemen, pharmacists, and, in my mother's case, librarians; her flawless command of Latvian, rare among her set, did nothing to help. Anti-Semitism, meanwhile, swooped from the state level down to the street; when my great-aunt died the same year, her funeral had to be postponed for fears of a pogrom. Just the previous summer, the entire Zilberman family had stood in a "human chain" that stretched from Vilnius to Tallinn, holding hands with strangers in an affirmation of all-Baltic unity in the face of Soviet oppression; now, my father and I were getting jumped by street hooligans for looking Jewish. The family, which had resisted the idea of emigration for decades, finally applied for refugee status in the United States. I packed away my cassette tapes and, in my imagination, a brilliant literary career (a month earlier, a local newspaper had published a sci-fi story of mine). I had just turned sixteen.

On August 20, 1992, the Zilbermans arrived in Cleveland, Ohio, where, within two weeks, I was flipping burgers at McDonald's and getting called a "commie" at Mayfield High School.

My English, while more functional than most Soviet newcomers', thanks to eight or so years of after-school lessons, was cramped and airless, and comically formal for an Ohio teen whose family was on food stamps; I had been taught to answer a "thank you" with "not at all."* I must have sounded just as stuffy in Russian to the fellow immigrant kids, who mostly hailed from provincial Ukraine and were a bit on the rough side. It was my first encounter with blue-collar Jews: back in Riga, I didn't even know this type existed outside Isaac Babel stories. Their music of choice was a mix of Russian prison ballads and West Coast rap. Since I had as little desire to associate with them as they did with me, even less to join the religious community (despite, or because of, its pushy courting of fresh arrivals), and felt no real affinity with the United States yet, Russian rock remained the focal point of my cultural identity.

E-mail was still three or so years out, and so Garros and I spent small fortunes exchanging reams of typed-out lyrics: I would mail him homemade rhymed translations of my new discoveries, like R.E.M. and Suzanne Vega, and he would keep me up to speed with DDT's or Aquarium's latest. At Mayfield High, for a multimedia presentation in speech class, I subjected my poor classmates to Nautilus Pompilius's "Like a Fallen Angel" and submitted Boris Grebenshikov's "Rock 'n' Roll's Dead" for the school poetry almanac.

These quixotic fits of proselytizing continued into college. I went to the University of Michigan and took dramatic writing, on the logic that my English wasn't yet good enough for prose but just sufficient for mimicking dialogue. Other immigrants of my vintage were busy studying things like computer engineering and econom-

---

*My basic vocabulary came almost entirely from C. E. Eckersley's *Essential English for Foreign Students*, a four-volume set published between 1938 and 1942, fitfully supplemented by the lyrics to *Jesus Christ Superstar* and Pink Floyd's *The Wall*.

ics, leaving me to play catch-up to the putatively cooler film-student crowd. Even as I discovered the music of, say, Will Oldham or the Silver Jews, and with it a comfy new identity as a corduroy-wearing, Williamsburg-prefiguring Midwestern indie kid, I was obsessed with making my indie-kid peers admit that Russian rock was *just as good*. I would draw mostly imaginary links between DDT and the Pixies, or compare Auktyon to Pavement. I tortured my first American girl-friend with this nonsense, shuffling CDs in and out of a car deck to point out some minute similarity between a noisy passage in Aquarium's "Fighter Jet" and Sonic Youth. "Why are you so insistent that I like this stuff?!" she finally snapped. "I don't even like Sonic Youth all that much!"

"You don't get it," I said. "I don't need you to like it. I need you to acknowledge that they both exist on the same plane."

"Why is that important? What do you care?"

"What do *I* care?! Um, let's put it this way: the day a Russian rock band has a hit song in the U.S., I will run through the streets naked, singing that song out loud."

"So wait," she said, "am I standing in for the entirety of the U.S. here?"

I paused. "Well . . . yes." She was right. Somehow, my entire sense of belonging had gotten snagged on this one dumb kink. I needed validation that my former self wasn't a waste of time—and then and only then, for some reason, could I retire it and move on with the business of being a new American.

As school went on, I fell in with a tight group of fellow film students, wrote my first play and script in English, and began to review movies for the *Michigan Daily*; slowly, gradually, any need to maintain a separate Russian self was receding. The play was about the young Orson Welles putting on *The War of the Worlds*, seen through the prism of his fraying friendship with John House-man; the screenplay took place in the greenroom of a fictitious late-night variety show. That was where my fascinations lay—in the seams and stitches of the American pop culture. On occasion, I would drive to a bootleg Russian CD store in Southfield and pick up the latest records, but outside validation for that habit was no longer required. If anything, my tic had reversed itself: now, when I listened to the sleek Britpop of Mumiy Troll, Zemfira's crypto-lesbian anthems, or the nascent, naive hip-hop of Bad Balance, I was fishing for hints of, respectively, Blur, Ani DiFranco, or Wu-Tang Clan.

Time and again, a professor would gingerly ask why I never drew on my "immigrant experience" or wrote a Russian character: *But your life must have been so colorful!* The very idea infuriated me. All immigrant literature is essentially two plots, I would sputter in response: "my first hamburger" (where the hero is seduced away from parochial values by postmodern America) and "my last babka" (where the second-gen hero loses his way and has to re-ground himself in the authentic shabbiness of the old country). I thought both were crap, for two reasons. One, they obliterated the specificity of the culture being discussed: you can be Finnish or Vietnamese, it's the same fucking narrative. Two, they treated American whiteness as an *absence* of background—where, to my relatively fresh eyes, it was as specific as anything, with its own complicated codes. The idea that being from *anywhere else* was automatically dramatic felt to me patronizing and orientalist.

The Zilbermans, meanwhile, were crossing off every line on the American-dream checklist with an almost alarming swiftness. My father had found work in his field at Ford Motor Company, testing new cars for noise and vibration; the family's cream-colored ranch house stood at the end of a quiet cul-de-sac. The only missing part was a doctor or a lawyer for a son—but, to their endless credit, my parents never once tried to steer me toward anything more lucrative than my vague ambition, at the time, to become a film critic.* In May 1998, I graduated from Michigan a would-be city sophisticate with a head full of movies. By August, I was occupying a friend's couch in Brooklyn and interning at the *Village Voice*. For all I knew at the moment, my entire history with Russia had been successfully relegated to trivia status: a factoid I might trot out at parties, an accent I might lean into to charm a girl. Nothing more.

At the very same time, in August 1998, a rash of black-and-white billboards popped up over Moscow, all bearing a severe inscription: IN RUSSIA. AT LONG LAST. They were heralding an event that, in the barely emergent post-Soviet story line, felt like a milestone: the launch of Russian *Vogue*. Condé Nast—the world's grandest lifestyle upseller, the publisher of *Vanity Fair*, *GQ*, and *Glamour*, and, through its London-based Condé Nast International silo, their countless localized editions from Paris to Tokyo—was coming to Moscow. Russia, it seemed, had officially arrived.

These days, it might take some effort to understand how so much social significance could attach itself to the arrival of a fashion mag. For one thing, you'd need to consider the since-diminished role of the print media, which, perhaps, has nowhere been more outsize than in the Soviet Union in its last years. The so-called thick magazines—essentially, literary journals—were the wellsprings of glasnost, publishing not just crucial condemnations of Stalinism, such as Alexander Solzhenitsyn's *The Gulag Archipelago* and Yevgenia Ginzburg's *Journey into the Whirlwind*, but samizdat hits

*Somewhat miraculously for Soviet immigrants, whose experience in a socialist bureaucracy tends to push them rightward, they also became committed Democrats—with my father going so far as to canvass for Obama in 2008 and 2012.

like Vassily Aksyonov's *The Island of Crimea* and cutting-edge foreign stuff like *A Clockwork Orange*—in an interesting translation that replaced the droogs' Russian-derived Nadsat slang with English. As a result, for instance, the drab monthly *Novyi Mir*'s circulation hit 2.7 million copies in 1990. (The magazine still exists; its print run in 2015 was 3,000.)

Even more important was the Yeltsin-era Russia's touchingly anxious impatience to acquire the trappings of a "normal country." *Normal*, the key word of the era, meant anything and everything, and was being applied with the same pleading intensity to every facet of life, from crucial to mundane; *normal* was WTO membership and daily deodorant use and a professionalized army and good pizza and a functioning parliament—and, yes, fashion magazines. One can argue that if 1990s Russia had gotten the bigger things on this wish list more readily, the world might be spared its current foreign policy. As things stand, it got *Vogue*.

It would also be useful to remember how profoundly *not* normal Russia was at the moment. The crumbling empire that my family left in 1992 was no more; among the ruins, new species scurried. Out of crooked privatization auctions that had redistributed the Communist state's riches to the redistributors themselves and their cronies, a class of oligarchs rose within months. Smaller business swelled in a grotesque symbiosis with a criminal underworld feeding off it, and a security apparatus feeding off that. The top predators in all three categories soon needed a place to stash the gains; Russia became the land of short-lifespan banks and even shorter-lifespan bankers.

Most industry, science, and culture stopped cold or thrashed around in mad disarray. Those without entrepreneurial and/or criminal proclivities felt left behind; their discontent swelled the ranks of the Communist Party, now presenting itself as a scrappy underdog, back up. By the time of the 1996 presidential elections, the threat of an across-the-board Communist comeback became so great that Boris Yeltsin had to rely on oligarchs' collusion, mercenary American advisers, tightened media control, International Monetary Fund loans illegally funneled to his campaign, libel against the other contestants, voter intimidation, and finally good old ballot-stuffing to keep his job. The original sin of the new Russia—placing stability over democracy—had been committed, invisibly paving the way for Putin and, in the long run, providing a moral-equivalence justification for Russia's own meddling in the U.S. elections.

But for now, in the summer of 1998, the worst seemed over. The party was back on. And a good party needed organizers, stylists, and chroniclers. There was no one better suited to all three roles than Condé Nast.

The company's top executive in the new market was a colorful East German named Bernd Runge, who had previous experience running glossies in France and the reunited Germany. Like many born in the DDR, Runge spoke Russian and had been to the Soviet Union before—in fact, he had studied at the Moscow State Institute of International Relations (MGIMO), a storied diplomat mill. A few years later, *Der Spiegel* would reveal Runge as a former agent of Stasi, the East German secret police. Code-named "Olden," even as a student he would report back to Berlin on his MGIMO classmates. So, ironically, the man charged with spreading the gospel of cosmopolitan glamour came from the same stock as the men who would recently jail you for same. Runge's pick for *Vogue*'s first editor in chief, the brash and worldly Aliona Doletskaya, came with her own plume of KGB rumors; though she denies them, her biography certainly had a touch of the Bond girl about it, complete with diamonds (once married to the Soviet ambassador to Botswana, she had worked as a media consultant for De Beers).

Condé Nast's two nicknames in Moscow's media circles were

Condensate, a pointless play on words, and the Fur Fridge. The latter alluded to the publisher's headquarters at Bolshaya Dmitrovka 11, which sat atop a huge cold storage for furs. The largely windowless building was one of the very few Moscow establishments to have stayed in business since the czarist times, persevering through wars and revolutions: the merchant grandes dames, the Stalinist inner-circle wives, the gangster mistresses—all needed someplace to stow their minks for the summer. The newest iteration of that elite tribe were the women *Vogue* would now target. The location was wickedly perfect.

On August 17, 1998, with the magazine's premiere issue at the printers, Russia defaulted on its debt obligations. The ruble cratered overnight, falling to one-third of its dollar value. Fortunes were wiped out, banks mobbed and then shuttered. Foreign goods, to which the Russians had just grown accustomed, vanished from the shelves. The country reentered crisis mode; *Vogue*'s lush launch party underwent a hasty scale-down. Those AT LONG LAST billboards now acquired an ironic ring. The *Moscow Komsomolets* tabloid predicted that *Vogue*'s first Russian issue might become its last, and that the entire publishing house would pull out of the market it had barely begun to crack.

The Fur Fridge, however, survived. If anything, the crisis made *Vogue* even more of an aspirational beacon, and its dazzling editor into a huge celebrity.

In the loosey-goosey world of Moscow media, where half the people were winging it half the time, Runge's Condé Nast acquired a mythical reputation as the place where German discipline met ruthless Manhattan ambition. Doletskaya was said to turn away anyone "spoiled" by previous Russian magazine experience. All intra-office e-mail correspondence was supposedly conducted in English. Rumors spread of employees going crazy from overwork and Byzantine intrigue.

By 2000, the magazine was riding high enough to test out a supplement called *Men's Vogue*: the newly monied Russian business-men, after all, needed as much acculturating as their wives and mistresses. The experiment was so successful that, just a couple of issues later, *Men's Vogue* spun off from the mothership. In March 2001, with a cover featuring Monica Bellucci's hard nipples above the slightly odd exhortation TO BECOME A WINNER, *GQ Russia* was born.

GQ's original editor in chief was the mysterious Ram Petrov, whose name sounds like a Dolph Lundgren character from a straight-to-VHS movie. Petrov had put out only a few issues before being sacked by Runge and replaced by his deputy. No one in today's Moscow appears to know what he's up to now.

The deputy was a corpulent, red-bearded intellectual punk named Alexei Zimin, who couldn't be more different from the Fur Fridge stereotype of a high-strung workaholic. He and his gang of friends were young and talented, and had no fucking idea what they were doing. Zimin decreed that a real Russian "men's maga-zine" (a novel concept at the time; its only real competition was Artemy Troitsky's highbrow take on *Playboy*) should champion a kind of aestheticized dissolution. His crew were fans of the rising rock band Leningrad, which plied the same trade—boorishness with a meta wink. A representative early lyric of theirs: "Damn right I'm a wild man / Balls, tobacco, vodka fume, and stubble." Calculatedly naughty and cynical to the core—even the band name was a fuck-you—it was as far removed from the earnest, romantic Russian rock of the 1980s as the country itself had become.

Zimin's men took not just stylistic but also behavioral cues from Leningrad. They'd roam the halls of Condé Nast swigging whiskey from the bottle. The staff music writer played occasional percussion in the band itself. Leningrad, for their part, proclaimed themselves to be "gentlemen of the new millennium." The two sides finally consummated this relationship when Zimin declared Leningrad's vocalist Sergei Shnurov *GQ*'s Man of the Year. At the party, the band smashed their instruments and pissed into a potted ficus. Upon witnessing this, the English overloads from Condé Nast International had Zimin swiftly removed. The entire staff walked out with him. Zimin went on to edit a cooking magazine, co-own a wildly uneven restaurant named Ragout where I would get food poisoning twice, and finally open a vodka bar in London, called Zima, which would become a smash success.

A third editor, Nikolai Uskov, was brought over to clean up the place. Under him, *GQ* became professional, properly glossy, breathlessly enamored with wealth, crypto-gay in its fashion pages, and closer in tone to *Vanity Fair* than to the American *GQ*. Uskov reigned over the magazine for eight years, running it competently enough for the Fur Fridge brass to look the other way as he sucked up to oligarch after oligarch in search of a better gig. In late 2011, he would strike gold and depart to take over *Snob*, a rudderless media project lavishly funded by billionaire Mikhail Prokhorov. Uskov's first *Snob* cover was a portrait of Prokhorov.

The event that would make me his successor had meanwhile already happened: I published my first novel, *Ground Up*. It was a slight satire about an obnoxious yuppie couple who destroy each other's lives when they open a coffee shop on the Lower East Side. Once again, as I had in school, I was writing in specific defiance of the idea that people should write about their own heritage. And, once again, the editor suggested I make the male protagonist a Russian immigrant. This time, I grudgingly complied. It was a three-page, one-day rewrite.

At that moment, an entire wave of immigrant writers were being loudly feted in the press for what I increasingly felt were very wrong reasons. In the ancient *Saturday Night Live* skit "Toonces the Driving Cat," a couple put a cat at the wheel of their car ("Look, he's driving! He's driving!"), which the animal then proceeds to crash off a cliff. The punch line: "Toonces: he *can* drive, just not very well." These first-gen novelists were now getting the same fawning treatment for the very act of writing in English. Gary Shteyngart, Lara Vapnyar, Anya Ulinich, Irina Reyn: *Look, they're writing! They're writing!* For *Ground Up*, I prohibited the publisher to mention in any press materials that English was my second language. To me, getting reviewers to *not* notice this fact was the highest honor I could achieve. I didn't want to be Toonces. I wanted *Ground Up* to be judged on its merits. And so it was, and was found perfectly average.

There was, however, one place in the world where a book conceived as a strident disavowal of Russianness could become a bestseller. You've guessed it. In the summer of 2010, I got a call from Uskov. *GQ Russia* was naming me its Writer of the Year.

Had I bothered to put "walk through Moscow in a tuxedo" on my list of things to do in this life, I could now safely check it off. The side street in front of the theater was a static maze of Benzes and Bentleys, with no place to pull up. The jam gave me a face-saving chance to get out of my regular taxi around the corner and hoof it to the red carpet from there.

GQ had rented out the theater, a hideous 1990s-built edifice glowing at the side street's end, to hold its Man of the Year awards: "the unofficial start," in the breathless tabloid formulation, "of Moscow's social season." In New York, I didn't get into such events without a reporter's pad.

A few months earlier, *Ground Up* had come out in Russian, translated by my wife and myself and rechristened *The Coffee Grinder* for want of the needed pun in the language. It sold only a few thousand copies at first, but they seemed to have been the *right* few thousand copies. New York–obsessed young Muscovites glommed on to the book's yuppie couple and their Lower East Side misfortunes like it was *Sex and the City*—a guide in the guise of a novel. Given the demographic, the ratio of readers to reviews was nearly one to one.

The other nominees in the Writer of the Year category were Serhiy Zhadan, Roman Senchin, Mikhail Elizarov, Aleksandr Terekhov, Pavel Pepperstein, and Andrei Astvatsaturov (whose last name I, in case I got the chance to thank the other nominees from the stage, had practiced for hours). They comprised a remarkably accurate cross-section of modern Russian literature.

Though I had lost track of the state of the Russian belles lettres in my Midwestern 1990s, I had been making up for it lately, especially after I got the notion to translate *Ground Up* into what still sort of qualified as my mother tongue—it would have felt a little strange to release a book into a cultural context I knew nothing about. To my surprise, as I read on, I discovered that there were two kinds of serious novels in the new Russia: "extreme" and phantasmagoric. The first kind dealt with the most wretched dregs of society, who by implication stood in for society as a whole. The reader, trained by decades of Aesopian Soviet satire, knew that if the novel's action took place in a mental ward, that mental ward was Russia; if it was in a prison, the prison was Russia; if it was in a tiny Siberian village populated by, say, cannibals, the village was Russia and the cannibals were the government.

The second kind was a conspiracy fable, devoted to the thesis that the world is run by shadowy magic forces. Supernatural cabals figured in a staggering percentage of post-Soviet highbrow prose— Pavel Krusanov's *Angel's Bite*, Vladimir Sorokin's *Ice*, and just about everything by the bestselling Viktor Pelevin, whose 1999 satire *Generation P* (published in the United States as *Homo Zapiens*) explained that the world leaders were CGI cartoons. In Pelevin's three subsequent novels, the world government was revealed to be, respectively, a gay mafia, werewolves, and vampires. This mode of thinking had a rather touching teenage tinge. Earlier that week, when the culture portal OpenSpace.ru had asked prominent Russian intellectuals to respond to Osama bin Laden's killing, half of them dutifully answered that bin Laden had never really existed, or was a projection of the "naively dualist American consciousness."

Pelevin and Sorokin (whose prose qualified as *both* extreme and phantasmagoric) were seen as the top of the heap. A popular theory about the Russian ruling class divided the government into "the Pelevin guys" (drugged-out nothing-is-real types) and "the Sorokin guys" (preaching a heavier, gloomier kind of postmodernism). Interestingly enough, neither of the two literary superstars participated in Russia's civic life in any appreciable way, ceding the "public intellectual" mantle to lesser authors such as Boris Akunin, a merely competent writer of stylized detective stories. Sorokin refused most interviews; Pelevin, for his part, led a fully Pynchon-like existence, living, per rumors, either in Thailand or in an anonymous apartment block in southern Moscow.

Making up for their reticence—and then some—was Eduard Limonov, a scandalous and sometime brilliant author of Henry Miller–esque confessional novels, for whom books had long fallen by the wayside and public activity became the main means of artistic self-expression. In the 1990s, disgusted, like many in Russian bohemian circles, with the creeping conflation of "freedom" and bourgeois normality, he put together the National Bolshevik Party, an exercise in reflexive contrarianism and shock iconography that was as much a political movement as an art project. The party members were supposed to greet one another with the words "Yes, Death!" For a while, the NBP actually became a valid voice of the nationalist left, or at least the part of it that loops all the way around into hard right, until their Baader-Meinhof–lite high jinks got them banned in 2007. Limonov's literary output had since dwindled to slim and increasingly weird essay collections, but his dashed-off shock-jock columns were everywhere—including *GQ*.

Earlier that week, I had reconnected, after almost twenty years, with Alexander Garros—my childhood friend and now one half of the Garros-Evdokimov writing duo. While my big debut wrung comedy out of croissant prices, his and Alexei's, a psychedelic tour de force called *Headcrusher*, was about a man whose life morphs into an ultraviolent computer game: a pretty wide thematic split for erstwhile best friends brought up on absolutely identical literary diets. I couldn't help asking Garros about it. How, in his opinion, did this happen? Why, instead of Tolstoy and Dostoyevsky, or even our childhood idols Aksyonov and the Strugatsky brothers, did the Russian writers in the twenty-first century find bedrock inspiration almost entirely in Gogol?

Garros and I were standing with our drinks on the rickety balcony of his Stalin-era apartment building, overlooking a dark bight of the Moskva River. "I mean, don't *you* want to write a novel," I pressed, "about, jeez, I don't know, some group of idealistic Muscovites slowly getting corrupted by the 1990s' crime and the 2000s' money?"

"Sure I do," said Garros. "But you see, when you start writing out the details of everyday Russian life, the absurdity just overwhelms you. At some point, you give up. Your characters start flying around, they sprout fangs and tails. Because that's the only way to stay true to the material. Russian reality is too phantasmagoric to fit into realist logic."

My fellow nominees for Writer of the Year provided a good illustration of his thesis. Senchin and Elizarov were realists, but only in the Russian sense. Elizarov once wrote a novella called *Nails*, which culminated in the main character (an adolescent mental-hospital patient) eating his dead friend's (another patient's) fingernail, and dying from cadaveric poison. In interviews, he and Senchin showed a brutally nationalistic bent and were considered "fascists" in the more genteel literary circles. "For instance, I hate gays," said Elizarov in an interview. "I'm not going to stand up and cheer when the TV tries to convince me that they're good and talented. My job is to uphold the right of the people to say the same. But since I'm craftier than our government, I can do it in craftier ways." Pepperstein was also "anti-American," but in the kind of sniffy French fashion that tends to mask a total obsession with the United States. He was as famous for conceptual paintings of Uncle Sam and Pepsi cans and American flags as he was for his avantgarde novels, which bore titles like *Mythogenic Love of Castes* and *The Swastika and the Pentagon* and jumbled fairy-tale, propaganda, and pornography archetypes. (His contribution to OpenSpace.ru's bin Laden discussion: "I listened to Obama's speech. Charmingly childish. Very *Lion King*. I didn't like it. It could have used more gags, like *The Simpsons*.") Terekhov, for his part, wrote an eight-hundred-page historical novel about a Stalin-era murder case that one reviewer called "fantastically unpleasant, not to say revolting." It was meant as praise.*

Among this bunch, *The Coffee Grinder* looked like a city dandy arrested for jaywalking and thrown into a holding cell with hardened criminals: skinny, overprivileged, and profoundly hateful. This is probably why it won, too.

I had known about the results for three months. The Man of the Year winners were supposedly decided by readers' online votes right up to the day of the ceremony; the vagaries of the long-lead

---

*Lest this quick rundown come across as too dismal, allow me to quickly recommend a couple of twenty-first-century Russian novelists I adore and admire: Sergei Bolmat and Evgeny Vodolazkin.

publishing cycle, however, meant that in order to get the winner's photo and profile into the right issue, the magazine needed to interview and shoot him well before the official end of the voting. "You have a commanding enough lead," the magazine's marketing director had told me. She sounded a little embarrassed.

I tried to play along, but judging by friends' winking commentary, the cat had been completely out of the bag for weeks before the awards. It thus felt crushingly fake, the whole thing—but, as I was quickly learning, this was the way a Russian felt about every public surface of life: politics, media, table manners. In the Russian mind, and more often than not in Russian reality, things like awards and elections were mere paper plastered over a yawning chasm, lies to distract from the Real State of Things, which was unspeakably tragic and accessible only by chucking social convention (and thus accessed nightly, through drink and cocaine and hash, by everyone around me). This, perhaps, was what my accidental competitors were writing about, and what Garros meant. They were right—and, pretty soon, I would reap the benefits of my collusion with the absurd. I may not have been about to grow fangs, but I'd already sprouted tails.

■

"Now Yuri is a real star," said someone loudly. A big black Mercedes behind me had just disgorged Yuri Nikolaev, the wizened former anchor of a Soviet song-and-dance program called *Morning Mail*. "Anyone can roll up in a Benz nowadays. Yuri had one twenty years ago"—when it required staggering amounts of financial, political, and social juice. The platoon of red-carpet photographers turned around to snap Yuri, and I was able to sneak inside the theater unmolested.

The vast foyer crawled with what I assumed were celebrities.

The women were dressed impeccably; the men, forced into tuxes, looked miserable. I imagined them clawing at their bow ties when nobody was looking, like a cat in a new flea collar. The bar proffered a muddy "exclusive" variation on the Bramble cocktail, called the Black Tie. I took one and watched the crowd. Every once in a while, a ghost of my Soviet childhood would flit by—a face half-remembered from television or an LP cover, plus twenty years of hard living, minus the same in plastic surgery.

The rest were someone's children. Sofiko Shevardnadze, the socialite granddaughter of the last Soviet foreign affairs minister, strolled in a scarlet dress past Ksenia Sobchak, "Russia's Paris Hilton" and the daughter of the Leningrad mayor who'd given Vladimir Putin his start. Sobchak waved to Fedor Bondarchuk, the actor-producer-director who happened to be the son of Sergei Bondarchuk, the Soviet filmmaker who'd once been given a blank Kremlin check to shoot *War and Peace*. Here we were at the tail end of 2010, with Russia rounding up its second decade of capitalism, and every diamond in every earlobe was still traceable back to the great big trough of government connections.

I was relieved to see Valeria Gai Germanika. A wildly talented young filmmaker, she was a nominee in the dubious Woman of the Year category.* Germanika was much more interesting than all the heiresses and scions around her. Hailed as a genius after her very first picture—the minimalist, shaky-cam high school film *Everyone Will Die Except Me*—the twenty-four-year-old was feted so much that she immediately went into full diva mode, throwing tantrums and walking off sets and dressing like Lady Gaga before even starting her second film. In a way, she would not even have to

---

*For Man of the Year, the Russian *GQ* used "Chelovek goda"—essentially "Human of the Year"—instead of the proper but awkward "Muzhchina goda." As a side effect, the undoubtedly well-meaning new category cast women out of the human race altogether.

start it now: she had fully found herself as an all-purpose celebrity. That night, Germanika came in massive diamonds and a baggy metallic dress that showed off her bicep tattoo of a treble clef. She brought along a shivering Chinese crested named Moni. The dog wore a casual denim ensemble.

I came up to Germanika to tell her that I really wanted her to do *It's Me, Eddie*. This was, I knew from interviews, her dream project: a film adaptation of the 1976 novel that made a celebrity of Eduard Limonov. *Eddie* was a chronicle of New York a-go-go decadence as experienced by a Russian outsider. The main character, a broke and horny poet living in a grim SRO, mostly details his sexual conquests. It culminates with a scene forever seared into every reading Russian's brain: a tussle with a black street robber that somehow turns into oral sex. (In France, the book's title was *Le poète russe préfère les grands nègres*; the Germans published it as *Fuck Off, America*.) It wasn't a coincidence that the book came out the same year, and wallowed in the same milieu, as Martin Scorsese's *Taxi Driver*: in Eddie, Russians had their own Travis Bickle.

And it was a perfect fit for Germanika's sensibilities. But ever since Limonov had become a political outsider, no producer in Russia would lend a kopeck to a screen version of one of his novels. This detail hadn't even occurred to me: the faraway prancing Eddie of 1976 and the National Bolshevik blowhard Limonov hardly even seemed like the same person. The novel was thirty-four years old, and Limonov wouldn't even get paid for the rights—he waived his fee for Germanika so she couldn't be accused of enriching him. And still she couldn't find the funding.

"Take me to New York with you!" Germanika cooed as soon as I told her I was from the city and I really wanted her to shoot it there. "Marry me and whisk me away from here!" She had a manner about her, grande dame inching toward drag queen: a kind of ironic hyperfemininity at the edge of the vapors. It was a fun performance. "I'll do anything! I will wash your floors! I will babysit your children!"

"Well, maybe not that last one," I said. "But I'd love to help out somehow. I'm a big fan. I'd tell you all sorts of compliments, but I suspect compliments are not your thing."

"My thing," said Germanika, "is black bogs of despair."

At this point, not a second too soon, we were ushered from the hot lobby into the somewhat cooler theater itself. The awards got under way.

The opening montage, set to a live suite conducted by Vladimir Spivakov, was a quick refresher on the main events of 2009–2010. It was an idiosyncratic mix of the tragic and the trivial, and a pretty handy document of what the Russian view of the year was. President Medvedev's first tweet; James Cameron's *Avatar*; a militia officer slugging a protester in Triumfalnaya Square; an Icelandic volcano belching smoke; the Gulf Coast oil slick; smog over Moscow.

Ivan Urgant, the event's young, slightly Middle Eastern–looking emcee, started with a bit that merited transcribing. "We have gathered here tonight to celebrate," he began, stumbling on the magazine's title, "the whatchamacallit—I forgot. And why, come to think of it, should I remember? All these ceremonies have melded into one in my mind. Same two hundred people in every auditorium. You're all showing up in my dreams by now. I know everything about you, and you about me. Must we keep this up? I didn't go to college for this crap—I'm an artist! Uskov," he continued, addressing the magazine's editor in chief in the front row, "aren't you a historian by education? And what have you done with your life? Why are we lying to each other right now, acting like we don't know who's going to get these awards? Everyone knows everything! Do something genuine for once. Skip a shave. Buy a shirt from Zara. Christ."

The laughs were scattered and tentative. Just when I thought Urgant's scripted freak-out was over, it revved up in earnest. "Enough! Admit it, we're all sick of this! Let's all get up and march out of here! Come on! Do it!" he bellowed, pacing up and down the stage and eventually descending into the audience to grab a female plant's designer clutch and tear it apart. (The punch line: a Federal Security Service officer's ID tumbled out.) The bit ended with a rotund older sidekick stepping from the wings to remind Urgant how much he got paid for his appearance. "There, there," the sidekick cooed. "Think of your country house. Think of your BMW."

If the routine wasn't very funny, it wasn't really meant to be. It was disgust masquerading as a bit masquerading as disgust, and it infected the entire evening. The first two presenters, actress-director Renata Litvinova and ballet star Nikolai Tsiskaridze ("the only ones who would get on this stage for free," Urgant said, belaboring his point), caught the same bug and could barely make it through announcing the nominees. Their derisive snorts and blatant eye rolls accompanied every name.

The second duo, announcing TV and cinema categories, was a stranger one: Sergei Selyanov, a big-time movie producer, and Irina Khakamada, an opposition politician. Ironically, Khakamada had been blacklisted by the state-owned Russian TV since 2002. "Television doesn't like *me*," she deadpanned when Urgant asked her whom she liked out of the five nominees in the category.

"I would like to add that I'm also working for free tonight," she then ad-libbed.

"I got paid for the both of us," said Selyanov.

It was that kind of night. But then again, every society night in Moscow was like this. The air thrummed with collective self-loathing, the only remedy for which was cynicism: one could fully relax only when everyone around was impugned equally and there was none left to judge. The meshing gears of contempt and complicity, with me a passive cog.

My category's presenters were Igor Krutoi, a shaven-headed pop composer and impresario with the look of a retired thug, and Ksenia

Sobchak in a fire-red dress. Sobchak's last name put her as close as the new Russian society got to old money, and her exhibitionist streak did the rest: she was now a self-perpetuating tabloid fame-ball, covered today because she was covered yesterday, her every dalliance and feud spelled out in smeary block type. Instead of pop celebrity, however, Sobchak's ambition ran to more complicated ends. Her dream was to be taken seriously, in any medium. She gave public talks. She hosted TV shows. A month or so earlier, she had put out a book called *The Encyclopaedia of the Lokh*, a satiric taxonomy of the titular creature. (*Lokh* is a Russian slur whose meaning resides somewhere between "sucker" and "loser.") "The sweet lokh," she wrote, in not-bad prose, "is the main ornament of our social skyline. It is in him, for the lack of anyone better, that our nubile kind finds an inexhaustible wellspring of genuine and unmediated experience." She also flourished as an ace interviewer, coming on as a naïf and then asking sharp questions. (It is admittedly easy to be fearless when your dad gave Putin his first job.) Still, intellectual Moscow was wary of her and eyed her as a weird intruder, like a group of high-school misfits unsure why the prom queen wants to sit with them at lunch. Once, while trying to say the word "existential" on air, Sobchak had tripped up and said "existentional." This innocent malaprop caused squalls of mirth. In a way, the bohemians were as nasty to Sobchak as the tabloids; she was dead stuck between two worlds. "I consider her a tragic figure," Andrei Loshak, an opposition TV reporter, once told me, without a trace of irony.

Even knowing the award was mine, when Sobchak announced the seven nominees for best writer, I experienced a combo of goose bumps, sweats, and dry mouth. I wasn't afraid of a last-minute switch; I was more worried about what I was about to do myself. The thing was, minutes earlier I had decided to use my time onstage to lobby for Germanika's *It's Me, Eddie*. Why the hell not, I thought. Might as well make this memorable. Plus, the venue seemed receptive to mild dissent. The evening's opening montage had included shots of the Triumfalnaya Square protests, which was far more subversive than what I was going to do.

"And the writer of the year is Mi—" said Krutoi with zero enthusiasm.

"You look like you've read all of those books, Igor," interjected the emcee.

"Oh, yeah, right," scoffed Krutoi. "So, anyway, the writer of the year is Michael, uh, Michael Idov."

I trotted onto the stage, accepted the Plexiglas letters G and Q and an expensive watch that came with them, and launched into my spiel. At first I concentrated on one task: thanking all six other nominees, one of whom, I repeat, was named Astvatsaturov. "And finally," I said, breaking out in sweat once again, "I'd like to think that there's a person in this room with enough bal—uh, guts, to finance Valeria Gai Germanika's next movie, *It's Me, Eddie.* Thank you all." Hey, that went well! I turned to leave the stage with my loot.

"Wait, where are you going?" said Sobchak. "Haven't they told you?"

"Michael, it's a trap," said Urgant. "Go. Go now. The dragon has chosen her victim." Little puddles of laughter were pooling in the crowd. I knew I was walking into something, a skit of some sort.

"As many are aware, Michael," continued Sobchak, "I have a certain tradition here at the *GQ* awards. Every year I pick the best-looking man and bestow upon him my kiss. This year, I have picked you."

With these words, Sobchak grabbed me and kissed me on the mouth. Dozens of cameras snapped away, ornamenting the periphery of my vision with silvery flashes. The center, meanwhile, was taken up by a red-and-blonde blur with tongue. It was not unpleasant. In fact, she initiated the withdrawal, as this lokh kind of got into it. The whole thing lasted seven or eight seconds.

"Well," I said into the microphone, catching my breath and rather unphotogenically wiping my mouth, "at this point I think I should also thank my wife, Lily." The line killed. I happily retired backstage to pose for a line of photographers with my prize and, as a courtesy to the evening's sponsors, a bottle of French vodka. Then I came back to watch the rest of the show, which for some reason ended with a live reggae musical number.

As we pushed toward the exits in the narrow aisle, Alexei Kazakov, an executive at the channel that would be broadcasting the awards later in the week, slapped me on the shoulder. It was not a friendly slap.

"Thanks a fucking lot, man," he said. "Thanks a whole fucking lot for the Eddie thing. You really fucked me on this one."

"I'm sorry. I had no idea," I said.

"Limonov's name is one of, like, five taboo words on TV."

"I didn't say Limonov's name!"

"Doesn't make a difference."

"You can cut it out of the broadcast."

"Yeah, well, I don't want to cut it. But you've put me in the position where I have to be the asshole and cut it."

An hour later, though, Kazakov cheered up. From the after-party chatter, it was fast becoming clear that the Sobchak kiss was the highlight of the entire evening. The crowd, whittled down to fifty or so of the luckiest invitees, had moved over to a restaurant called, with remarkable simplicity, Meat Club. Before me stood a plate with a filet mignon the size of a fez; sitting across the table was Sergei Minaev. He was the first Russian author to wangle a million-dollar advance. I knew this because he had just told me, between bites of steak.

Minaev's novels were about Moscow nightlife: cocaine lines off toilet bowls, that sort of thing. They all had half-Cyrillic, half-English titles, which must have telegraphed worldly sophistication:

Духless (Soulless), The Телки (The Chicks), Videоты (a pun on Idiots), etc. Before becoming a bestselling writer, he was a successful businessman, and he immediately parlayed his fame into a small empire of media properties: Minaev owned a publishing house and hosted talk shows on television and radio. Throughout it all, he had kept his day job, which was importing cheap liquor and marketing it as high-end. (Come to think of it, this appeared to be his literary modus operandi as well.) The award, and Sobchak's kiss, had clearly elevated me to a whole other stratum. Forget Astvatsaturov and Pepperstein. Now I got to hang out with writers like Sergei Minaev.

"You know, Misha, right now you have a chance to make a very decent career," Minaev said with a godfatherly inflection. He wiped his hand with a napkin, finger by finger. Then he gave me his business card.

The next morning, a hungover Yandex search for "idov + sobchak" netted seventeen hundred hits. The kiss was everywhere. The morning after that, it reached print. "Ksenia Throws Herself on Married Man." "Ksenia Sobchak Pushes Writer to Cheat on Wife." "Sobchak Kisses Another Woman's Husband." "Sobchak Seduces Married Writer in Front of Spouse" (my wife was two thousand miles away). For some reason, today's two trashiest and most vicious Moscow tabloids used to be Young Communist publications in the Soviet era: the Komsomol Truth and the Moscow Komsomolets. Neither has changed its old title (Komsomol un-portmanteaus into "Union of Communist Youth") or logo, which in the case of the Truth incorporates an Order of Lenin. Except now Lenin, in an ordeal somewhat similar to the one my parents' fridge has put him through, presides over such items as "Fresh Pix of Planet's Hottest Butt."

The Komsomolets even included a fabricated quote from me. I supposedly told them, "in an exclusive interview," that my wife was intelligent and reasonable and she'd understand. I suppose that's how tabloids get away with it: by having you say things you'd feel idiotic refuting. Was I going to claim that I never called my wife reasonable?

▪

The establishment was embracing me as a sort of plaything. I was invited to an event thrown by Vladislav Surkov, Putin's "gray cardinal" who famously liked to keep tabs on "culture." An FM station called Love Radio nominated Sobchak and me for Kiss of the Year; we lost out to Lady Gaga and Harry Potter (kissing their respective partners, that is, not each other). I went to a channel called TVC and taped a groggy interview for their morning show. "No questions about Sobchak, please," I overheard my publisher's PR woman instruct the segment's producer.

My friends, meanwhile, were uniformly disgusted. In the circle of young New York–obsessed liberals who formed *The Coffee Grinder*'s initial readership, people like Minaev were deemed *nerukopozhatnyi*—a great synthetic word that means, literally, "unshakehandswithable." Shakehandswithable people ate at Mayak Café, not Meat Club. TVC was a despised channel: a slush fund, someone indignantly explained to me, for the Moscow mayor Yuri Luzhkov and his buddies. My new patron Nikolai Uskov, the editor of the Russian *GQ*, was suspect, too, for reasons unknown. In short, Sobchak's toxic aura had rubbed off on me. I was doing everything wrong. Back in New York, my wife, Lily, while every bit as understanding as the *Moscow Komsomolets* had presumed, was not exactly delighted either, objecting less to the hoopla itself than to the horrifyingly fake aw-shucks attitude I had adopted in response to it. In short, everyone agreed that it was a good idea for me to lay low for a while.

So I did just that. I even went off social media. Before I did, however, I wrote one Facebook post that only I could see, as a kind of confession into the void. *"If I were to be absolutely honest with myself,"* it read, in Russian, *"my entire Russian persona is based upon the idea that I don't need a fucking Russian persona. But the farther I go, the less convincing this pose becomes. Because when you start getting career advice from Sergei Minaev, you can, of course, keep pretending that it's all one big art experiment, but only for so long. By even tangentially brushing against that whole scene, I am afraid I'm risking the friendship of dozens of likable people, most of whom exist in direct opposition to the 'glamorous Moscow.' So, resolved: from here on out, I focus on English-language work only. Let's consider this chapter of my life closed."* And, with that, I suspended my Facebook account.

This turned out to be a terrible idea. Because, a year later, the very same dozens of likable people would use the very same Facebook to start a revolution.

Chapter Two

The New Decembrists

On a late December night in 2011, at Les amis du Jean-Jacques Rousseau, known simply as Zhan-Zhak, a tiny island of faux Frenchness in the center of Moscow, Christmas garlands fringed the bar. An accordionist was doing his best Brel. Wooden tables held a mosaic of wineglasses, whiskey tumblers, and iPhones lighting up every few seconds with new bits of excitement. I looked up from my own phone, taking in the scene for the story I was writing for *New York* magazine. The bistro teemed with revolutionaries.

Granted, they didn't yet know whether they could call themselves that. They used the word with a crooked little grin fastened to the last two syllables, as if apologizing to one another for being so pompous. In the late 1980s, the writer Sergei Dovlatov had noted that his generation of Soviet dissidents lacked a lexicon—all good and noble words had already been co-opted by the Communist Party. The next generation of Russian liberals, then, was stuck with a vocabulary—of justice, liberty, hope, etc.—disemboweled twice, by communists *and* dissidents. Idealism of any kind was perceived as embarrassing. As one friend of mine put it, no one wanted to "disgrace themselves with unironic indignation."

Instead, a new language of cynicism had flowered. Over the aughts, there came into being an extraordinary number of energetic new slang terms for various subspecies of fraud: *raspil* (embezzlement), *otkat* (kickback), *otzhim* (government-assisted hostile takeover). Every protest, every public opinion, was assumed to be *zakazano* and *proplacheno*—"ordered" and "paid up." The most fashionable pose was that of a conspiracy theorist: belief in a shadowy world government, be it the KGB, the CIA, the Jews, or a coalition of some or all of the above, became as commonplace in the Russian kitchens as it was in the Russian novels. Whatever opposition to Putinism remained, it was a leftover stew conflating social liberals with near-fascists, Randians, Stalinists, "edgy" aesthetes drawn to the fringe, and so on, in one of the least organic alliances in history.

Apathy, not oppression—this is what the New Decembrists were up against. A few prominent ones were seated across the table from me: Ilya Krasilshchik, the editor of the biweekly *Afisha* (a sort of hipper *Time Out*); Filipp Dzyadko, the editor of *Bolshoi Gorod*, a magazine that used to trade in harmless municipal-interest stories and was now running cover lines like "Send Both into Retirement";* and Katya Krongauz, an editor at *Bolshoi Gorod* and Krasilshchik's wife (which technically made her and her husband competitors). I knew all three, which made writing about them a little awkward.

Then again, who knew things would turn out like this. Less than two weeks before, on December 10, 2011, acting mostly through Facebook, they and a handful of friends had somehow managed to get some sixty thousand people out to Bolotnaya Square to protest a parliamentary election rigged in favor of the ruling United Russia party. Come tomorrow, December 24, they'd have to top themselves.

"Bolotnaya," as the December 10 rally was already known, was by an order of magnitude the largest public demonstration Russia's capital had seen in more than a decade. It was already being credited— overcredited, really—with instantly giving birth to a new civil society and ending the era of corrupt complacency that marked the Russian aughts. Tomorrow's gathering, on the larger Sakharov Square, needed to make an even bigger impact. Otherwise, the official narrative would write the Bolotnaya protest off as a fluke.

"*Fuck*, I'm freaking out." Krasilshchik, twenty-four and handsome in an NHL-goalie kind of way, complete with a severe bowl haircut, ordered a Stella Artois. Zhan-Zhak was out of Stella. Krasilshchik asked for a Leffe instead. "No," he suddenly said, arguing with some internal monologue. "No. I'm not getting depressed unless there's drastically fewer people. Like, *half*."

"I think *twice* the number will show up," said his friend Filipp Dzyadko. Despite having five years on Krasilshchik and a scraggly beard, Dzyadko looked even more boyish. *I am the only thirty-something here*, I absently thought. Dzyadko's confidence in his

---

*You didn't have to explain to the Russian reader who "both" were: then–prime minister Vladimir Putin and -president Dmitri Medvedev.

prediction lasted exactly to the end of the sentence. "Or . . . not. I don't know!"

"Maybe one hundred and fifty percent," offered the fourth person at the table, Ilya Faybisovich, the only one I didn't personally know. Faybisovich was a twenty-five-year-old translator and London School of Economics graduate who happened to be the admin for the rally's Facebook page. Bespectacled, dandyish, and intense, he was the zealot of the group. When the others talked about the protests, their speech still whiffed of a collegiate bullshit session. Faybisovich was dead serious. He owned those scary words— *revolution* and the rest—in a way the others hadn't yet mastered.

"But one hundred and fifty percent of *what?*" parried Krongauz, alluding to the fact that the Bolotnaya head count was still being debated. All four shared a nervous snicker. What the hell had they gotten themselves into?

The entire point of Putin's meticulously constructed "power vertical," a concept that essentially disabled all levers of governance except the president's, was that spontaneous mass protests could not and would not happen. Between 2001 and 2004, all major television networks had gone under some form of state control. After 2004, governors and big-city mayors were no longer elected but appointed by the Kremlin. The formerly boisterous Parliament turned into a rubber stamp, and the United Russia party assumed almost as much of a monopoly on the political process as the Communist Party of the Soviet Union used to have. A handful of puny alternative parties—the so-called systemic opposition—soldiered on as parliamentary window dressing. Vladislav Surkov, the ruling party's ideologue, dubbed this arrangement "sovereign democracy." Everyday Russians quickly redubbed it "souvenir democracy."

The regime's most ingenious feature was a built-in tolerance for a certain degree of dissent: not enough to matter, just enough so that Western journalists would have something to write about. In retrospect, the West had largely bought into this con. If you leaf through articles about Putin's various pre-2011 crackdowns, most sound like the state is crushing a potent revolt. "The editors always want us to give the 'opposition viewpoint,'" I remember one former reporter for *The New York Times*' Moscow bureau saying with a laugh. "*Where's the opposition? More opposition!* We were like, 'It's really not about the opposition here.'" A tyrant suppressing the people's will was a more familiar and dynamic narrative than the people's will simply petering out. To a people with still-fresh memories of Soviet oppression and 1990s' chaos, disenfranchisement was a reasonable price to pay for full grocery stores, freedom of travel, and no more exploding bankers' limousines. Thus, for most of Putin's first two terms, the Russian public and its government remained largely incurious about each other. Any kind of enthusiasm for the business of governance was seen as either naive or venal.

Remarkably, all this was achieved with very little in the way of actual hard censorship. Heads of TV channels' news divisions received weekly *temniki*, or "topic memos," from Surkov's offices, and a couple of topics (war crimes in Chechnya, Putin's personal wealth) were unambiguously off-limits, but in most cases the media were left to divine the boundaries of their freedom for themselves. To put it bluntly, the system was held together not by top-down oppression but by bottom-up cowardice. Within this system, glossy lifestyle magazines such as *GQ*, seen as a steam valve for the wealthy, got away with infinitely bolder content than the big daily newspapers—as long as they weren't read beyond the Westernized chattering classes.

And the Internet, by 2011, remained wholly uncensored: despite having penetrated over 42 percent of Russian homes, it was still thought of as a toy for the elite. As a result, sites like LiveJournal and, later, Facebook and its homegrown cousin, VKontakte, gradually began to function less as social networks in the Western sense than as alternative mass media for a whole new class growing up right under the government's nose: those who barely remembered the Soviet Union at all.

"Stability's children," as the Putin-era twentysomethings were jokingly called, matured into a world of total political apathy. Many sublimated whatever civic urges they had into the so-called theory of small deeds. Originated by the 1880s essayist Iakov Abramov and publicized by his rather unlikely heir, Vasily Esmanov—the founder of LookAtMe.ru, at first a hedonistic youth portal focusing on hipster street fashion—the theory posited that thinking Russians, instead of trying to influence the government, should devote themselves to small, local, achievable change. Things like the cleanup of the long-neglected Gorky Park and the founding of Strelka, a Cooper Union–like design institute, were seen as points of national pride. A whole tribe of young Muscovites—many of whom would soon be on the streets, yelling for Putin's ouster—set the limits of their imagination at what the writer Oleg Goncharov would dub "Stockholm in the Sky": a dainty dream of bike lanes and stylish cafés. These were the same people who made a bestseller of *The Coffee Grinder*, whose satire of yuppie New York they seemed to mistake for aspirational lifestyle porn.

Krasilshchik, Krongauz, Dzyadko, and the other December 2011 activists all more or less belonged to this group. All were heirs to notable families of Moscow intelligentsia; all acquired their media megaphones at a remarkably young age, thanks largely to the Afisha Industries publishing house. In the mid-aughts, Afisha's brass, Ilya Oskolkov-Tsentsiper and Yuri Saprykin, gambled on the idea that youth-oriented publications could be edited by the very demographic to which they spoke. Krasilshchik became the editor in chief of the eponymous magazine, which had a hundred-thousand-copy run, at twenty-one years old. Dzyadko took the reins at *Bolshoi Gorod*, which used to belong to the same house, at twenty-five.

Krongauz has been a reporter since the age of twelve, when she rang the bell at *Afisha*'s predecessor, *Stolitsa*, and said into the intercom, "I think you should have a children's affairs correspondent." Even Faybisovich, not a journalist, used to freelance for *Bolshoi Gorod*. In other words, the revolution was being brought to you by the same people you would have relied on, weeks earlier, for restaurant picks.

Faybisovich snapped open his laptop and checked the latest projections for tomorrow's rally. The number of RSVPs had jumped from 35,000 to just over 51,700. He looked again in fifteen more minutes: 51,891. This was not a bot attack, of which they'd had several. Different pattern. This was really happening. Faybisovich grew giddy. "Any of you guys having vodka? No?"

I felt their excitement infect me. Nominally, I had come to Moscow as a reporter to write about the next day's rally. In reality, I was drinking with its organizers. It was harder than ever to stay impartial.

━

I had met Krasilshchik and the rest the previous time I had been in Russia for a political story: March 2, 2008. This was the day Vladimir Putin, president since 2000 and constitutionally barred from seeking a third term, replaced himself with a hand-picked successor. Dmitri Medvedev was a mild, slight, puppy-headed technocrat, at five feet three even shorter than his patron. He handily won the election; the only people permitted to run against him were Communists, who are a perennially useful bugaboo, and clowns.

I spent that day running around Moscow, covering the election for *The New Republic*. Hundreds of billboards hung along the city's main thoroughfares, yet none came from a specific candidate or party, and their design was unvarying: a flat reminder, against the backdrop of the federal tricolor and the two-headed eagle, that "March 2 is the Presidential Election." The same image graced every municipal-controlled surface, including the backs of Moscow Metro tickets. It didn't endorse Dmitri Medvedev, and it didn't have to. At this point, the flag and the eagle did it naturally. He was the only candidate with free access to the imperial imagery. As the man himself put it when refusing to debate his opponents on TV, "I have no need to prove my superiority in a verbal battle with those who never stood at the helm of the state apparatus."

The question was not whether Medvedev would win; Moscow bookmakers, a gambling friend told me, didn't even accept bets on the election's outcome. They offered an over-under on his getting 71 percent of the vote instead. The only unknown seemingly bothering Russia's bureaucrats was turnout. In Novosibirsk, the authorities were letting loose with both the carrot (free blini for everyone!) and the stick (a director of a factory there allegedly held all employees' February salaries until they voted). The head administrator of a Moscow hospital told me that he had been entrusted with making sure "all doctors and all patients" voted, a tableau I had trouble visualizing. In the provinces, the elections were being treated as a kind of forced holiday. In Kamchatka, folk dancers performed in front of the precinct. In Samara, people received soccer-fan-style scarves for voting.

In another bid to drum up excitement, state TV covered the evening's returns with a dash of American style: giant screens were set up at the Central Elections Committee HQ to flash figures from the nation's six thousand precincts (and a few hundred makeshift precincts abroad). In lieu of any mystery about the winner, however, the networks were left to wring out whatever suspense they could from the turnout question. That morning, Channel One cut into a documentary about fashion designer Vyacheslav Zaitsev (he met Pierre Cardin personally!) to announce that "sixteen percent of the electorate has voted so far." Gazprom-owned NTV ran similar turnout updates at the bottom of the screen. It looked about as exciting as seeing one half of a sports score.

Among my friends, their friends, and friends of their friends, I hadn't found a single person planning to vote that day. A few briefly considered voting for the Communists—the only semi-credible opposition—in a show of defiance, but in the end no one bothered to go through with it. (It was understandably hard to work up any enthusiasm for the Communist candidate, Gennady Zyuganov, as this was his fourth presidential campaign.) Instead, many of them coped with Medvedev's preordained victory via a kind of transference, developing a sporting obsession with the American Democratic primary fight between Barack Obama and Hillary Clinton. "We're just watching it like a Latin American soap opera," explained Garros. "*What did Juan Alberto say to Maria Luisa today?* That sort of thing."

The day's viral hit was "They Will Be Punished," a song by a novelty rapper named Kach. "The elections are over, I couldn't be happier," Kach intoned over a sampled swish of a lash landing on someone's back. "Orthodoxy rules the land, it's the Russian jihad." The rest of the song consisted of a jokey list of people and institutions that would be "punished" come March 3, including Ksenia Sobchak and "everyone at *Bolshoi Gorod.*"

At noon, I poked my head into Precinct 2074, inside the Centre Pompidou–like headquarters of the Russian Academy of Sciences. Hours earlier, President Putin, the most comfortably walking lame duck in history, voted here, dunking his ballot into a transparent box rendered invisible by a simultaneous explosion of a hundred flashes. It looked, appropriately enough, as though the box itself became an orb of white-hot light—aglow with the will of the people, or something—as Putin made communion with it. Now the press was gone, and uniformed militiamen (not yet rebranded as the "police," as they would be under Medvedev) plainly outnumbered the voters. Gorgeous girls guarded a spread of free fish sandwiches, both apparently meant to entice the electorate.

My dismal glimpse into the state of the Russian liberal opposition, three years before Bolotnaya reinvigorated it, came in the final hours of March 2, at a party thrown by the dissident website Grani.ru. Old-school opposition eminences milled about Mayak Café—which had the same owner as Zhan-Zhak—cracking jokes about Putin's agents infiltrating the evening. The atmosphere was that of a Brezhnev-era Soviet kitchen: smoke-swathed intelligentsia exchanging fatalistic quips about how screwed they are. Most of the guests were old enough to have sat in those kitchens.

For a gathering with at least two viable candidates in attendance—Mikhail Kasyanov, former prime minister, and Vladimir Ryzhkov, former deputy chairman of the Duma—notably absent was anything resembling a plan, a platform, a blueprint for moving on. The organizers screened a satirical cartoon instead. A woman moved through the crowd distributing plastic bags that said "I'm Taking No Part in This Farce," made famous hours earlier by Garry Kasparov, who toted one to a photo op in St. Petersburg. Then they showed the cartoon again.

At 9:00 p.m., when the last polls closed, everyone whipped out a mobile phone and checked the results: Medvedev in a landslide—shocker. A new round of unfunny jokes followed. (*It's 2026, and Putin says to Medvedev: "Wait, I forget, who am I this time, prime minister or president?" Medvedev: "I think I'm prime minister. You're president." Putin: "Then fetch me a beer."*) The event's official peg was the launch of a new opposition website, GraniTV.ru, which, activist Yulia Berezovskaya explained, was meant as a riposte to the lavishly funded pro-Putin site Russia.ru. That it was being launched on the night of the election, and not, say, three months earlier, spoke volumes.

"I had a shot," Kasyanov told me. Both he and Ryzhkov had

wanted to run against Medvedev and were barred on sadistic tech-nicalities. "I had a shot, and this is exactly why Putin gave the order to create the bureaucratic obstacles that resulted in my removal." Standing ten feet away, Viktor Shenderovich, a former TV star now blacklisted from all but one network, placed Kasyanov's chances in a hypothetical squeaky-clean contest at 10 percent. The opposition had no one to offer up: Kasparov or Kasyanov weren't it. "Our very way of life has to change before that person even has a chance to emerge," said the sculptor Lidia Gandlevsky when I asked her if there was anyone, anywhere, capable of outweighing a Putin en-dorsement. Many added that the last person capable of inspiring (and financing) a liberal movement was oligarch Mikhail Khodor-kovsky, a political prisoner since 2004.

By 1:00 a.m., the party was down to two journalists, the editor of the daily *Kommersant*, his best friend, the movie star Mikhail Efremov, and Mayak's owner, all uproariously drunk and singing folk songs. A mile or so away, on Red Square, a triumphant state-sponsored victory concert was winding down. Staggering into the street, the dissidents could hear a faint thumping and see the dif-fused glow of the floodlights rising over the Kremlin. The election was over.

At first, everyone blithely if logically assumed Medvedev would just be a Putin mouthpiece. The intelligentsia, however, also hoped against hope he would develop his own ambition. Just as Putin's every facial tic was once examined for hints to the extent of his severity, Medvedev's most workaday initiatives (like his order to curtail surprise inspections on small businesses) were being parsed for signs of a thaw, codes signaling new freedoms. Finally, a year or two into Medvedev's term, something interesting happened. Whether due to Stockholm syndrome or in a rare case of paying it forward, the young and the successful began, slowly but surely, to *like* him.

Medvedev kept saying all the right words: *liberalization,*

modernization, court reform. The fact that little ever came of his rhetoric was almost beside the point. He was compact, presentable, English-speaking. He used Twitter. (Putin, meanwhile, kept vanishing deeper into his strongman image: riding horses bare-chested, tooling around in race cars, shooting tigers with tranquilizer darts.) By the summer of 2011, many of the "hip" mass media—most notably *Bolshoi Gorod*'s corporate siblings, cable channel TV Rain and business web portal Slon.ru—began positioning themselves as Medvedev's base for his reelection campaign. The president's personal visit to the TV Rain headquarters, in the trendy Red October district, sealed the deal. In the hypothetical matchup between Medvedev and Putin, Medvedev could increasingly count on the vote of the "small deeds" crowd.

All this came to a rude end on September 24, 2011, when Medvedev got up in front of the United Russia congress and simply announced Putin was coming back. There would be no competition from within the party, no primaries, no campaign. There would be, for all intents and purposes, no real election. In March 2012, Medvedev would just step aside, revealing himself for the seat-warmer that he, it was now clear, had been all along.

The "Medvedev liberals" were understandably crushed. But no one felt more betrayed than the young people who had just allowed themselves their first-ever iota of political engagement in what turned out to be a farce. Facebook filled up with teens and twentysomethings calculating how deep into middle age they would be when Putin finally leaves his post. The fuse of "unironic indignation," that shamefully direct emotion, was lit.

The two factors that made Bolotnaya possible were Facebook and Navalny. The social network, seen as somewhat "elite" in comparison with its wildly popular local equivalent, VKontakte, connected young Westernized Russians in a more immediate way than Live-Journal and other blogging platforms. And Alexei Navalny, who was thirty-five in 2011—and a month or so older than me—became Russia's first Internet politician.* More important, he was the first would-be challenger to Putin whose fame didn't predate the Putin era.

A lawyer by education and trade, Navalny entered politics in 2000, through the ineffectual-by-design "systemic opposition" party named Yabloko. By the mid-aughts, he struck out on his own, trying on several populist messages to see which one would stick. Among them was a nationalist one; Navalny was involved with the so-called Russian March, an annual gathering whose mildest slogan was "Russia for Russians, Moscow for Muscovites," and he co-founded a "democratic nationalist" organization that ended up merging with a full-on fascist group called Movement Against Illegal Immigration. It is not impossible that Navalny viewed all this in purely realpolitik terms, as a necessary way to amass muscle for a broad revolutionary coalition; in any case, he has been evasive on the subject, and it didn't endear him to the intelligentsia. In 2009, Navalny hit upon a much more effective and unifying anti-corruption message, coining the instantly viral term "party of crooks and thieves" for the ruling United Russia. His original M.O. involved shareholder activism—Navalny bought tiny shares in publicly traded oil and gas companies, then began showing up at shareholder meetings to demand more accountability. When his profile rose enough, he started RosPil (a good pun on *raspil*, "embezzlement,"

---

*Ironically, Navalny eschewed Facebook; his main media platform was the already out-moded LiveJournal. Since then, he has also amassed enormous followings on Twitter and YouTube, for which he makes well-produced investigative video reports and tapes a weekly talk show, but LiveJournal (now wholly owned by a Russian company) remains Navalny's preferred communication method. Roskomnadzor, the Internet censorship body, blocks his page for Russian users, to little effect.

that made the word look like the name of a state agency), a kind of local WikiLeaks devoted to publishing confidential documents proving government corruption. Navalny was energetic and media savvy, possessed of a Kirk Douglas–grade chin dimple, and, literally alone among the Russian opposition, seemed to have a thought-through long-term plan. (Even if this was an illusion, the very ability to cast this illusion *still* put him ahead of the Kasparovs and Kasyanovs of the world.) Though he'd deny it in 2011, everyone knew where this was heading: in a few more electoral cycles, he'd be in prison or president.

On December 4, 2011, Russia held a parliamentary election marred, as usual, by crude fraud designed to tip the felt for the ruling party. Unlike in 2008, however, this time the high jinks were documented by myriad smartphone cameras. United Russia operatives were seen being bused from polling station to polling station to vote multiple times, in a process called "carousel." Institutions such as schools, army bases, and, in one infamous case, a mental hospital, delivered nearly 100 percent of the vote to Putin's party. United Russia's numbers magically swelled two- and threefold in hand recounts. Observers saw neat stacks of prefilled ballots shoved into boxes. Those who tried to point out the irregularities were shown the door.

One of those thrown out was Ilya Faybisovich, the translator. Fuming, he left the precinct, headed over to a book fair where most of his friends had congregated that day, and found everyone talking about the election. "By late afternoon, it was beyond obvious that we got swindled and that this time there would be ample proof," he told me. "The Internet was full of video clips." He went home and wrote an angry post on Facebook, tagging about 250 people in it, as many as he could manually do on an iPad. In the ensuing exchange, he found out that a friend of a friend named Roman Dobrokhotov ("I don't even know his political affiliation,"

Faybisovich said) had secured a permit for a December 5 rally at Moscow's Clear Ponds park.* At 7:00 p.m., with polls still open, Faybisovich called Dobrokhotov. "Hi, I hear you have a permit. Let's give it some PR," he said.

The Facebook event for the rally had already been created by yet another activist, Denis Belunov. Faybisovich got a hold of him, too, and asked to add him as the event's administrator. They tried a personal approach. Instead of endlessly reposting stuff to one another's walls, they sent out personal invitations to friends, asked them to do the same, and even called a select group on the phone. "I don't even know why we decided we'd be good at this, but there we were," Faybisovich said. By the next afternoon, the rally had gone from 2,000 invitees and 180 RSVPs to 25,000 invitees and 2,700 RSVPs. VKontakte picked up the cause. Echo of Moscow, the radio station, did some last-minute outreach as well. Some 5,000 people showed up.

The night became known as the Ruined Shoes Rally, because the protesters stood ankle-deep in mud. There hadn't been anything like this in Moscow for years: a pure show of grassroots solidarity, no leader, no clear demands. Its closest equivalent was Occupy Wall Street. Both groups had come together less to advance a specific agenda than to vent raw feelings. There were no designated speakers except for the quick-on-his-feet Alexei Navalny. Navalny yelled something about "ripping out the bastards' throats" and promptly got arrested when the legal rally turned into an illegal march. With just one day's preparation, however, the organizers felt that the protest hadn't reached its full potential. That night, they found out that a hard-left activist named Sergei Udaltsov, by that point already in jail for *another* protest, was holding on to a gold mine of a permit:

---

*This, it needs to be explained, is what Russian opposition organizers did: they randomly applied for rally permits, just in case, for weeks and months ahead. The permits then became a kind of commodity.

December 10, Saturday, a large central square. Perfect. With anger over the election mounting, it was clear that this band of amateurs would have to take the December 10 rally much more seriously. An organizing committee, or Orgkomitet, began to fall together.

At first, it existed only online. A young man named Ilya Klishin, the editor of the youth-politics portal Epic-Hero.ru, created an invitation-only Facebook chat devoted to the rally's logistics. Faybisovich invited his stepfather, Sergei Parkhomenko, an influential editor and publisher, to join it. Over the next weeks, the twelve-member "secret revolutionary chat," as Krongauz jokingly called it, generated more than eleven thousand messages. The chat, which I've glimpsed, reads like a brain scan of a collective adrenaline rush. Written in heartily filthy language (it was an all-male group, Krongauz pointed out), the discussion veered from strategy to tactics, from gossip to frank back-channel communication with Putin's and Medvedev's staffers. "These guys have gone crazy," Krongauz said, needling her husband, who was well within earshot. "They have wound each other up so much they think they're these global puppet masters." Then she got serious. "Someday, it should be published as a book."

The first offline session of the Orgkomitet, which now included famous writers and a sprinkling of actual politicians, including Navalny, was held at the *Bolshoi Gorod* headquarters. "We didn't ask for permission," said Krongauz. "We didn't even tell [the magazine and TV Rain's owner, Natalia] Sindeeva. If you don't want to hear no, don't ask the question!" Krasilshchik's *Afisha* published first-person screeds by its star writers and editors giving their personal reasons for going to the rally. Masha Gessen, the former editor of *Snob* and a frequent *New York Times* contributor, organized weekly meetings at Masterskaya (Workshop), a bohemian club where people could brainstorm ideas for the rally: flash mobs, posters, slogans, stickers, performances. On December 8, with two days to go before the Bolotnaya event, Vasily Esmanov called a sub-rosa meeting of Moscow's editors in chief at Strelka. (He had by now renounced his small-deeds theory in a new manifesto called "The State as a Service.") The editors agreed to waive all photo copyrights for the day. *Bolshoi Gorod* and OpenSpace.ru, a culture website, pledged to set up a hotline for arrestees. ("Thank God, there were no mass arrests," admitted Krongauz, "because the six clueless girls on six phones that we were able to put together would have been totally useless.") In the end, no phone rang. A sixty-thousand-strong rally came and went without a single pair of cuffs on a single pair of hands.

The Orgkomitet had agreed on, and the crowd upheld by acclamation, five demands: freedom for political prisoners; forfeit of the election results; investigation of the head of the Central Elections Committee; the ability to freely register opposition parties; and a blueprint for new, fair elections at an unspecified point in the future. The most popular chant in the crowd was simply "Re-e-lection!" A few people held up variations on "Down with Putin," but they were in a minority. The rally's real point was to broaden the movement's appeal, and it worked. Self-described fascists in black stood next to LGBT activists with rainbow flags, society ladies next to steelworkers. State-controlled television, apparently emboldened by what it saw, overrode its own internal censorship mechanisms and covered the protest in a neutral, newsy tone.

It was a PR defeat the Kremlin had not seen since the nineties. But it was also a rebuke to the "old" opposition luminaries: Kasyanov, Kasparov, Boris Nemtsov, and the rest. Nemtsov spoke from the stage that day, but the terrible PA system assured that no one beyond the first few rows heard anything. It didn't matter. The people had come out to feel strength in their numbers, not to listen to leaders. Navalny, for his part, was still in jail serving out his fifteen days for the previous protest. National Bolshevik Eduard Limonov, who tried to hold his own alternative unsanctioned demonstration, failed to get arrested, drove home, and wrote a bitter blog post.

The protest was quickly becoming professionalized, and with this came inevitable tension between the old and the new guards.

On the eve of the next rally, which would be held at Sakharov Square, I made it to the final session of the Orgkomitet. It took place in a cramped conference room, whose chalky white walls reminded me of the Soviet classroom where we'd endured our Tolstoy tortures. With hours to go before the protest, Kasparov and Nemtsov were still squabbling with the new kid Navalny, already the most popular face of the movement. Sure enough, Navalny wanted a nationalist faction to be represented onstage. The old guard was scandalized.

Krasilshchik and Dzyadko, invited in an advisory capacity, hung back in slight disgust with both parties. "The old-school guys still think they're the ones getting the people out," Krasilshchik said. "But you have to feel for them, too. They ate shit off a boot for ten years. And now something's finally happening, and they're not controlling it." A compromise was struck at the last minute.

Next, Krasilshchik and Dzyadko met up with Faybisovich and guested on Echo of Moscow, a slightly stodgy liberal radio station, repping the new breed of protester there as well. The program's co-host Vladimir Ryzhkov, a former member of Parliament whom I remembered from the defeatist 2008 election party, was firmly of the old school. "Ahh, hipsters!" he boomed, entering the green-room where the trio waited. "I was promised hipsters. Are you hipsters?" The program itself was little different. The hosts interrogated the youths as if the latter were, as Dzyadko put it later, "from another planet." *Why are you doing this?* was the recurring question. Krasilshchik paused, then nailed the answer: "Because being able to go to a good restaurant is no longer enough."

At ten in the morning the day of the big rally, I sat in the tiny kitchen of the one-bedroom that Krongauz and Krasilshchik shared in a Soviet apartment block building, above a low-rent beauty salon.

Their son, Leva, ten months old, crawled from the living room to the tiny kitchen and back, periodically crossing paths with Couscous, the family cat, and Fena, the dog. In four hours, the movement would either rise to a new level or begin its decline. Moscow was quiet and frigid; bluish winter light slowly came up over the boulevards. The streets were deserted. Many people had left town for the holidays. Who knows how many more would stay in because of the cold.

We donned our sweaters and gloves and hats and scarves. "This revolution has been sponsored by Uniqlo," Krasilshchik quipped. Our first stop was to drop off the baby at Krongauz's parents, an intellectual couple who poured us coffee and didn't say much, though their nervousness was palpable. Krongauz hadn't gone to the December 10 rally because, had something terrible gone down, she wanted a guarantee that Leva would not be left without both parents. This time there was no such fear. If anything, the protest was almost *too* sanctioned. The big question was whether the city government would provide protesters with cisterns of hot tea, as a city staffer had promised to do over the secret revolutionary chat. Krasilshchik worried that the rallies were becoming "protestainment," as he put it. "I was at Strelka the other day," he said, "and I overhear this hipster kid telling a girl, 'Turns out, going to rallies is so much fun! I'll be going all the time now!'"

At quarter to one, the cab in which Krasilshchik and I were riding entered the traffic jam he had helped create. With more than an hour to go before the official start of the rally, a few thousand people were already waving flags in front of the stage. The rock-concert-quality sound system, procured by *Afisha*'s Yuri Saprykin, was banging out a playlist he himself had compiled: "Long Happy Life," by cult punk band Grazhdanskaya Oborona; "Freedom," by St. Petersburg rock veterans DDT; "Uprising," by Muse. Coming closer to the stage, I suddenly heard a familiar loping rhythm. It was the intro to "I Want Change," a perestroika-era anthem by my childhood idols Kino. I stopped, listened, blinked back a freezing tear. "In our laughter and our tears and the pulsing of our veins," sang Victor Tsoi, dead for twenty-one years. "Change! We're waiting for change." There it was again, the uncynical, elemental language of protest, freed from the suffocating layers of irony.

The revolutionaries, meanwhile, were taking Instagram snapshots of one another on the stage, backs to the crowd. Saprykin paced, glowing. TV Rain was broadcasting live from its own sleek platform, as if covering the Oscars. *Kommersant's* radio station was attempting to interview the journalist Oleg Kashin in his capacity as one of the rally's organizers. "Guys! I'm your correspondent!" he finally said in exasperation.

At twenty minutes to the start time, the square was full. A brownish porridge of heads and hats stretched to the horizon, squeezed on two sides by monstrous Brezhnevite architecture. The police were moving the line of metal detectors back to accommodate more protesters. At least one hundred thousand people had come. Nothing else needed to happen. This already was a triumph.

But something else did happen—politics. The speeches started, and right away you could see the crowd's enthusiasm flag. Saprykin's crystal-clear PA was, in fact, a liability: unlike at Bolotnaya, the people were forced to listen this time, and they didn't like what they heard. Boris Nemtsov tried, and failed, to rouse the crowd with chants. Alexei Kudrin, Putin's former finance minister and confidant whose appearance here was a likely olive branch from the top, spoke mildly of incremental change and got booed for his trouble. To the younger protesters, both were usurpers of the cause at best. The crime novelist Boris Akunin and the all-purpose public intellectual (critic, radio host, poet, lecturer, novelist, biographer of other writers, and, inevitably, *GQ* columnist) Dmitri Bykov did better; with the atrophying of Russian public life, entertainers retained the ability to relate to crowds that politicians had lost. Then a goateed nationalist named Tor took the mic to push the "Russia for Russians" line, met, thankfully, with jeers and disapproving whistles.

The disconnect between the stage and the square reached its apogee when the next speaker strolled onto the stage. To my surprise, I knew her quite well. It was Ksenia Sobchak, the socialite/journalist who had kissed me on a different stage a year before. Sobchak suggested a "dialogue" with the Kremlin, to a squall of derision. Once again, her attempt to bridge the gap between the moneyed elite and the hipper media crowd, with which she clearly felt more affinity, fell through. A government functionary, a fascist, an heiress—these were not the potential leaders Krasilshchik and his friends had in mind.

Next up, however, was Navalny. Fresh off a résumé-burnishing fifteen-day stint in jail, the blogger was in extreme populist mode. "There's enough of us here to storm the Kremlin right now!" he yelled.* "But we're not going to! At least not yet!" His speech was an absolute hit. Its simple rhetorical refrain, *Yes or no?!,* was pure crowd heroin. "Even I got this little thrill when Navalny was speaking," Krasilshchik confessed later. "And I'm very skeptical about him."

Navalny finished to square-rattling applause and returned backstage, where a trio of female activists, including Sobchak, flanked him angrily. A star may have been born on the square, but not here. "Lesha, are you fucking nuts?" they yelled. "What the fuck are you talking about, storming the Kremlin?!" Navalny laughed. "I don't know," he said. "It just kind of slipped out!"

Meanwhile, at the deserted *Bolshoi Gorod* offices, surrounded by half-eaten vending-machine detritus, Katya Krongauz was performing the journalistic equivalent of juggling chain saws. She was

---

*Judging from the numbers of riot police around the square, he was not the only one to whom this scenario had occurred.

updating her magazine's Twitter, Facebook, VKontakte, and stand-alone blog feeds at the same time, while watching the rally on a Rambler TV online feed. She hated what she was seeing. "The people came out to the square in such numbers because they've been promised they won't have to see the same old faces that always show up at these things," she said. "Precisely because they're not a political force but a *civil* force. On Bolotnaya, there were no heroes. Now everyone's pushing his own line already."

The protest was still wrapping up on Krongauz's monitor when her husband arrived at the office. Krasilshchik was buzzing with the live energy of the rally; his wife sulked in response.

"All these politicians . . . ," she said.

"I dunno," said Krasilshchik, scarfing down a vending-machine sandwich. "I also have this weird aftertaste left. I'd love to understand exactly what has just happened. Because I'm not sure I do."

"Why is your voice so hoarse?" asked Krongauz. "Were you screaming?"

"Yeah," Krasilshchik said meekly. "I was yelling, 'Go away,' at Tor."

Once again, the revolution had an after-party. One by one, the group that had gathered at Zhan-Zhak the night before slowly re-congregated at a communal table in Bontempi, an Italian restaurant a few doors down and owned by the same man, Mitya Borisov. At first, everyone just excitedly recounted the events of the day over wine and grilled fish. Eventually, however, the euphoria began to wane.

"I'm worried about the nationalists," Krasilshchik said. "There was no festive feeling this time around. Bolotnaya was a festival. This was a political rally."

"I'm not going to the next one," said Dzyadko.

"I can easily imagine our entire little group going out and voting for Putin," said Faybisovich, "if he's up against a Communist in the runoff."

"Navalny's the only one who knows how to work a crowd," said Krasilshchik. "Which sucks, because I am now worried about him."

"Well, yeah, he studied at Yale!" joked Krongauz. "The Americans taught him!"

Just then, the problematic Navalny walked in with his friend Oleg Kashin and sat down a few tables over. Everyone at our table stopped talking for a second. Then the din began anew.

In the next day's morning papers, the December 24 rally looked far more impressive than the December 10 one. The head-count consensus came in around one hundred thousand. The Putin regime appeared alarmed. Flacks began to distance the prime minister from the United Russia party he created. Within two weeks, Putin would try presenting himself as a liberal reformer, of all things: "We need to . . . stop the extremely repressive tendency [of the security forces]," he would write. This was the same man who once took visible pleasure in saying protesters should "get smacked upside the noggin with a truncheon." Even more tellingly, this mild message would appear on a brand-new, specially created website soliciting the electorate's advice. (Before moderators scrubbed it, the highest-rated bit of that advice read, "I strongly urge you to remove your candidacy from the presidential election.") In a few more days, Putin would even express willingness to meet with Bykov and Akunin, the two nonpolitician members of the Orgkomitet.

In the younger crowd, however, no one was celebrating. Many felt the movement had hit a wall. Faybisovich had grown dark. He was sure he was being watched, predicted arrests and purges, and tried to convince me to take the existence of the secret chat off the record. "I fear for the safety of the common cause," he said over pasta carbonara at a restaurant called Mi Piace, dressed in a smart charcoal wool blazer. "Sorry I have to be talking like this."

Afisha's Yuri Saprykin went down with an unexplained fever. Among other things, he was disillusioned by the old-school faces of Nemtsov and Kasparov horning in on the new movement's momentum. "If Nemtsov calls me tomorrow and says, 'Yuri, could you organize the stage for us once again?' I will not do it," he told me.

The question of what's next hung over the group. Perhaps a rock concert! Rock for Clean Elections. Someone tried to contact Peter Gabriel and Manu Chao. Someone else suggested Pink Floyd. This did nothing to alleviate the main emerging problem: revolution did not pay. "If this story goes long and gets real, with all the delegations and negotiations, it will become incredibly hard to do this part-time," Faybisovich said. "And the only people ready to do it full-time are assholes."

After December 10, a few editors at *Afisha* had indeed discussed quitting their jobs and going into community organizing, but in the end it just wasn't feasible. Everyday lives were taking over. Filipp Dzyadko was getting married on February 4, the day of the next scheduled rally. And everyone was leaving town for New Year's, as Muscovites do, through at least January 10. It was not clear how fired up one could remain after two weeks in Bali. And then—then what? Since the movement's main slogan was "For Fair Elections," a relatively clean Putin win on March 4 would leave it without a reason to exist.

I felt much more upbeat. In my mind, the protests had *already* done their job. (On this, I turned out to be right; on the rest of this paragraph, not so much.) I figured that the most likely eventuality was a steady drip of incremental change over the next several years, patterned after the Soviet Union's collapse and most of it improvised at the city or region level. Since Putin's brand of oppression was built on a kind of systemic self-hypnosis—there were never any mass purges, just a handful of show trials and corporate takeovers after which everyone else has gotten the message—it was uniquely susceptible to the reverse process: people spontaneously deciding, en masse, that defying Putin's will wouldn't cost them too much.

Late on Christmas Eve, the night of the Sakharov Square rally, I decided to walk back from Bontempi to the place I was staying, a ten-minute stroll. As I was ready to cross the Garden Ring, a vast avenue that circles and psychologically defines the city's center, I saw a multicar cortège make its way from the Kremlin to the Parliament. Traffic in all directions had been stopped by the police. It could only be Putin or Medvedev. Two years earlier, reporting on Medvedev's election, I had the quintessential Moscow experience of getting stuck in the kind of power traffic jam these closures can cause, waiting for at least thirty minutes before that black G-class Mercedes whipped by. My cabbie suffered silently, muttering to himself every once in a while. So did everyone around us. Not tonight. As the presidential posse turned toward New Arbat Avenue, a vicious chorus of horns, pressed at once by seemingly everyone from where I stood to the horizon, greeted it head-on. A frozen symphony of hate and frustration hung in the air. The traffic did not move an inch—but at least there was the noise.

I took out my phone to capture it. As the recorder rolled, inscribing the sound into a spiky waveform, I marveled, for the hundredth time that day, at how lucky I was to be right here, in Moscow, at this particular moment. The horns kept wailing. Could this really happen? Could the regime, one that imprisoned or exiled its few real opponents and bought off the rest with derisive ease, be undone by a few Facebook event invites? What would the *next* new Russia look like? Navalny as president, Yuri Saprykin as minister of culture, TV Rain on every screen? And where would *I* be in it?

When the recording was done, I decided to treat myself to a quick e-mail check. Into the in-box slid a new letter from Karina Dobrotvorskaya, the president of Condé Nast Russia. It was an offer to fly to Moscow to discuss the idea of taking over the Russian *GQ*.

"Actually," I wrote back, "I'm a few blocks away. And yes."

Chapter Three

The Lokh

O n February 4, 2012, hours before my first official work-day, I landed in Moscow on a one-way ticket. I was trav-eling light; the rest of our stuff would arrive with Lily and Vera a month later, once I had set up a beachhead. My only suitcase contained a dozen variations on what I imagined my *GQ* uniform would be from now on, a dutiful distillation of the Man-hattan media-bro style of the moment: checkered shirt, knitted tie, cuffed jeans, heavy-soled pseudo-working-class boots, and a tweed blazer. No one in Moscow wore tweed blazers, so I had decided to make them my signature. They telegraphed just the right degree of self-aware nerdiness, repped a certain kind of Americana, and would help set me apart from my ultra-slick Armani-wearing predecessor, Nikolai Uskov. I was lugging three or four of them, with elbow patches and without, all bought in secondhand shops around St. Mark's Place for less money combined than one Armani pocket square.

I bounded out of Sheremetyevo's brand-new swan-shaped international terminal and into the brutal cold, searching for my ride. At minus five degrees Fahrenheit, the frost seemed to make one's nose hairs jingle. An absolutely white sun hung in a white sky—just a disk of slightly cleaner white, as if a clock had been taken down from a wall. The formerly notorious Aeroflot, which a friend of mine once anagrammed into *Fear Tool*, had blossomed into a very respectable airline, so I had landed in relatively high spirits. I was also looking forward to meeting *my own personal driver*, apparently one of the perks of the job. Chauffeurs were not that uncommon in Moscow, where labor ran cheap, but I—my lagging soul still in New York, like Gibreel and Saladin's in Salman Rushdie's *Satanic Verses*—found this an unimaginable luxury. Hell, just a few years earlier I had been bartending at Lucien, on the corner of First and First in the East Village, to supplement a trickle of two-digit freelance writing fees. If Uber existed then, I might have driven one myself. *Started from the bottom, now we here.* In my mind, ascents like this happened in hip-hop, not in goddamn journalism.

On Christmas Day, responding to Karina Dobrotvorskaya's magically timed e-mail, I had visited her at her immense apartment on Petrovsky Boulevard, decorated almost exclusively with rabbit figurines. Dobrotvorskaya was recuperating from pneumonia but looked as impeccably put-together as she had at the Man of the Year awards. She sliced me some cheese and hard salami; there was no bread, but she had matzos, interestingly. "Karina used to be a pudgy intellectual Jewish girl with the last name Zaks who loved theater," one mutual friend said, laughing, when I mentioned that detail. "She went over to the dark side of the force."

The offer itself sounded tentative—less like Dobrotvorskaya worried about my ability to do the job and more like she was concerned I'd be put off by it. Some of the editor in chief's duties did admittedly sound a little scary, especially the need to deal with advertisers, which I had naively assumed was the publisher's job. "After the crisis [of 2008], all our magazines spread their legs for the advertisers and haven't crossed them since," she said with a smirk.

Dobrotvorskaya also warned me that most of the editorial team would up and leave with Uskov. "It's a Russian thing," she explained. "There's nothing we love more than teary drama." Even if the handoff would be pointedly amiable—with a photo op of me and Uskov shaking hands, etc.—Karina softly recommended that I stop reading blogs for a while after the announcement. The Russian Internet made Gawker look toothless, she said, once again revealing a gift for precise phrasing. "People rip each other to shreds discussing a pasta recipe." She then told me I had six days to make up my mind.

I walked outside, gulping cold air, called Aeroflot, cut short my reporting trip, and flew home to New York to figure things out. I spent most of the flight tapping out an old-fashioned pros-and-cons list. Both columns started with the word *Russia*.

I had decided right away that there would be two people with full veto power over my choice—Lily and my agent Amanda "Binky" Urban—but also a panel of "experts" I would consult: Nelli Konstantinova, a Russian Condé Nast lifer and a family friend;

the Gawker czar Nick Denton, because he had done the expat thing as a reporter in Hungary, knew everything about the magazine business, and had no dog in this fight; and, finally, my parents. The truth was, however, that I already knew I was going to do this. So, when almost everyone on the list told me to go for it, I was merely relieved, not encouraged.

As for my parents, well, I didn't give them veto power, did I?

Once I had formally accepted the job, Dobrotvorskaya asked me to do two things right away. One was to make a gentleman's agreement with Uskov to embargo our respective career moves from the press until January 10 (when our employers would announce the switch). The other was to contact Ksenia Sobchak, who was—surprise!—*GQ*'s most treasured contributor, despite writing for half a dozen other magazines, and whom I was instructed to keep at all costs.

I called Uskov on January 3. He was nervous and tense, as Dobrotvorskaya had predicted, and seemed rather hilariously upset that the magazine was continuing at all without him. "I am glad for you, though I shouldn't be," he said.

"Did you have a different successor in mind?" I asked, confused.

"No, not really," he said. "In fact, I recommended you."

Uskov talked a big game: he had been going to quit for years; Prokhorov had wanted him for years; he was now going to create "a competitor to all of Condé Nast." He was, however, civil, and I politely listened. We reiterated our agreement to avoid all publicity until January 10, and even made a lunch date in Moscow we both knew we were not going to keep.

I then e-mailed Ksenia Sobchak, asking her not to make up her mind just yet. She was on holiday in Courchevel (I knew this from the tabloids, of course). Sobchak responded by leaking the news of my hiring to her two million Twitter followers: "The new editor of *dzheekew* is the novelist Michael Idov," she wrote. "Perhaps it was my kiss at the *dzheekew* awards that brought him luck." With one tweet, the story became about her and her scoop. I could see why she was such a valuable asset.

What had been a relatively open secret was now no secret at all—freeing Uskov to immediately announce his move to *Snob* and give a dozen boastful interviews about how he was going to take the entire *GQ* "family" with him, but let the new guy get his sea legs first. (Over the next months, he would indeed pick off the magazine's old staffers one by one, while sending me simpering e-mails about how much it hurt him to do so.) He seemed to want to be seen as running *Snob* and still calling the shots at his old job at the same time.

Not knowing what to do, I stupidly kept my end of the bargain and stayed mum until the embargo ran out. By the time my own barrage of interviews with the Russian press began on January 10— at 4:00 a.m., Moscow being eight hours ahead of New York—Uskov had thoroughly salted the earth: I hadn't even arrived yet, and I already looked like a loser.

The gist of my plan for *GQ*, or whatever I'd inherit of it, involved "democratizing" the magazine's scope—its current version, for instance, barely covered sports, food, or the booming world of serialized TV. I also wanted to beef up the feature well, which mostly consisted of Q&As, with deeply reported long reads. In other words, I wanted to rid *GQ* of its cheesier high-society pretenses and to make it palatable to the younger *Afisha* and *Bolshoi Gorod* crowd—roughly along the lines of what Adam Moss was doing with *New York* magazine, which had been a stodgy read for Upper East Siders when I started working there in 2006. I was planning to keep the fashion department operating quasi-independently until I figured out the intricacies of the local market. Finally, I wanted to make the magazine more Russian, as funny as it might sound: no homegrown celebrity had been on its cover in six years, which seemed insane to me. This last intention, in a bit of double irony, struck my interviewers as very American. It seemed that I wasn't getting something fundamental about the Russian media world's view of itself.

Most of the reporters dispatched to interview me were people I already knew; some were friends. But our conversations, one after another, struck a newly tense note, one I had never heard from them before. The questions brimmed with self-loathing (*Why would you even come to this awful place?*), which manifested alternately as ironic pity (*Boy, he has no idea what he's in for*) and suspicion (*There's got to be something wrong with him if he is stooping to our level*). Even *Afisha*'s Ilya Krasilshchik, whose magazine I genuinely admired, began his interview by asking how much Condé Nast offered me, disparagingly compared Russia to Africa, and mocked my belief that I would find any worthwhile contributors there. "I hope I'm wrong. I mean, I still disagree with you [that there are good writers in Russia] and you'll still eat a ton of shit," Krasilshchik wrote to me in a private message after the interview ran. In his mind, I'm pretty sure, this was an apology.

As the only possible response to this relentless dourness, I adopted a kind of rah-rah positivity. The double bind—of not only making sure I didn't insult my interlocutors but also not allowing them to gleefully flagellate themselves about how terrible Russia was—forced me into a stereotype: I was the soulless Yankee technocrat, setting himself up for a pratfall. The Russians take inordinate delight in thinking of themselves as hilariously broken, and an American makes for a perfect straight man for that routine. So, the more the interviewers treated me as a naïf, the harder I leaned into the image myself. *Of course I will find new authors. Of course the old ones are great, too. Things in general are great! You guys are terrific!* "This is an interview of a Decepticon to the Autobot Monthly," wrote one commenter on the *Afisha* site.

So that's how I made myself feel as I stood outside the terminal, waiting for my driver. Unflinchingly upbeat. Unerringly positive. Teflon. Now if only the car would come.

Those minus five degrees, meanwhile, were really making themselves felt. The roots of my wisdom teeth frosted up. Finally, someone texted me: "I'm here. Vasily." After sucking on my index finger for a few seconds to make it recognizable to a touchscreen as a human digit and not a frozen frankfurter, I called back. (No texting: the cold allowed me the time window for one push of one button.) Nearby, a man leaning on a beat-up Volkswagen Golf raised a phone to his ear.

I gingerly approached the car, which was encrusted with shimmering frozen dirt. The round-faced Vasily, in a parka atop what looked like another parka, began by explaining that he was not, in fact, my driver: mine couldn't start his car today, on account of the cold. I asked what kind of car it was. A Subaru, said Vasily with a touch of envy.

Turned out that Condé Nast's actual company cars were quite modest: they were there to courier around clothes and documents, not editors. It was up to me to wangle a freebie from an advertiser, Vasily explained. Uskov, for example, had a Jaguar from Jaguar, which he kept in a garage across town. Every morning, he made his driver go there and switch cars before picking him up to go to work. This seemed not just ethically questionable but also downright silly.

Vasily's Golf, meanwhile, had adequate heating and a working radio that was, at the moment, playing the song "Wisdom" by the band the Guggenheim Grotto. To its calming la-la-la chorus, I started to put together my first day's itinerary as a Russian.

The presidential election was a month away, and Moscow was churning under the ice. As we drove from the airport, three political rallies were happening at once. One was an anti-Putin march to Bolotnaya Square, where most of my friends were. This was a big one: the official opening of the new, 2012 season of "protestainment," the one Ilya Faybisovich had fretted about. It was also the first time the protesters were allowed to *march*, not just to stand in one place; back on December 4, Navalny had been arrested precisely for an attempt to lead the crowd away from Clear Ponds. The new arrangement seemed to show the authorities' growing willingness to accommodate protest.

Unable to make it there on time from the airport, I followed the rally's progress live on Twitter. In another new development, the marching crowd broke into four sectors. The first and largest, dubbed the "general civic column" without any party's insignia, was headed by the publisher Sergei Parkhomenko and the Communist politician Yevgeny Dorovin. They were followed by the so-called liberals (the term meant pro-capitalist free-market types, with no civil liberty overtones); "the right," meaning nationalists and headed by Tor; and "the left," led by Sergei Udaltsov. One of the main speakers was Olga Romanova, whose businessman husband had recently been jailed. "Freedom to everyone who's in prison!" she declared. "Prison is a place for thieves. They tell us we're lokhs because we don't steal. Putin is a lokh!" The lokh taxonomist and purported Putin godchild Ksenia Sobchak, meanwhile, was sitting this one out after getting booed the last time. "The same people can't keep speaking at different rallies," she tweeted.

The second event was a pro-Putin counter-demonstration on Poklonnaya Gora, to which thousands were bused in—some on orders from work, some for money. (It must be as exhilarating to volunteer one's presence at a street rally in minus five degrees as it is miserable to attend one for cash.) The official police tallies for the Bolotnaya march and its Poklonnaya antipode came to 36,000 and 138,000 people, respectively; flipping these two numbers would get you much closer to the real head count. The Poklonnaya gathering's somewhat rattled-sounding central slogan was "We Have a Lot to

Lose." A similar pro–status quo rally had been staged there on December 24, too, to balance out the Sakharov Square one. This was fast emerging as a new Kremlin tactic: the authorities tapped aimless youths, retirees, and *budzhetniki* (public-sector employees) as extras for astroturf pseudo-events while the state media, using the Big Lie technique of accusing your opponent of your own sins, spread the libel that the Bolotnaya protesters were paid directly by the U.S. State Department.* ("We're supposedly acting in the American interests? Lies, fucking lies, and provocation!" yelled Udaltsov from the stage at Bolotnaya, before putting the Communist spin on things: "You lying bastards, I've been wearing this jacket for three years while you've got villas!") No matter; once again, the Putin propaganda was not about providing a provable version of events but about making you mistrust all versions equally. And once you've stood in a shivering crowd for a few rubles, would you ever imagine anyone doing the same for free?

The third rally of the day was a sideshow on Pushkin Square, right past which we drove, presided over by Vladimir Zhirinovsky— the garrulous right-wing carny barker whose rather incoherently populist Liberal Democratic Party of Russia has been the Kremlin's designated protest-vote lightning rod for going on twenty years now. He drew about a thousand diehards. Finally, an entrepreneur named Konstantin Borovoy also spoke at Sakharov Square to about 150 cold souls.

I barely had time to photograph the blue-and-yellow LDPR banners flapping around the rueful Pushkin statue before we arrived at my brand-new home. I had rented a small apartment in a neoclassical Stalin-era slab at 4 Tverskaya Street; Tverskaya is Moscow's Fifth Avenue—if Fifth Avenue led straight to the White

---

*In 2017, Donald Trump would, of course, use the exact same tactic to smear the protesters marching against him.

House and held an annual tank parade. Next door was the very same State Duma whose bungled elections had triggered the entire protest movement. The Kremlin, its walls the color of frozen beef, lay right beyond. It was, in short, a show-offy address, but also a kind of lokh one: only a fresh Western expat would fall for the Kremlin view. True Muscovites of means preferred quiet side streets around Patriarch Ponds, Yakimanka, or the Arbat. I would discover one of the reasons as soon as April, when the tanks began to rumble under the windows in preparation for the parade.

Too excited to stay in and unpack, I dropped off my tweed-filled suitcase and headed straight to Bontempi, where I immediately ran into Yuri Saprykin and Filipp Dzyadko. Both were fresh (or rather frozen) from Bolotnaya, and thawing themselves out with vodka. The rally appeared to have gone very well. The extreme weather adversity ended up giving it an emotional boost. After the December 24 demonstration, which Krasilshchik had complained had felt like work, the heady air of a citywide holiday was back. The mood was strangely playful: the "general civic column" included Hare Krishnas, clowns, and a cardboard crocodile operated by several men. "And the speakers were much better this time," Saprykin added. The absolute highlight, he said, came when the 1980s' rock star Yuri Shevchuk, of DDT, played a frozen-fingered rendition of his perestroika hit "Motherland." Another anthem of a previous revolution, rendered relevant again:

Motherland
Let them scream "she's hideous"
She may not be beautiful
But we like her anyway
To the scum she's gullible
But to us—

The chorus purposely ended like this, an interrupted thought. Twenty-three years later, the degree of the Motherland's trust in "us" (i.e., not-scum) remained an open question.

I wondered who would come up with this song's equivalent for 2012, and how soon: the new movement was still looking for a language, trying things on. So far, it had succeeded only in creating a visual symbol—a white ribbon. Many protesters had worn it pinned to their lapel since mid-December; by January, it began showing up on car antennas. But the ribbon's meaning, beyond expressing general disagreement with the status quo, was a blank slate. (Putin, if nothing else a master of on-the-fly meme creation, glibly claimed to have mistaken it for a condom when he first saw it—"I thought, how nice, people are out campaigning for a healthy lifestyle.") As the newly splintered "right" and "left" columns demonstrated, the marchers agreed on what they were protesting (electoral fraud and political repression) but, two months into the revolt, had come no closer to rallying around a leader, a policy, a martyr, a demand, or even a slogan. An animating jolt could thus come from anywhere. The search was on. And it occurred to me that, starting today, I might even be a part of this search, not just an observer.

At that point, my reverie was interrupted by Mitya Borisov— the owner of Bontempi, Zhan-Zhak, Mayak, and the rest of the opposition drinking holes, as well as an enthusiastic consumer of his own booze supply. Borisov pulled me aside to propose going into a partnership on a *Ground Up*–themed coffee shop. (He wanted it to somehow be both a café and a reality show; the details were not clear.) Remarkably, the opposition's restaurateur was the soberest I had ever seen him. When I got back to the table, Saprykin explained to me that Borisov was starting up his own political career—beginning with a run for the mayor of Moscow. In the anything-can-happen fog of the moment, it didn't even strike me as a long shot.

Exhausted and exhilarated, I went back to the empty apartment and, in an attempt to reboot my circadian rhythm before Monday, took melatonin for the first time in my life. It was supposed to prevent jet lag. (While the Moscow–New York time difference is beatable by powering through one extra-long day on arrival, the New York–Moscow jet lag would sometimes take me weeks to overcome.) The pill gave me a whole suite of nightmares, complete with false awakenings, kidnappings, melting faces, and scary babies. At some point, I dreamed of walking through a Moscow subway station, totally dark, the darkness alive with the stirring of homeless men huddled in its recesses. Then two of the men grabbed me, roughly lifted me by my armpits, and carried me while running outside. The wooden station doors swung open, saloonlike, and there I was flying into a dark and flat field, held upright between my unseen captors so that my feet were barely skimming the ground. Faster and faster we went, toward the jagged black wall of forest at the far end of the field. I made a titanic effort to wake up and finally did, gasping as they do in the movies. It was time to go to work.

The building really was a fur fridge. The Condé Nast entrance stood to the left of the main one and was far less prominent. I got to the tenth floor, unlocked the empty *GQ* newsroom with a key borrowed at reception—I was the first to arrive—and, having nothing better to do, went into the editor in chief's office and sat down at my new desk.

The room remained as Uskov had left it, with fuchsia walls and framed covers of every issue *GQ Russia* had ever put out. The desk was blond wood with a galaxy of cigarette burns. In its center stood a bottle of Armenian cognac with a note that said "Good luck, Misha!" The window opened up to the unpretty back side of

Tverskaya. At 9:00 a.m., the octopus ink outside was just beginning to pale. Out of the murk came yards heaped with violet snow, black garages, a checkerboard of rusted metal roofs.

My first conversation of the day was with Maria Uspenskaya, the head of the company's HR. She was tasked with explaining to the clueless American the most important intricacy of the Russian labor code: I was not to fire anyone, ever. To be more precise, I was banned from using the words "you're fired," or anything that could be construed as having the same meaning. In Russia, no one got fired because, by law, a firing got you a twelve months' salary as a parting bonus. Only so-called black companies—the ones that paid their employees mostly in cash and kept tiny salaries on the books—could afford to do it, because even twelve months of those official salaries added up to peanuts; but Condé Nast was, of course, a "white" company. Even accidentally saying something like "you need to leave" in front of an employee immediately opened it up to an unwinnable lawsuit.

Furthermore, the fired person could sue at any time for the next *three years*. There have been cases, Maria told me, of people getting fired, suing two and a half years later, and getting their jobs back *and* the lost wages for the whole amount of time they've been away. It was an interesting holdover from the Soviet times when the law tended to side with the worker in nearly every employment dispute. It also created an absurd situation where employees, instead of quitting, could just keep doing a terrible job in the hope of getting bosses so angry that they'll say the magically actionable words. The head of HR was thus a position akin to a hostage negotiator: her job was to calmly talk people into quitting.

As a veteran of Manhattan media (I was once booted from *Time Out New York*, where I had briefly held the improbable title of "Eat Out Writer," with fifteen minutes to collect my belongings), this left me agape. As a lifelong confrontation avoider, however,

I was also a little relieved: it meant that whenever I wanted to get rid of someone, the only thing I could and should do was send them up to the eleventh floor to see Maria.

At this point, though, I was far more concerned with hiring new people. The first thing the decimated magazine needed was a deputy editor. I wasn't deluded enough to think I could just parachute into Moscow and hit the ground running. I may have known Russia better than most Americans, but there were still huge gaps in my knowledge of its television, arts, sports, etc.—exactly the things I was going to refocus the magazine on. Just a few days earlier, I had confused Nikolai Svanidze, a bespectacled TV host, with Nikolai Tsiskaridze, the fiery Bolshoi Ballet dancer. I needed a strong deputy, one who could not only guide me through the scene but also swiftly take over where I failed. Alexei Munipov, my friend and an extremely talented writer and editor at *Bolshoi Gorod*, was a natural choice and my first call.

It hadn't even occurred to me that Munipov would say no to this promotion—until he did, at Café Pushkin, sourly filling me in on what Moscow's "cool" press thought of *GQ*. Not much, it turned out. To the Zhan-Zhak crowd, Uskov's magazine was sending all the wrong signals with its wealth worship, and they had stopped paying attention to it years ago. (Many still couldn't forgive Alexei Zimin's 2002 ouster, his slapdash issues now mythologized as the "golden age" of the magazine.) Munipov and friends were afire with revolutionary fervor over at *Bolshoi Gorod*, which, after its epochal "Send Both into Retirement" cover, had turned into a full-on conceptualist tool of the opposition. For one recent issue, the entire editorial team, with spouses and children, had gone to Georgia, which Russia had recently invaded and still demonized; another issue, meant to combat Putin's stealth rehabilitation of Stalin, consisted of the names of Muscovites who perished in the 1937 Stalinist purges: no ads, no stories, just 9,780 names over 72 pages. Their idea of a celebrity interview was the sixty-five-year-old poet Lev Rubinshtein.

I obviously couldn't offer such total freedom, if only for the fact that *Bolshoi Gorod* was a free giveaway and *GQ* needed to sell copies. (Neither, it would turn out, could Alexander Vinokurov, the owner of *Bolshoi Gorod*, who later fumed to me: "I literally beg them to put *a face* on the cover. Not asking for Brad Pitt, just a human being. They say, 'Sure, boss.' I pick up the next issue—it's a fucking pair of deer antlers." The print edition of the magazine was finally discontinued in February 2014.) My plan to install Munipov as my second-in-command and eventual successor failed miserably. What bothered me even more about this conversation, however, was the feeling that I was somehow, unbeknownst to myself, getting reassigned to the other side of the barricades by the very people I was trying to join. This must have been how Ksenia Sobchak felt at the last rally.

Sobchak, meanwhile, was my next quest. The instruction was to try to keep her contributing to *GQ* by any means necessary. I felt a little conflicted about this. I could see her value: she was everywhere. I could also see the drawback: she was *everywhere*. I'd open Munipov's *Bolshoi Gorod* and there was Sobchak, on page 36, interviewing some ex-Marines who had recorded an anti-Putin song. And there she was on page 53 of the same issue, hawking a new restaurant she had just opened. Sobchak was launching some new product, some new partial iteration of herself, seemingly every week. Along the road to Rublevka, the ultra-rich enclave west of Moscow, her face stared down from dozens of billboards, advertising some luxury or another; at the same time, her new political talk show on MTV, *Gosdep* (The State Department), was the toast of my Twitter feed. She had also just premiered yet *another* talk show, on TV Rain, this one tied to the upcoming presidential election, where she was going to interview all the presidential candidates—except

Putin. ("My connections have been exaggerated," she'd dryly tell me.) All this was in addition to her primary gig: hosting a long-running *Big Brother* knockoff on the TNT channel. Her reach was truly staggering.

She was a familiar type, I thought, and a very American one in fact: an insatiable media workaholic. A Martha Stewart. No outside employer would ever be able to buy more than one-tenth of her focus. What if we pooled our resources, though? I had six Condé Nast titles behind me; perhaps, in exchange for not going over to *Snob*, she'd be interested in staying on as some sort of star contributor-at-large to the whole empire. This would be my pitch, then. Short of turning *GQ*'s website into her personal webcam feed, I didn't know what else to offer.

I called Sobchak and asked to talk in person. In this case, it meant my tagging along to the taping of her radio show (one of several she hosted) on a rather tasteful music channel called Silver Rain. When I showed up at the station hoping for a greenroom chat, it proved impossible: even there, Sobchak was being tailed by a reality-TV crew from Channel One, making yet *another* show. It finally dawned on me what her plan was. We'd have to talk in the studio. Live on air. With me as a guest.

The show was an hour of forced unstructured banter. Sobchak's heavy-lidded cohost Sergei Kalvarsky, who bore some resemblance to a younger Rodney Dangerfield, suffered through my Yankee Decepticon stump speech about how I—perhaps with Sobchak's help—was going to take an already-great thing and make it even greater, then launched into a remarkable protracted riff about my future in Russia. It was a joke, but a chilling one. "Let me tell you what will happen to you over the next few years," he drawled. "First, you will stop jogging. You will get fat like me. You'll stop wearing whatever the hell you're wearing right now and get normal big-boy suits. Then you will start accepting bribes for articles. Next, you will start hanging out with Gazprom managers. You will go to saunas with them, drink heavily, move to Rublevka, take a lover, beat her . . ." It went on and on. "None of this will happen," I finally said. "Your prediction is all wrong. You know why?"

"Why?"

"Because I don't jog."

Sobchak laughed, and we moved on to the next topic, but Kalvarsky's little oracle act had rattled me. Backstage with Sobchak after the show, free for a blink before the reality-TV crew would beset her again, I bungled my pitch to her, speaking in a tentative stammer and looking mostly at my shoes. (It was also the first face-to-face conversation Sobchak and I'd had after sucking said face at the Man of the Year awards.) I did, however, notice, and enjoy seeing, her media persona vanish as soon as no cameras or mics were trained on her. Left alone, Sobchak looked tired and spoke fast, impersonally, and to the point. She said that she'd think about the offer, and even added that she'd be interested in developing a video component to her *GQ* columns (*How would she find the time?*). The conversation lasted for about forty-five seconds. Then she jumped into her bodyguarded and chauffeured black SUV and left, followed by the reality-TV crew. I went home feeling cautiously upbeat.

Three days later, Sobchak announced her new position as *Snob*'s director of special projects. Evidently having alchemized my Hail Mary into even greater leverage, she was now back in Uskov's employ and giving interviews about how *GQ* "didn't have enough" to offer her. It was true. I didn't. No one did. Within three months, and without leaving *Snob*, she became editor in chief of another magazine at a different publishing house.

The one hire I did manage before my first day of work was an executive assistant. To break with the sexist Russian tradition of male editors with eye-candy secretaries (and, frankly, to avoid possible complications myself), I was set on hiring an older lady or a guy, a move that Maria from HR clearly considered insane—"a man's not going to bring you coffee!"—but, to her credit, allowed me to make. The best candidate I found, Sergei, was a willowy, whispery creature, with something of a Tim Burton cartoon character about him, who immediately began tweeting about his new job before even starting it. This should have been a red flag. I was so proud of my bit of affirmative action, however, that I had forced myself to look past it.

It was around 11:00 a.m. when the hollow-eyed Sergei was installing himself at the desk outside my office, and the newsroom beyond was slowly filling up with staffers. In the nook where graphic designers sat, rows of large monitors blinked to life. It was time to address the troops.

My style as a magazine editor, inasmuch as I had one, was based on two concepts I had learned from my betters. One was the "package approach" perfected by Adam Moss's *New York* magazine: take a near-random topic, like breakfast or circumcision, and gloriously exhaust it by attacking it from five, six, seven different angles. Always be on the lookout for subcultures to discover and tribes to taxonomize—and when you do, throw so much coverage at them that the competitors will feel silly even broaching the subject for years.

The second key notion came from Jim Nelson's American *GQ* and its relentless quest for the service component in everything: *What's my takeaway? What do I, as a reader, get out of this?* Before leaving for Russia, I had the pleasure of shadowing Jim for a day that included two editorial meetings: a middle-of-the-book meeting, devoted to an Iraq War story, and a fashion-well meeting, about a page that depicted a leaning tower of sunglasses. Both lasted for about two hours, and he brought the exact same intensity of scrutiny to each. This, undoubtedly, was something to emulate.

By contrast, the established way of doing things at *GQ Russia* was to fill the magazine with one-page columns by celebrity authors and kick back. I wanted to institute an actual feature well, and to shift the money the magazine was currently handing public intellectuals for random armchair musings over to younger authors who could use it to get up and chase an actual story for a few weeks. But I also wanted to move some of the fashion pages up to the front, by giving them a no-bullshit instructional tone: here's your tool kit for the month, that sort of thing. Most of all, I was interested in building up the magazine's website. The country to which I had just arrived could change at any minute, lunge in any direction. A magazine with a ninety-day lead cycle was not the ideal instrument for covering it.

I called an all-staff meeting and said some of these things. As with almost every other instance of public speaking in my life, my memory of the actual speech is a blur. I then took a core group of editors to lunch at a nearby Chinese restaurant and said some more of these things.

The team, which ranged from sleekly styled guys just out of college to a fifty-two-year-old cackling cynic in a torn fisherman's sweater (there's one at every magazine), struck me as nice enough. They all had an easy rapport with one another and didn't seem somnambular or defeatist. There was just one problem I could see with these editors: they didn't, well, edit. They wrote up a storm themselves, they acted as liaisons between columnists and production, they worked contacts, they organized things. But when it came to their most literal job—taking other people's texts and making them better—most drew a blank. (Turned out that this kind of editor was called a "rewriter" here—in English, no less, *reraiter*, that's how exotic the concept was.) Part of it had to do with the magazine's reliance on columnists, few of whom expected anything they submitted to ever be challenged or cut. The other culprit was the faulty structure: since the magazine was chopped up into tiny, unchanging one-page sections, everyone just filled their slot and that was it. There was never a plan B. If a story didn't pan out, it left a gaping hole in the issue and everyone went into panic mode. I suggested what I thought was an easy fix: flexibility. "How about, if there are two good restaurants opening and no good movies released, we don't *have* to have a movie review that month?" I said through a mouthful of bad lo mein.

The editors looked at one another. I thought for a second that they seemed impressed.

"Right?!" I pressed on, encouraged. "Maybe not every issue should have a fragrance page!"

The editors looked at each other again. This time, I read their expressions correctly. It was pity. I had a lot to learn.

As I would find out soon enough—in about an hour, in fact— half of these one-page sections in the front of the book were there to serve the content of the opposite page: that is, the ads that ran next to them. They were the *spetspozicii*, "special positions," and the reason that these single pages were more expensive and prestigious to buy ads next to lay precisely in their total predictability. The last thing a luxury advertiser wanted to see was their product opposite something unexpected.

The other half of the one-pagers masked advertiser favors. An airy article on yachting I tried to cut turned out to exist for the sole purpose of pleasing Beluga, a vodka client, whose logo was on one of the yachts' sails. The advertisers carefully measured the amount of "editorial support" their brands received and threatened to pull their ads if it wasn't deemed sufficient. It wasn't payola, but it also wasn't *not* payola. (The casuistic equivocation that luxury publishers like to use states that their choice of "partners"—advertisers—is selective enough in and of itself, so they take money only from the brands they'd want to cover anyway.) In other words, pulling a pageful of Swiss watches from one issue just meant I would have to run two pages of Swiss watches in the next one.

My least favorite, and least movable, spetspoziciya was the editor's letter. I hate the genre with all my heart. Most editor's letters sound as if they've been dictated to a butler during a hot-stone massage. They depict the author either as some kind of retired British Army major, musing idly on the issues of world import from an ancestral country seat, or a weather-obsessed New Age loon, maniacally enumerating the signs of the season. To this unenviable choice Russia added a third option: a monthly manifesto on why everything is going to hell and Russia is the worst place in the world. (Philip Bakhtin, the editor in chief of *Esquire*, especially excelled at this one.) But I couldn't get rid of the damned thing, for the abovementioned reason that advertisers loved placing their ads next to it.

To make things even more baroque, there existed no real reason why ad space next to the editor's letter should have any special value. Few people of sound mind read the editor's letter. It was the matter of intramural bragging rights: a show for competitors, who'd open the magazine and think, "Whoa, Gucci's spending hard these days." Brands even had their own legacy spots—for instance, Prada on the fifth spread.

But even *that* wasn't enough of a reason, since any competition here, just as in Russian politics, was all but imaginary. Most of the brands that advertised in *GQ* came bundled into massive holdings like LVMH Moët Hennessy Louis Vuitton, which were in turn represented by their Russian partners: the Mercury Group, which owned TsUM stores, and Bosco di Ciliegi, which operated the competing department store GUM on Red Square. So, in essence, up to 90 percent of our advertising came from two clients.

All this I would learn, at lightning speed, during my next two scheduled meetings: with Igor, the fashion director, and with Katya, the *creative* fashion director. He was a Balmain-wearing dandy with a working command of Korean from his days as a fashion buyer in Seoul; she, a Gothy bohemian I had once met in New York, sardonic and given to black-and-silver ensembles. The only thing the two shared was an all-consuming sense of being underappreciated. Their titles were a parting gift from Uskov; now each considered him- or herself the other's boss and wildly schemed to have the other removed. (Just in case things were beginning to seem easy, I had inherited a little *Game of Thrones*.) My meek hope to stay above this particular fray lasted for another fifteen minutes: both were already feuding with Calvin Klein about their seats at the upcoming Milan Fashion Week (each wanted the one front-row seat), and the marketing department needed my decision. Mentally conjuring the spirit of King Solomon, I said I would sit there.

It was now close to 5:00 p.m. I had been paraded in front of three separate advertisers' reps in three separate, though equally deserted, luxury restaurants; each time, a big point was made out of them being "the first we're having Michael meet." Another hour flew by in the company of two agitated International Watch Company reps, who, through the marketing department, were forcing some Russian athlete down my throat for a photo portfolio. The concept was up to us, as long as the guy wore an IWC watch. The only thing I knew about this athlete was his very public membership in United Russia. I pushed them back about one-tenth of the way by promising to feature the watch sans the athlete.

Next came the meeting with the editor in chief of the soon-to-launch Russian *Allure*. She wanted Kate Moss on the inaugural cover, but a rep for Kate Moss allegedly demanded that, in return, her personal trainer (the rep's, not Moss's) get editorial coverage in all other Condé Nast Russia titles. Yes, *all* of them. I politely told her off. "But he's a *mirakl vorker!*" she kept saying again and again, in English, with rising desperation.

I went back to my fuchsia office, past the sticklike Sergei, who was fighting in a whisper with a female editor whose name I hadn't learned yet, locked the door from the inside, and collapsed at the cigarette-burned desk. I was beginning to doubt whether I'd make it. This was a job for two men—two men with unrelated, not to say mutually exclusive, skill sets: one to represent the magazine to an endless stream of marketing clients, and the other to actually run it. Combined with the fact that I had to find a new art director, oversee a full redesign, basically teach a team of editors to edit, and revamp the website, this was getting scary.

Ah yes, the website. I gathered the strength to lift my head off the desk and type "GQ.ru." Staring back at me was my own glib mug. The goddamned site was running a homepage story about my first day, accompanied by an already outdated interview I had given it back on January 10. A full-on slideshow of my portraits. It looked not just immodest but obscene. Forget Solomon; I was Onan. I darted out of the office and half-ran to the section of the newsroom where the Web department sat.

"Hi, guys. I know we haven't really even met yet, but, uh, please take this down."

"We can't."

"I'm pretty sure you can."

"No, you don't get it, chief. Marketing sold this as a special feature to Glenfiddich. We have obligations now."

I took a pause to compose myself. Not only was I not in charge of my own magazine's website, but I was now unwittingly shilling Scotch.

"Well," I said, "hope I get a lifetime supply." I was beginning to feel I'd need it.

Over on Twitter and Facebook, to which I, against Dobrotvorskaya's best advice, reflexively dashed next, my former *Afisha* and *Bolshoi Gorod* friends were already exploding in derision. In their eyes, the life of corrupt glamour had swallowed me whole on day one. I could feel the glee of the Zhan-Zhak crowd. *We knew he'd be just like the rest of them!* One more lokh, proven *unshakehandswithable*.

All right. All right. So this was a false start. I just needed a new one.

And for this, I would need an all-new team. A team neither complacent nor doctrinaire. Neither Rublevka-glamorous nor Zhan-Zhak–ascetic. I'd need men and women, smart and young and funny and above all with a healthy appetite for the absurd, for the absurd was all around me. A team optimized for craziness and change. I pulled off my itchy wool tie, hung it on the desk lamp next to me, and went to work. By 8:00 p.m., I had burned one side of the tie. I also had something like a plan.

The only people left at the office were me and Sergei, the willowy assistant, pecking at his computer across the wall. I gathered my things and, before leaving, opened Twitter one more time, to masochistically check the abuse pouring my way. In the expected avalanche of fresh mockery, one tweet stood out. "Idov's still here," it said. "Looks rather endearingly pathetic in his dumb brown sneakers." It was about an hour old. It came from Sergei's account.

I took a few seconds to consider the Russian labor code. Everyone has to quit voluntarily. No words or phrases that could be construed as termination of employment. Just send them up to Maria on the eleventh floor.

"Hey, Sergei!" I finally called.

Sergei stuck his Jack Skellington head in the doorway. "Yes, boss?"

"I'm firing you. You're fired. You need to leave."

▪

A week later, I was sitting in a café called Dodo (which would soon share the fate of its namesake bird). Squinting at me across the table through a curtain of Gitane smoke was my new deputy editor, Roman Volobuev.

Volobuev was a film critic by trade, but not like any film critic I'd known. Trailed by groupies online and off, he was something of a star himself, hung out with young actresses, and, despite a lazy eye acquired as a consequence of a brutal street beating, had dated and/or briefly married every specimen of a certain kind of beauty (French gamine) in town. Like me, he had begun publishing in newspapers well before finishing high school; unlike me, he didn't bother to finish it once he had. Volobuev had an affected yet amusing air of rakish disgust with everything around him, and a habit of burying his head in his hands and mouthing, "Oh God," in a stifled voice when he laughed. His resting pose was a face-palm.

Despite a clear ambition to write and direct films—another thing we shared—Volobuev was a print-media lifer. In his teens, he used to work with the famed investigative journalist Anna Politkovskaya, assassinated for her reporting in 2006. He had also been part of Zimin's "golden age" *GQ*; this would be his second tour at the magazine. Two days before our meeting, he up and left Krasilshchik's *Afisha*, where he had worked for almost a decade, offering up in the way of an official explanation that he didn't like the smell of the paint at its new offices.

"Look," Volobuev said, stubbing out the Gitane. "Fair warning.

I'm probably going to be a terrible deputy editor, because I hate work and I hate people."

"Little do you know," I replied, "that's exactly what I need right now."

I was, in fact, convinced he'd make sense at my *GQ*. Volobuev was intimidating—hell, I was a bit intimidated by him—and would be a ruthless authority to authors, which was the point. I was trying to build the first Russian magazine where the editors would be held in higher esteem than the writers. His tone would help push the magazine where I needed it to go. And, finally, he was neither a Putinist nor a zealot obsessed with the purity of the protest at the expense of common sense. We shook hands, Volobuev lit another Gitane, and I was off.

My next hire, Gosha Birger, was Volobuev's polar opposite. A balding, bespectacled manboy of vast intellect and magnificently self-aware geekery, he came from Vasily Esmanov's LookAtMe constellation of hipster websites but had clearly outgrown them. Birger was a brilliant pop-culture theoretician. His obsessions included regional hip-hop, obscure computer games, alternative porn, coding, meme curation, and dachshunds. He was pen pals with the lead singer from the National and turned cyber-squatting on absurd domain names into an art form. He was also a walking comic relief whose very presence swept all of *GQ*'s innate macho pretension right out of the room. In other words, he seemed like the perfect editor for our website.

Birger and I began by coming up with two blogs: *The Inspector General*, a culture news stream that Birger would mostly write himself, and a political blog that I had wanted since day one. The presidential election of March 6 was now less than a month away, and somehow not a single Russian magazine had a blog devoted to the daily pre-election ticktock. (Instead, everyone just kept pouring out columns, essays, and manifestos.) We called ours, in the mock Soviet style, Politblog. It would be written by Andrew Ryvkin, a twentysomething St. Petersburg native who had spent his formative years in Boston and seemed to me, from his online posts, to be a media star in the making; he was sharp and mordant but without advocating too hard (which was the chief failure of almost all Russian political writing). I told him that the tone of Politblog had to be "slightly agape at the absurdity of it all," and that's exactly how he wrote it. Later, when we became friends, I found out that Ryvkin was a son of Mikhail Zhvanetsky, the Soviet Union's most famous stand-up comedian and satirical writer, a lineage upon which he admirably avoided capitalizing. Politblog immediately brought eyeballs and Facebook links to GQ's moribund website. This was especially great since my first issue of the actual magazine was still two months away. (The March issue, now at the printers, was all Uskov's.)

Finally, I hired a new assistant, Masha Limonova. She was everything I had originally been trying to avoid—tall, blond, slender, and almost parodically beautiful in a 1940s Marlene Dietrich way. Masha exuded competence and almost too much poise; it was immediately clear that her career at Condé Nast would outlast mine. (Indeed, she is now the society editor at the Russian *Tatler*.) I was now down to my last meeting of the week, and the most important one.

I walked into a mazelike backyard off Karetny Ryad, located an unmarked black door, and trotted down the two flights of stairs leading to Delicatessen—a windowless basement bistro that would soon become my new favorite place in Moscow. (The chef, Ivan Shishkin, had apprenticed with Blue Hill's Dan Barber; the bar turned out things like barrel-aged Manhattans, a rarity in the city of a million mojitos.) For the moment, however, the drinks were irrelevant. I was there to meet my two new writers. Which was admittedly a bit of a task, since I didn't know their names or what they looked like. There were maybe eight people in the world who did.

One of the eight was my friend Julia Ioffe, who had set up this blind date. Julia, at that point a roving Moscow reporter for *The*

New Yorker, The New Republic, and other publications, had recently befriended the anonymous authors of @KermlinRussia, a mega-popular Twitter account that had started as a parody of Medvedev's but soon veered off in its own direction, becoming, in essence, a successful independent media project. The account's creators were known only by their purposely half-ass pseudonyms, Sasha and Masha. "The Kermlins," as Julia called the duo, had given only two interviews to date and had worn disguises for both: she was a cat; he was Batman. I scanned the room half-expecting to see the masks.

"Sasha and Masha" turned out to be Arseny Bobrovsky and Katya Romanovskaya, an unexpectedly gorgeous yuppie couple from the intersection of media and finance. Arseny owned a small PR firm; as he and Katya put it, most of their clients were mid- to high-level entrepreneurs whose ultimate PR goal was to be seen next to Putin or Medvedev in a news report from a business conference or factory visit. The firm provided this service by slipping envelopes of cash to TV crews: ten thousand dollars, split between the cameraman and the editor back at the studio, would buy a cutaway shot to the client. "The @KermlinRussia project was my fuck-you to all these assholes who just wanted to be noticed 'up there,'" Arseny would tell me later. "It was like, here, watch me live your dream: I'll create a publication out of nothing that the people 'up there' will be forced to pay attention to."

On June 23, 2010, he saw his opening. That day, then-president Medvedev registered, to a great deal of fanfare, his own Twitter account: @KremlinRussia. In retrospect, this stunt marked the beginning of the honeymoon Medvedev would briefly enjoy with the same liberals who'd march against him two years later; even the skeptical Russian blogosphere went uncharacteristically gaga over it. "I came home that night and started reading Lepra [Leprosorium, a legendary invite-only online forum], and even Lepra was in this full-on loyalist frenzy," said Arseny. *"The President's on*

Twitter! It's a new era! We can write to the President directly! The government is finally listening to us!" Within seconds, Arseny had registered an account nearly identical to Medvedev's.

At first, @KermlinRussia was Arseny's private time-waster, and looked for the most part like your average exercise in Internet fakery: the point was to get people to confuse the parody for the real thing. "I hated that he kept calling it his 'project,'" Katya recalled. She got on board, however, when she realized that the growing number of followers would soon make this parody project more successful than Arseny's actual ones. To their credit, they quickly steered the account away from trolling and in favor of pithy, sticky, lightning-quick satire. Their best lines sparked hundreds, sometimes thousands of retweets. (When Putin said that the Russian policy on some issue or another "doesn't have to be all stick and no carrot," @KermlinRussia immediately clarified: "We can fuck you up with a carrot, too.") Sometimes one sentence would take hours to craft; in effect, they were now going through the same process as a late-night talk show's staff writing jokes for the host's monologue, the difference being that no talk show in Russia would ever touch jokes like these.

Well, *I* would. By the end of the evening, I made the duo a slightly insane-sounding offer: they would unmask themselves in an exclusive interview with me, after which they themselves would become *GQ*'s regular star interviewers, replacing in that role Ksenia Sobchak. Oh, and they would also do a back-page comic with underground cartoonist Egor Zhgun.* Perhaps a number of barrel-aged

---

*Zhgun was perhaps most famous for crashing an open-call design contest for the upcoming Sochi Olympics' mascot with a psychedelic drawing of a furry blue toad named Zoich. Zoich had a ski pole in his mouth, the Russian Imperial Crown on his head, and Olympic rings floating in his eyes, and naturally proceeded to win the poll, putting the games' organizing committee in an awkward situation. This being Russia, however, it was later revealed that the committee had paid Zhgun to submit the toad in the first place, as a way to drum up viral excitement for the poll itself.

Manhattans did influence the decision, or at least the speed of it. Regardless, the Kermlins said yes. And, with that, I had my team.

A Casanova film critic, a polymath nerd, two masked stars of the new opposition, and a fellow-American son of a Soviet comic. (In my elation I failed to notice that I had accidentally put together an almost entirely Jewish crew, with Volobuev the sole Slav.) In just two years' time, none of us would be working in journalism, and not all of us would be on speaking terms; more remarkably, the Russia we'd inhabit (or, in half the cases, leave) by 2014 would have been barely recognizable to us that evening.

For now, however, this was beginning to look like a magazine.

Chapter Four

The One-Two Punch, Part One

A s the winter of 2012 wrapped up, the upcoming presidential election of March 4 looked, at least on the surface, a lot like those of 2004 and 2008. Vladimir Putin's third term as the president, and fourth as the de facto leader of the country, was all but assured. Arraigned against him was the usual crew of pseudo-competitors: Gennady Zyuganov, whose Communists, with 13.7 percent of the vote in 2004 and 17 percent in 2008, were the closest to a challenge the ruling United Russia had ever allowed; the perennial right-wing rodeo clown Vladimir Zhirinovsky, now on his fifth go at the polls, whose numbers invariably landed between 3 and 10 percent; and finally a designated "liberal" spoiler to siphon off the attention of those city elites who still, for some unfathomable reason, bothered to vote. In 2004, this role had gone to Irina Khakamada. In 2008, with Garry Kasparov and Mikhail Kasyanov barred from running, their near-parodic replacement was one Andrei Bogdanov, a corpulent Freemason (he was the Grand Master of the Grand Lodge of Russia) with the hair of an aging heavy-metal drummer, who got 1.3 percent of the vote.

This time, the liberal flavor of the year was Mikhail Prokhorov, the gangling billionaire owner of *Snob* and the Brooklyn Nets. No one knew what, exactly, it was that Prokhorov wanted, and even who he truly was. In the mid-aughts, Prokhorov enjoyed a seemingly self-constructed reputation as a playboy ("It used to be that you go to certain clubs," recalled one Muscovite friend, "and if at some moment fifteen barely legal girls show up all at once, you could tell that Prokhorov is about to stop by"), though he also projected a remarkably asexual, ascetic vibe. Well after he had become a billionaire, he and his quiet intellectual sister, Irina, shared a relatively small Moscow apartment; he also reportedly worked out for up to six hours a day and wore loose Brioni suits that billowed off him like sails from a spar because, as he once told a stylist, he wanted to be able to drop-kick people while wearing one. Prokhorov's interests varied wildly. He invested in low-cost hybrid cars, nanotechnology, and banks. He flirted with the governorship of a far-flung Russian province, going so far as to establish tax residence in a tiny Siberian village.* He had also endowed a lavish literary award, a publishing house, an arts festival, and, finally, *Snob*, which at

---

*In 2009, Prokhorov—then Russia's richest man—paid his income tax of 16 billion rubles, or roughly $550 million, out of snowy Yeruda, population 2,300.

least made sense as a way of buttering up—when not downright employing—the opinion makers on whose support he could lean for the presidential run. In 2008, this was a smart move. By 2012, however, the situation had changed—the elites, electrified by the mass protests, demanded a more muscular detractor to Putin. Prokhorov had made a halfhearted attempt to stay hip to the new tone—on December 24, he even visited the protest rally on Sakharov Square (where a number of young jokers gathered in a circle around the six-feet-six candidate and chanted, "You so fucking tall"). Still, the limitations of his appeal were obvious. While Navalny roared from the Sakharov stage about Putin's "crooks and thieves," Prokhorov's campaign speeches, of which he'd only given five or six, didn't even dare to criticize the record of the man he was ostensibly running against. It seemed increasingly obvious that the billionaire was fulfilling his end of the usual backroom deal with the Kremlin: to campaign but not too hard.

The election's main intrigue was thus not about who was going to win, as it hadn't really been since 1996. Instead, the question bedeviling everyone—including those in charge of answering it— was whether Putin's new government would incorporate the protesters' demands into its program or strike back.

And, indeed, there was a brief moment when the Kremlin seemed rattled enough to offer concessions. On December 22, right between the big Bolotnaya and Sakharov rallies, Dmitry Medvedev had given his final presidential address to the Federal Assembly— the Russian equivalent of the State of the Union speech. In it, he directed the Duma to simplify the process of registering new parties: the required number of signatures would be dramatically reduced, from forty-five thousand to five hundred.* Medvedev also

---

*Ironically, the biggest outcry in response came from the Duma's "systemic opposition," Communists and Yabloko, who now feared real competition for their designated second and fourth places in every contest.

advocated the return of direct gubernatorial elections. Both of these things were on the actual list of protesters' demands. Even Putin, who in December had demurred from any dialogue with the opposition, saying that it lacked a defined agenda, by mid-January suddenly offered to meet with its "nonpolitician" leaders, such as the novelists Boris Akunin and Dmitry Bykov.

Most strikingly, on December 27, Vladislav Surkov, the chief ideologue of Putinism and the architect of "souvenir democracy," got demoted from first deputy chief of the presidential administration to deputy prime minister "in charge of modernization," which above all meant a move from the Kremlin to the Parliament building just when Putin was preparing to hop the other way. Surkov responded by giving an unexpected, not to say bizarre, interview to the *Izvestia* daily, in which he lavished nearly obsequious praise on the protesters and seemed to call the system corrupt.

"The best part of our society, or, more correctly, its most productive part, demands respect," Surkov said. "They are saying: *we exist, we matter, we are the people.* One can't haughtily wave their opinion away . . . To concede to the reasonable demands of the society's active segment is not a forced maneuver by the government, it is its duty and constitutional obligation. Of course, any crowd may put forth unreasonable demands, or follow the lead of provocateurs. But we have the laws to deal with provocateurs, while the government's job is to protect the basis of the constitutional society. And here, a question arises: what are we protecting? Who would want to protect corruption, injustice, who would want to protect a system that's deaf and growing dumber in front of your eyes? Nobody. Not even those who are part of this system. Because they wouldn't feel that the truth is on their side."

His language was so incendiary that a few of us, for a brief moment, thought that Surkov might want to head up the protest movement himself and ride it back into the Kremlin. (He possibly could have, too, were that his real intention; he was smart enough and the opposition rudderless enough.) A flamboyant insta–conspiracy theory even had him financing the opposition, somehow for the benefit of Medvedev, through the Skolkovo Innovation Center. Looking back at Surkov's statement, however, the one clause that glares back at me in pulsing neon is "we have the laws to deal with provocateurs." Indeed, *this* was the tack the Kremlin was already gearing up to take: recrimination, libel, demonization, and vengeance, all cloaked in the kind of quasi-legality that would soon have state prosecutors in the Pussy Riot case reaching back to A.D. 692 for the Quinisext Council church laws, and the Duma inventing ad hoc ones whenever someone new needed to be jailed, broken, or spooked into flight. We didn't know it at the time, but we had just seen the peak of the protests' success. There it was, with the grinning Surkov perched atop it.

The pushback began within days. On February 7, in what was to be the first swallow of a dismal spring, *Gosdep*, Ksenia Sobchak's freewheeling political talk show on MTV, got canceled right after the premiere, despite bringing in a rating three times the average in its time slot. Navalny was to be a guest on the second episode. Twitter filled up with jokes suggesting other shows Navalny could kill by visiting, like *Dancing with the Stars*.

Though Sobchak was able to move the program to TV Rain, where it would survive for a few more episodes as *Gosdep 2*, she couldn't have picked a worse title for it. The U.S. State Department had been cast as the central villain in the counternarrative upon which the Kremlin settled: It was Gosdep that was trying to overthrow Putin, like it had done with Yanukovych in Ukraine in 2004. The leaders of the opposition were its agents or stooges. Hillary Clinton personally signed off on the rallies.* The phrase *pechen'ki*

---

*I had long noticed Russia's intriguing tendency to assign female secretaries of state their own agency (Madeleine Albright, Condoleezza Rice, and Clinton all entered Russian popular culture as fairy-tale witches) while treating male ones as faceless functionaries. In the John Kerry years, the Russian state media cemented this pattern by inexplicably fixating on the State Department's *spokesperson*, the poor Jen Psaki, as a nemesis.

Gosdepa, "State Department cookies," became viral shorthand for the supposed funds the United States was funneling to the protest movement. (In response, counter-counter-demonstrators called the Horizontal Resistance Group trolled Putinists by distributing "One Hillary" banknotes, made to look like dollar bills with Clinton's portrait, stamped with a Gosdep seal and marked "legal tender for all operations pursuant to the buying and selling of the Motherland.") And Clinton's main henchman, her enforcer on the ground and liaison to the opposition, was without a doubt Michael McFaul, the brand-new U.S. ambassador to Russia.

Montana-born McFaul, forty-eight at the time, with the sandy hair and square jaw of a retired NFL quarterback or movie detective, couldn't be more different from his predecessor. Ambassador John Beyrle, a career diplomat and a Bush-era appointee, had been fairly unknown to the Russian public at large, despite—or perhaps because of—the relative calm in the U.S.-Russian relations on his watch. In contrast, McFaul, who had come from academia and was one of the architects of 2009's "reset" policy toward Russia, was to be an avatar of the Obama age: cool, available, informal—a walking Ask Me Anything.

Obama's overture to Medvedev, inviting him to wriggle out of Putin's shadow, had gotten off to the worst imaginable start when Hillary Clinton handed Foreign Minister Sergei Lavrov a symbolic red button with the word *peregruzka* ("overload") instead of the intended *perezagruzka* ("reset").* This faux pas was nothing compared with McFaul's nightmarish debut as the ambassador. Two facts about the new arrival instantly struck the Russian imagination: McFaul arrived in Moscow on January 10, 2012, right after the

---

*The button is currently held under glass in an internal, appointment-only museum at the Russian Ministry of Foreign Affairs. I had the privilege of seeing it. It is truly a stunning example of idiocy.

first wave of big protests; and he had written his Ph.D. thesis on the U.S. role in global revolutions and freedom movements. Taken together, this all but proved that he had been sent here to foment unrest.

Granted, McFaul made himself an easy target. As befit the hip young ambassador, he took to Twitter, where he kept a running commentary on his life in Moscow, feuded with his former friend turned histrionic Putinist Sergei Markov, baited Ksenia Sobchak, fed all manner of troll, and gamely answered readers' questions in terrible Russian (somehow rendered all the worse for McFaul's fearless embrace of memes; he started one tweet with "Чят," a rough equivalent of "Wazzzuuup"). On January 17, *before* officially handing his ambassador credentials to Putin, he invited Alexei Navalny, Boris Nemtsov, Yevgenia Chirikova, and other opposition figures to his new residence at Spaso House; a mind sufficiently inflamed could see this as an indication of who Obama's envoy saw as Russia's next leaders. At the Spaso gates, a gang of pseudo-journalists beset the arriving and departing guests and barked leading questions at them. The resultant video made it to YouTube under the libelous title "Receiving Instructions at the U.S. Embassy," where it still sits, with more than a million views and counting. (Amazingly, even after the brutal assassination of Nemtsov, who's prominent in the footage, many of the Russian comments under the video call for the other "traitors" and "kikes" to be murdered as well.)

Things escalated from there. On January 20, former foreign minister Igor Ivanov was gently tut-tutting McFaul in the government daily *Rossiyskaya Gazeta*; by early February, the ambassador was being slandered online as a pedophile in coordinated bursts of disinformation (the Russian language has a great word for this tactic—*vbrosy*). Privately, McFaul would tell me later, the Kremlin kept back-channeling him to assert that all the *vbrosy* were "just a show before the election" and begging him to bear with this torture for just a while longer.

Once the cacophonous propaganda machine got going, however, it was hard to stop. The pestering would continue well after the election. Unaccredited "journalists," mysteriously armed with the U.S. embassy's detailed and up-to-date schedules, lay in wait at every turn. On March 31, one of them, a nameless redheaded woman, would pounce at McFaul as he exited a building where he had just met with human rights activist Lev Ponomarev; there was no earthly way a reporter would have known about this meeting without the aid of the Russian security services. "I'll gladly sit down with you for an interview," McFaul would tell her, in shaky Russian, trying to keep his composure. "But like this . . . I mean, every time I go somewhere . . ." The video then shows him falling silent just long enough to realize that he can't take it anymore. "This turned out to be a *dikaya strana*!" he suddenly sputters. "Nowhere else do they do this! Not in the U.S., not in England, not in China!" Imagine, if you will, the distress to which a U.S. ambassador had to be driven that he'd call Russia a savage (wild, uncivilized, uncultured) country, on camera, within three months of arrival. NTV, the state channel most openly tasked with hounding the opposition, would play the clip on the news that very night, while denying that the redhead worked for them.

I admired McFaul from the start—even related to him, to a degree. He and I had arrived in Russia almost simultaneously; like me, he was not the obvious choice for the job—a scholar, as opposed to a Foreign Service lifer; like me, he was trying to distinguish himself from his predecessor and perhaps overdoing it a bit; and, like me, he was getting bullied for his trouble. God knows I had called Russia worse things than *dikaya strana*; there just hadn't been any cameras around—yet. So I knew what I wanted for my first issue of *GQ*: an exclusive interview with the scandalous ambassador.

I figured that my being an American would open a few extra doors at Spaso House, and at first it did. For the actual story, I happily recruited Julia Ioffe: she'd met McFaul before, in his capacity as Obama's special adviser, and they had ongoing communication. Within a week or so, Julia had sat him down for a long talk, as frank as McFaul's precarious situation would allow. (At that point, he was getting beaten up on Foggy Bottom as well; a faction at the State Department bristled at the amount of press he and his Twitter exploits were getting.) And then, at the eleventh hour, with myself and the *GQ* photo crew literally halfway to Spaso House to shoot the ambassador in the natural habitat, McFaul canceled.

At first, I thought this had to do with the snow blanketing Moscow. ("It's a nine out there," the driver said. "Nine of what?" I answered. Turned out that Yandex.Maps, the app everyone used to get around, had a ten-point system for rating traffic jams.) My second thought was that McFaul had been pressured by Washington to tone it down. I called Ioffe. She was spooked even more. "Something's deeply weird about it. And I wonder if it has something to do with the screw tightening all around," she wrote back. The crew trudged home. A ten-page hole blew open in the issue; we papered over it with a bland Hollywood photo portfolio from *Vanity Fair*.

I scheduled a dinner with Joe Kruzich, the embassy's press attaché, to figure out what the hell had just happened. We met at one of the grand restaurants on Kuznetsky Most, designed for people who like to isolate themselves from the crowd by paying seventy dollars for a piece of turbot. Kruzich, who looked like an older John Cusack and dyed his hair deep chestnut, came dressed in a beige camel-hair blazer and a blue tie with wiggly whimsies all over it. One of his favorite topics was how hot the Nashi (pro-Putin youth organization) girls were. I resolved to fantasize he was CIA, because this would at least give his shtick some sort of explanation.

There had been a threat against McFaul, Kruzich explained

between old-fashioneds, and the "ambo" had been advised to stay out of the public eye for a few months. The embassy wanted the story moved all the way down to July or August. Ioffe's follow-up interview with McFaul's wife, Donna, was also being canceled. I offered to photograph McFaul now and sign an embargo until May. No dice.*

With nothing left to discuss, I asked Kruzich about Mikhail Prokhorov. "Our feeling at the embassy is that he is a Kremlin project," he said sagely. Mostly, though, he wanted to talk about *Mad Men*. We made a pact to throw the next season's premiere viewing party at the embassy, inviting advertisers, media people, and expats. Glenfiddich could sponsor! (None of this would ever happen.) The famed film director Stanislav Govorukhin, who was at the moment Putin's reelection campaign manager—whatever that job entailed—was seated in a nearby alcove, dining with a shaven-headed former-bandit type. So this was the big time, I thought briefly. Eating seventy-dollar turbot beside Putin's inner circle while it torments the people you're trying to actually engage. Christ.

Now that the opposition's honeymoon was over and the election loomed weeks away, it was time to pick sides. "The best part of Russia's society" was quickly fissuring into two camps. Directors, novelists, artists, conductors, screenwriters, TV hosts, sculptors, pianists, restaurateurs, and, yes, magazine editors—there was now a "Putinist" and an "opposition" flavor of each. Boris Akunin, the country's most popular middlebrow novelist, stood fast with the protesters. So did Dmitri Bykov, Russia's widest-read public intellectual. Neither of them had taken Putin up on his proposal of a meeting back in January. (Later, in November 2013, Akunin would bow out of a literary conference at the Peoples' Friendship Univer-

---

*We ran the interview in May anyway, with bad photos. A year or so later, I would find out the real reason for McFaul's reticence: his wife, Donna, had thought *GQ* was a sexist lad mag that objectified women. It took a dinner at our house (during which my daughter spat up on her dress) to convince her that I wasn't a misogynist boor.

sity of Russia when it became known that Putin was going to drop by. "While there remain political prisoners in the country, I can't stand next to its ruler, even if it means simply being in the same room as him," he wrote on Facebook. In response, the Kremlin shruggingly accused Akunin of "nihilism." Bykov, for his part, said he had a more important lecture in St. Petersburg that day, and the liberal novelist Ludmila Ulitskaya wisely fell ill.) Was this the smartest thing to do? Could dialogue, back when the moment was right, have led to concessions down the line? *Should* it have? These questions were now, sadly, academic. The protesting intelligentsia's obsession with the purity of their own ranks was reaching an all-time high. Everyone's *shakehandswithability* was under daily relitigation.

This was no way to create change, I thought; it seemed apparent to me that whoever got in front of the new movement would have to work with the existing elites, and unite wildly disparate factions. It was obvious to Yuri Saprykin as well: "Isn't it odd," he wrote, "how the same stirred-up intelligentsia that managed to find common ground with [Communist] Sergei Udaltsov and [nationalist] Konstantin Krylov, now can't and won't understand a Putin voter? I might even suggest that calling Putin a demon out of hell and considering the issue closed might not be the best way of defeating him." Few liberal opinion makers, however, evinced any appetite for nuance. The next time I met Alexei Navalny, he was working on the idea of boycotting restaurants owned by members of United Russia.

On the other side of the literary divide, Sergei Minaev, he of the *Soulless* bestsellers and the lucrative liquor business, swung hard for Putin. So did Sergei Lukyanenko, the author of the blockbuster fantasies *Night Watch* and *Day Watch*, about the epic battle between the ageless forces of the light and the dark (the big twist being that both sides turn out to be equally corrupt). Even farther went Minaev's old friend and partner Eduard Bagirov, another popular writer with whom Minaev had founded an online publishing platform called LitProm. Bagirov became one of Putin's *doverennye litsa*, or "surrogates."

The doverennye litsa project was an interesting one. The title didn't quite mean what it means in the United States: the surrogates, 462 in total and pulled from such fields as science, business, and the arts, weren't expected to hit newsrooms or spin rooms and advocate for Putin. In essence, it was just a master list of VIPs who have declared that they like him. Some recorded pro-Putin videos. Others' only seeming obligation was to provide a profile to a web portal where they could occasionally blog. (A sample post by Eduard Bagirov—in his presumably official capacity as a Putin surrogate—on that site reads thusly: "The Ebola epidemic is impossible in Russia . . . A Russian will never shit into a plastic bag and toss it into his front yard . . . A Russian will dig a latrine. An African will never think of this.")

It is quite probable that most of these people genuinely rooted for Putin. But since being a cultural or scientific VIP in Russia almost invariably means having the state support you, and with the state being fully synonymous with a current administration, it's impossible to know whether their support came from conviction or calculation, avarice or fear. In America, if, say, a famous jazz saxophonist flaunted a political affiliation, the most he or she normally stood to lose is a gig at the White House. In Russia, this saxophonist, to use the example of Igor Butman, was a member of United Russia's Supreme Council and conducted a jazz orchestra created by government decree and financed out of the Moscow city budget. The state had a way of binding Russia's best and brightest to itself in ways that made dissent risky and support redundant. "I really wouldn't want to find myself in the place of anyone who's being offered to film a pro-Putin video or become his surrogate right now," wrote *Afisha*'s Saprykin, again the sardonic voice of reason. "The benefit is minimal—at most, they're not going to give you any trouble; okay, maybe they'll show you on the news one extra time . . . The drawbacks, meanwhile, are incalculable: your name will become a synonym for selling out, your photo will be studied for signs of dementia, and you will suddenly find the only resource you could lend to the candidate of your choice—your reputation— spent and irrecoverable." Indeed, hordes of enraged anti-Putinists vowed to boycott the doverennye litsa en masse—their stage plays, their concerts, their soccer teams.

In most cases, these threats meant little. The political fissure ran along the usual unspoken demarcation between Russia's two parallel cultures: a liberal "boycott" of, say, the schmaltzy crooner Stas Mikhailov would be unlikely to cost him a single pair of ears, since the liberals didn't listen to Stas Mikhailov. It was at the few points where these two cultures crossed—around, say, the star conductor Valery Gergiev, whose fealty to Putin couldn't (couldn't it?) overshadow his genius—that electricity began to crackle.

The biggest scandal rippled out of a single thirty-second video in the "Why I'm Voting for Putin" series. The endorser was Chulpan Khamatova, a very good actress (Western viewers might remember her from *Good Bye, Lenin!*) and by all accounts a great human being, who devoted most of her time off the set to charity: her foundation, Gift of Life, raised funds for Moscow's Center of Pediatric Hematology and other children's hospitals. The opposition had always seen her as a kindred spirit. Perhaps that's why the sight of Khamatova, tremulously exhorting people to vote for Putin because "he always kept his promises to the foundation" (the only reason she gives in the video) was so monumentally upsetting.

What followed was part online bullying campaign, part florid conspiracy theory. *She couldn't have done it on her own. They threatened to pull her funding.* "This feels absolutely like a hostage video," wrote Anton Krasovsky, Mikhail Prokhorov's campaign manager. The leading journalist Svetlana Reiter went ahead and titled her article about Khamatova "Hostage." "Yes, she was forced, she was threatened," an anonymous source at Gift of Life told Gazeta.ru. "They threatened the children. They threatened to cut the financing to the foundation and the center. She's crushed. She's taking it all very hard."

Somehow, Khamatova was emerging from the scandal even more helplessly angelic, equal parts Joan of Arc and a Mayan virgin tribute. Metaphors rained. "It's our common fault, one and all, that this saintly creature is being forced to . . . dance before Herod," wrote the journalist Olga Bakushinskaya. "We need to kill the dragon instead of impugning the girl who walks into its mouth to save the children," echoed the composer Alexander Manotskov. During a live broadcast of the Nika film awards, cohosted, naturally, by Ksenia Sobchak, the opposition's would-be muse sprung a got-cha question on Khamatova: "Would you still support Putin if you weren't involved in charity?" and was just as naturally pilloried for it online. Dmitri Bykov—and here, things cross decisively into the "only in Russia" category—then published a thirty-two-line poem about the incident, not quite defending Chulpan but at least assert-ing her agency in her own decisions. However, it was *another* poem, a much shorter one by Ivan Davydov, that went viral and provided the final word in this sad circus:

> *Mr. Putin, glory be,*
> *Ate four children with his tea.*
> *He'd have eaten five but one*
> *Had been rescued by Chulpan.*

Meanwhile, my own shakehandswithability was probably beyond repair. The daily life of a *GQ Russia* editor, I had quickly learned, consisted mostly of glamorous-looking tedium that belied various marketing obligations. My first appearance in the Moscow society in my new capacity was at the supermodel Natalia Vodianova's Naked Heart Foundation charity ball. Unlike Chulpan Khamatova, Vodianova enjoyed the luxury of not having to support or reject Putin out loud: she lived in the U.K. and was married to the son of Bernard Arnault, the head of LVMH. Despite her fame and the attendant baubles, she managed to stay almost preternaturally nice and overall human, which made Condé Nast's institutional genuflection before her into much less of a chore.

The event fell on the coldest night of the year, at minus twenty-six degrees Fahrenheit. I had been growing to enjoy extreme cold as a kind of cleanliness: it froze the fumes out of the air and the filth to the ground. At night, when traffic disappeared and you could whip unimpeded past the Sumerian walls of the Kremlin, ruby stars glowing vaguely in the yellow sky, the city was quite beautiful. From inside a chauffeured car, at least.

I was seated at the front table with Vodianova herself; her Russian factotum, who called himself Timon of Athens; the inevitable Ksenia Sobchak; and Sobchak's ex-boyfriend, the Chechen-born billionaire Umar Dzhabrailov, who once ran for president. In 2017, he'd be arrested for shooting up Moscow's Four Seasons hotel and blame his gunplay on a "nervous breakdown." This was the first time I'd seen Sobchak since she bolted for *Snob*, and she was nice enough to apologetically explain the move (she wanted to be more than a brash interviewer, etc.). Dzhabrailov kept swigging green tea, cup after cup, brought to him specially. "So what's so interesting about that dude, other than you Frenching him a while ago?" he finally drawled, without looking at me.

The evening's auction netted 1.6 million euros. The top lot was a large pixelated portrait of Vodianova, laid out in round pieces of glass. The flamboyant Dzhabrailov, who let Sobchak do the bidding for him as reporters' flashes exploded around us, duked it out with a dull-looking middle manager from Gazprom. The Gazprom man went home with the glass Vodianova for six hundred thousand euros. "This guy," Sobchak said in a low, angry voice. "How can he even spend this kind of money in public?! He is a functionary! It's because of people like this that I have to go to protest rallies."

Back at my actual job at the magazine, things weren't going great. All the cover ideas for my first issue had fallen through. As a budget offshoot of a media empire, *GQ Russia* syndicated most of its covers from its older U.S. and U.K. brothers, and these came laden with various embargoes. As someone who only a month ago lived in the epicenter of the magazine industry, I couldn't even *conceive* of reprinting someone else's cover. No one around me, including my new team, appeared to understand my obsession with original images; they just quietly humored it. To me, however, this seemingly mundane choice came down to an elemental clash of ideas that had bedeviled my entire double life: my insistence that Russia's pop culture is an integral part of the world's, and most Russians' seeing it as completely separate. The logical extension of the latter vision was that anything made outside of Russia could be borrowed, copied, or plundered with impunity. As Volobuev would say in an interview, "Nowhere else in the world would a TV series' editor be told to just lift the title sequence from *True Detective*: who cares, it's not like anyone will see it anyway. We actually pride ourselves on taking something from abroad and copying it well enough—because people don't feel that they're part of the same process." At the same time, this dependence on the West for cultural and aesthetic cues led to a gruesome side effect: any authentically Russian achievement was not considered "real" enough in comparison. Thus, no Russian star was ever big enough to appear on the cover.

I was realizing, with no small measure of horror, that the educated, Westernized Russians—the kind who would read my magazine—hated their own celebrities. To be more precise, they pretended not to know them; and now, this studied incuriosity toward the mainstream of one's own culture had been fortified a hundredfold by the country's political polarization. I was hardly prepared to deal with this: the WASPiest, milquetoast-iest American reader might not follow the exploits of Kim Kardashian, but he wouldn't begrudge *Vanity Fair*'s putting her on the cover: his certitude in his own privilege would cushion the blow. Here, readers would literally cancel their subscriptions if I acknowledged the existence of someone like Stas Mikhailov or his fellow celebrity crooner Grigory Leps—because half of *GQ Russia*'s job was to help the reader maintain the illusion of a world without them. The big thesis that governed the careers of journalism's two famous Browns, Helen Gurley and Tina—that you could write about stupid things in a smart way—didn't apply, because the smart in Russia felt too acutely ashamed of the stupid; as acutely as one could feel only about a close relative, or perhaps a part of oneself. To me, this desperate elitism seemed to be a kind of Russophobia. And I suspected that it would doom the revolution even if nothing else would. Were the people who were afraid of watching their own movies or listening to their country's pop music really ready to govern that country?

Out of sheer spite, I assigned a five-thousand-word story on Mikhailov to one of my best freelance authors—a write-around with the working title "Stas Mikhailov Has a Cold," after the famous Gay Talese profile of Sinatra. For now, however, the idea of putting a Russian on the cover was dead. So were suggestions such as Joseph Gordon Levitt ("Russians don't know him"), Leonardo DiCaprio ("sick of him"), Matt Damon ("no one likes him"), and Jeremy Renner ("who?"). The only cover subjects that always worked were apparently Monica Bellucci—who had been on *GQ Russia*'s cover four or five times now, starting with its premiere issue—and Hugh Laurie, whose Dr. House, at that point, was basically a national hero. (Addled genius who hates people and rules?

Sign us up.) But the show's run was over, and Laurie had no current news peg.

When I found myself forced to choose between Guy Pearce, whom few people seemed to know even within the walls of the publishing house, and a year-and-a-half-old photo of Rihanna, I gave up and leaned on whatever was left of my New York connections. Namely, I called the American *GQ* and begged them for an outtake I liked from a recent photo shoot of Keira Knightley, who had just starred as Anna Karenina in an excellent new adaptation of the novel. Marketing was not enthused ("flat chest equals flat sales"). But at least it would be an original image, of sorts. With a Russian connection, of sorts.

On February 23, Army Day, the cold finally let up. The city was a saucer of slush. The Russians are dead serious about this holiday, which functions as a kind of ersatz Father's Day, so all the men at the office got wine and flowers from the women. (The ritual would be reciprocated in a mere two weeks—on March 8, Women's Day, which the Russian society, exacerbating rather than canceling out 364 days of casual sexism, devotes to simpering adoration of women.) I also received a bumper crop of flack gifts, some of which clearly exceeded the official hundred-dollar value limit, especially a pair of ludicrous rhinestone-encrusted men's sneakers in the colorways of the Russian flag. I had them mailed back as instructed, probably making an enemy of another advertiser.

The Kremlin used the holiday to stage another giant pro-Putin rally at Luzhniki Stadium, with people bused in by the tens of thousands; the incumbent himself, speaking from the depths of a vast parka, quoted Lermontov: " 'Now let us die at Moscow's gates, like our brothers perished!' The battle for Russia continues! The victory will be ours!" On the revolutionary side, everyone was equally wired, though not for the election itself. It was hard to feel passionate about Prokhorov, and there was little suspense about the result. The topic on everyone's tongue was March 5—the day after. How would the movement react to Putin's coronation? Some suggested a rally at Lubyanka Square, a location the twentieth century had rendered doubly meaningful—first as the KGB headquarters and then as the site where the people felled the statue of Felix Dzerzhinsky on August 22, 1991, the closest the previous Russian revolution came to an iconic *Mauerfall* moment. Others advocated for Pushkin Square, a less nakedly confrontational spot. There were rumors of a tent city poised to spring up, like Occupy Wall Street or Kiev's Maidan.

Just in case, I got Andrew Ryvkin, whose columns over the past few weeks had already put *GQ*'s Politblog on the media map, to come down from St. Petersburg and switch to full-on reporter mode. Ryvkin's writing had been great so far; he was clearly one of my best hires. He also loved picking Twitter fights with a wild variety of subjects; his latest spat was with Sergei Minaev and his friend and Putin surrogate Eduard Bagirov, whose LitProm publishing portal Ryvkin had for some reason called a "whorish project." I didn't pay it much attention at the time. I figured that any noise was good for the website.

In retrospect, I may have been distracted. My wife and daughter and cat had just arrived in Moscow; oddly, it was the cat's presence—much more so than Lily's or Vera's—that brought home to me the reality of my slapdash commitment to Russia. Having around a toddler on a New York sleeping schedule also meant that none of us could count on much sleep for the next weeks, even under the best of political circumstances.

On the election's eve, I occupied myself with a round table about social media at which Yuri Saprykin had invited me to speak, held in a painfully hip new space called, in English, Digital October. The guest of honor was David Carr of *The New York Times*. Carr and I talked shop for an hour and bored everyone, including, I suspect, Carr; this was Lily's first outing with me in Moscow, and, in a preview of how I would feel for the next two years straight, I kicked myself for having dragged her there. Saprykin was equally restless because Solidarity, one of the opposition's many redundant moving parts, was pulling out of the Pushkin Square rally or some such. This was classic Moscow 2012: journalists doing their jobs while also haphazardly arranging logistics for a revolt. Finally, Saprykin took off early on some revolutionary emergency, leaving the panel without a moderator. Later that night, I saw his tweet from a Peter Hook concert.

For my part, I spent the last evening of the Medvedev era with a TV executive I'll call Leonid. You may notice that, in a book otherwise full of real names, this one is changed; that's because in a few sentences we're about to do a lot of drugs and talk treason.

I had been courting Leonid, whose online writing I admired, as a potential contributor to *GQ*. He appeared to be curious enough about me to agree to a meeting. We ate at a restaurant that Leonid co-owned (as is the wont among the Moscow media elites), then moved to his apartment for a nightcap: tea for me, a novelty vodka called Churovka for him. Vladimir Churov, the inspiration for the vodka's branding, was the head of the Central Election Commission, widely accused of finessing December's Duma election results in the ruling party's favor and expected to do the same for Putin come tomorrow. For this, the opposition derisively nicknamed Churov "the Wizard" and made him the butt of a myriad of unfunny memes. The vodka itself was the product of a protest-art outfit called Ovoshcham.net. Leonid bragged that this bottle had been gifted to him by Churov himself, so clearly the satire wasn't as withering as one would hope.

At his previous job, Leonid had run a major state TV channel; he described to me the main thrust of his activities there as *trupoedstvo*, or corpse-eating, meaning a relentless focus on cruelty and trash. Then, for vague indications of less-than-total loyalty to the regime, he was let go. Out with a hefty parting bonus, Leonid now had his pick of suitors from other channels, including TV Rain. Moreover, the League of Voters, the emergent operating center of the new opposition, had supposedly just asked him to head it up, or to create a brand-new political party on its behalf. My meek offer of a monthly column in *GQ* was not exactly competitive.

Churovka gone, Leonid sat down at one of the many pianos lining the walls of his bachelor pad and started banging out the theme from *17 Moments of Spring*, a TV classic about an undercover Soviet spy operating high up the Nazi food chain. He played extremely well, with classical flourishes. He then fired up two tightly rolled hydroponic joints, gave me one, and began explaining himself.

Leonid's political compass, as was the case with nearly every truly successful Russian, was fairly flexible. Just as with his TV job, he was mostly interested in maximum impact, without giving much thought to the nature or consequences of that impact. "I can do this," he said flatly, referring to the League of Voters offer. "But only if someone really stood behind this, like the State Department." He looked at me hopefully, as if I had the capacity to parlay his words to my Washington masters. "Look," he said, "if the State Department decided to defeat Putin—to really fuck him up good— I would totally do it for them, because I know how to destroy that guy. But they would need to seriously invest in Navalny. I would love to be a part of a big story. I can do this. But only if they played to win."

"How *would* you destroy Putin?" I asked.

Leonid went to the fridge, opened the freezer, and pulled

out a baggie with what looked like a year's supply of acid for the *Pet Sounds*–era Beach Boys and their studio orchestra. He offered me two blots; I declined, citing my neurotic fear of any and all hallucinogens.

"No opposition will topple Putin," he said. "But you know what will? A three-day general strike. The State Department doesn't know what they should be financing. If they finance a Metro strike in Moscow starting Monday, Putin's regime would be done by Thursday." He gave me that look again, perhaps expecting me to reply that I would promptly relay his proposal to Ambassador McFaul.

"All right," I finally said. "I'm going to go."

"Are you sure?" he said, brandishing the acid. "You really should try it. It makes you feel like a mythic Greek warrior standing on the oceanfront."

"I'm good."

Leonid then gave me two joints as a souvenir, and I was off. This was the last time we met in person. From what I gather, the State Department didn't take him up on his offer. At present, he runs a minor cable channel owned by Gazprom.

◼

The election day came and went. Lily and I went to a polling station across the street from our apartment, in the Central Telegraph building, where Lily, who had kept her Russian citizenship, dutifully voted for Mikhail Prokhorov. Filipp Dzyadko's brother Timofei, posted to the precinct as an observer, walked around filming everything on an iPad. As we walked out, a silent group of soldiers in uniform, marching in step, walked in. Moving as one pink-flecked khaki snake, they bypassed the line and were led straight to the ballot box. "Well," Lily deadpanned, "so much for my vote."

A few hours later, with only a quarter of the ballots counted, Churov's wizardly Central Election Commission called the election for Putin. The official result ascribed to him 63.6 percent of the vote. Stanislav Govorukhin, Putin's campaign manager, called a press conference and proclaimed the election "the cleanest in Russian history." The number's realism was indeed notable. Perhaps it was designed as a little show of humility—or, who knows, even reflected the real vote tally.

Even less manufactured-seeming were the results in Moscow, where Mikhail Prokhorov actually came in second, pushing Putin below the 50 percent barrier in the federal region for the first time since 2000. What felt, for a second, like a symbolic little win for the opposition was in fact a disaster. In Putin's camp, there were only two lessons to derive from the Prokhorov experiment: one, Moscow was irretrievably lost, and thus all of Medvedev's little flirtations with its Westernized middle class had been pointless; and two, if even a transparent Kremlin plant running the laziest imaginable campaign could end up consolidating the protest vote, someone like Navalny must never, in any circumstances, be allowed on the ballot.

At night, the victory rally filled the Manezh Square, where Tverskaya met the Kremlin, and the sounds of the celebration shook our windowpanes. It was strange to actually hear Putin from a couple of hundred yards away. The once and future president's speech would soon become famous for something we couldn't hear, and only TV cameras could see, at the moment: shortly before speaking, Putin's right eye suddenly watered and shed what the next morning's press termed "tears of happiness." A less romantic theory blamed the stinging wind. Whatever the reason, it certainly wasn't the speech itself, whose gist could be boiled down to "I told you we'd win, and we won." Its scant 195 words contained only one interesting thesis: "This was a test," Putin said, "and we showed that, truly, no one can impose anything on us. No one, nothing! We showed that our people are truly capable of distinguishing between a wish for renovation and political provocations aimed only at destroying Russia's statehood and usurping power." It was clear that he didn't mean his ballot competition—what could Prokhorov possibly "impose"? The only logical reading of this statement was the intended one: by reelecting Putin, the Russian people had beaten back Gosdep.

As with all of Putin's election events, this one was partly staged. One of the several spots where the rally's paid attendees lined up to receive their fee happened to be in an arch leading from Tverskaya Street into our building's backyard. The same backyard had a little twenty-four-hour shop for life's barest necessities, which included vodka, and that's where many revelers headed as soon as the cash was in their hands. By the morning of March 5, empty bottles of cheap booze and starbursts of vomit strewed the yard.

That day's inevitable protest rally ended up on Pushkin Square: Moscow's City Hall hadn't granted the opposition the permits for Lubyanka or the Manezh Square, two locations closer to the seats of actual power. The rally's official slogan, as before, was "For Fair Elections," but, for the first time in four months, it felt defanged. Despite the usual irregularities—the bused-in voters, the improbable 100 percent turnouts in places like Chechnya, the tales of workers and teachers and retirees pressured to give their votes to Putin under various respective threats—despite it all, nearly everyone knew that Putin's ingeniously un-dictatorial 63.6 percent reflected something like the actual state of things. Ever since December 4, 2011, the opposition's two main animating forces were outrage at having been demonstrably cheated out of its franchise and the thrilling hope encapsulated in one of the early protests' most memorable slogans: "There are more of us than you think." It was now time to start entertaining the idea that, even in the fairest of contests, most Russians would still prefer Putin—especially if their TV kept telling them that his alternatives were American stooges. They might not like the regime enough to go celebrate its successful self-perpetuation for free, or even enough to give their vote to it without an institutional stick-and-carrot combo, but they sure liked uncertainty even less. To grow beyond its elite base, the white-ribbon insurgency would now have to choose between two ancient strategies: turn more populist or go underground, become the Tea Party or the IRA. It was hard to say which option seemed more nauseating at the moment. The truth of it was, very few *hated* the regime enough, either.

All the more bewildering was the speed with which the regime provided a reason to.

The permit for the Pushkin Square rally was a picture of lordly largesse: for the protesters' convenience, the Boulevard Ring traffic was cordoned off, and if enough people showed up, the city had promised to close down Tverskaya as well. But it also had a time limit—it gave the square to the people until 8:00 p.m. sharp. The deadline came and went, but a core group of protesters didn't want to disperse. The presence of two Duma deputies—the father-and-son team of Gennady and Dmitry Gudkov—gave the crowd a kind of diplomatic cover under the Russian constitutional law, as a deputy's "meeting with the electorate" was a legal format for a spontaneous public gathering. The letter of the law only held for so long. At 9:40, the OMON riot police units moved in. Andrew Ryvkin, who was covering the rally for Politblog, managed to escape by clambering up the stairs to the Pushkin cinema with Joshua Yaffa of *Foreign Affairs*; their less lucky colleague Simon Shuster of *Time* ended up briefly arrested. Looking down into the square, they could see the riot police arresting Navalny. Sergei Udaltsov, the neo-Communist firebrand who had become a kind of Navalny for the hard left, climbed into the empty basin of a nearby stone fountain with a group of supporters and refused to leave; the OMON, ignoring hundreds of phone cameras trained on the scene, roughly dragged them out. An aide to Gudkov had his arm broken. The emerging picture left little room for interpretation: only twenty-two hours after Putin shed "tears of happiness" at his victory rally, two of his most popular detractors were (back) in jail. Anyone still dreaming of "forced liberalization" from above had their answer now: that window, if it was ever open in the first place, had just been slammed on their fingers. More important, those itching to mix it up with the "traitors" but temporarily reined in by the opacity of the big boss's intentions had received their green light.

The next morning, March 6, Ryvkin filed his eyewitness report from the *GQ* offices (key sentence: "No one expected the guy to go Full Gaddafi quite this fast") and left to do an interview at Interfax, a newswire whose Pushkin Square headquarters overlooked the site of the night's arrests. Ten minutes later, my phone rang. It was Ryvkin again.

"Hey," he said, sounding more perplexed than anything. "Minaev and Bagirov just beat the shit out of me."

"What?!"

"You heard me."

"Get the fuck back to the office."

Ryvkin came in disheveled and sporting a shiner. The "Interfax interview" was a ruse: the pro-Putin novelist duo Sergei Minaev and Eduard Bagirov had lured him out with it and then jumped him at the building's entrance. At some point, Ryvkin said, the police saw the beating and tried to intervene. Bagirov showed them a red ID card that made them immediately vanish. The whole thing was apparently payback for Ryvkin's tweet disparaging their publishing venture as "whorish."

It all seemed too bizarre to comprehend—but first things first. Volobuev and I put Ryvkin up in my office; all three of us, it needs to be noted, were giggling hysterically. I recorded Ryvkin's informal deposition on my phone, made him call the cops and a hospital, opened a bottle of an advertiser's whiskey, and poured us all a double. Masha, my assistant, came in with a first-aid kit and an ice tray to offer a cold compress; Ryvkin threw the ice into the whiskey instead. It was all very *Mad Men*.

Meanwhile, press requests streamed in, from the pro-Putin tabloid website LifeNews to the liberal Lenta.ru to *The Guardian* to, ironically, Interfax. For the rest of the day, Ryvkin was ensconced in my office running a bilingual junket. Ksenia Sobchak called in from one of her myriad radio shows. Navalny tweeted about it, apparently from jail. On a day with lots of other grim news to process, this idiotic fracas was somehow a number-one topic. The beatdown had transformed Ryvkin into my biggest commodity.

He was also enjoying this status a bit too much for comfort—to such extent, in fact, that I began to worry that he had made up the incident, or coordinated it with Minaev, with whom he had had some vague previous dealings. I still couldn't believe that a Putin surrogate, and the millionaire novelist who had patronized me at Meat Club, would be this dumb and careless. My unspoken worries went away when both gleefully incriminated themselves all over Twitter. Whatever that red ID was, these guys truly felt invincible. Their groupies cheered them on, calling Ryvkin a wimp and worse. A TV personality named Dmitry Gubin managed to call *me* a wimp for not joining the literal fight: "That's right, Mr. Idov, you're not in New York anymore," he wrote. "In Moscow the editors, when their colleagues are beaten, go after the offenders. Bakhtin [the editor in chief of *Esquire*] would have let them all have it." Russia's frozen machismo, as always, was a sight to behold.

I did, in fact, limit my comments to a short Politblog post in which I simply announced that we'd pursue the attackers in court. Some of the public reaction fell under the rubric of "those

PC Americans will sue you if you look at them wrong." But the assailants were clearly freaked out by the post's calm litigiousness, which was the whole point. Bagirov wrote a threatening tweet about me but quickly deleted it, having either lawyered up or grown sensible for a second. A friend wrote to me from a rock concert: "I am standing behind Minaev. He is typing on his iPhone, 'only if he is hospitalized. Otherwise you can get off.' I can accidentally spill some juice on him."

"Please do."

He did, and sent me a photo.

It took only twenty-four more hours for the police to drop Ryvkin's case against the duo. "You must understand," a detective told him, "they're famous dudes. Sorry, but that's the way the law works here." Bagirov immediately went back on Twitter and publicly promised to "break [Ryvkin's] fucking face again." And this time, there was nothing legal that could be done to stop him or, for that matter, anyone else emboldened by the new directives from the top. The only remaining question was how much more juice we had to spill, and how fast we could run after we spilled it.

Chapter Five

The One-Two
Punch, Part Two

O n any given day, a crew of Lenin, Stalin, and Brezhnev impersonators worked the underpass near my house. The walkway, humid from collective breath and filled with the sour smell of dough, gave Tverskaya pedestrians their only option for reaching Red Square, and was thus a literal tourist trap. Another Lenin could be found outside, by the Voskresenskie gates at the mouth of the square, competing for tourists' attention with a macaque in a tiny parka. The macaque wasn't trained to do anything special, except not die in the cold. The Soviet dictators took things equally easy. I don't think I ever saw them engage in active impersonation—they just milled about catcalling girls. All verisimilitude hinged on facial hair: the Brezhnev could just as easily stick his eyebrows under his nose and become a Stalin. Perhaps that's why Khrushchev was never included in this group. True tyrants are generally great at turning themselves into laconic logos, but all you needed for a Khrushchev impersonation was to be a bald man in an ill-fitting suit; half the passing crowd would qualify.

As I crossed Red Square on my grotesquely scenic grocery runs—it was a shortcut to the nearest decent food store—I fell into the habit of watching the dictators. On this particular March day, a lone Stalin was going about his business; a scene unfolding a hundred feet away, however, would warm the heart of the real McCoy. That's where a swarm of policemen were arresting a group of people for wearing white ribbons.

Granted, the cops didn't go full Stalin right away. They began with a somewhat abashed lie that the square was "closed for parade preparations," though the Victory Day parade was over a month away. Then they appealed to unspecified "technical reasons." It was only when neither lie had convinced the protesters to leave that they just started to haul people off, arresting thirty-four all in all. None ended up with any charges; a trip uptown in a drafty *avtozak* (prisoner transport vehicle) was punishment enough for now.

In the short history of the protests, this was a first. The protesters were carrying no banners, chanting no chants. Thus, costume was destiny. Dressing as a cop gave you authority—no more or less ephemeral than whatever law underpinned the arrests. Dressing as a murderous dictator gave you a free pass to solicit nearby. My tweed armor gave me enough invisibility to walk by unmolested. And pinning a white ribbon on any of the above landed you in jail.

The ides of March were here. On the fifteenth, Sergei Udaltsov, in jail for his fountain antics on Pushkin Square, began another in a series of hunger strikes. Alexei Kozlov, the businessman husband of Olga Romanova—the rallies' treasurer, whose so-called Romanova's purse had entered the white-ribbon vocabulary—received a five-year prison sentence for insider trading on a flimsy case. NTV ran a prime-time "exposé" titled "The Anatomy of a Protest," which used staged scenes to suggest that the opposition had been paying people to show up at its rallies (yet another straightforward case of accusing your opponent of the exact thing you've been doing). The liberal Internet reacted with fruitless calls for a boycott of NTV's Western advertisers—as if a Russian state channel's business model depended on Depends. Ignored in the day's noise was the writer Masha Gessen's left-field suggestion of a tourist boycott of the city of St. Petersburg: a brand-new law on its books would punish something called "gay propaganda," which seemed like minor lunacy at the moment. Looking back, I can't help thinking that focusing on the anti-gay law while it was local and defeatable would have been much more fruitful than tilting at NTV. A mere year after its mocked but largely unopposed test run, it would sail through the Duma and become a nationwide tool of oppression.

And what was I doing that day? Eating eclairs with 150 luxury marketers at Casta Diva, an absurdly opulent restaurant on Tverskoy Boulevard. My boss, Karina Dobrotvorskaya, had organized the "breakfast" as my official rollout in front of GQ's antsy advertisers, many of whom professed discomfort at the magazine's new direction; I was there to calm their fears about GQ becoming "populist" or "political." I did reasonably well; at least no one fainted, stormed out, or pulled their ads on the spot. Outside the restaurant, OMON buses and mobile jails were moving into position for another spontaneous protest on Pushkin Square.

Three of the advertisers were too high-level for this mass

approach and required one-on-one hand-holding. I had to meet them all the same day—Prada, Ralph Lauren, and Philipp Plein, the latter represented by Plein himself, a tan German in a leather-trimmed blazer and a black shirt whose four undone buttons showed off his waxed chest. He fancied himself the new Tom Ford. Plein's stuff was the absolute worst—pseudo–rock 'n' roll *schmatta* made in ostrich and crocodile leather, adorned with Swarovski skulls and such, and sold for the price of a midsize sedan. He knew what he was doing, though: this garbage appealed directly to the aging Rublevka oligarchs looking to recapture their edge. Plein handled all his ads himself, and took out plenty of them. Naturally, he had been great friends with my predecessor, Uskov. Plein, too, asked me if the magazine was about to reduce fashion coverage and "drop the luxury angle." He then proposed a great way to undo the damage to the brand: how about we, *GQ*, put him, Philipp Plein, on the cover, surrounded by sexy models and photographed by Terry Richardson?

I said something vague and left alongside my now openly panicking publisher. I had, in fact, increased fashion coverage by ten to fifteen pages off the bat. I just *looked* like a guy who would reduce it. That was the difference between me and Uskov—he genuinely loved this stuff, all of it, uncritically, as a lifestyle. With me, well, things were a little more complicated.

I like men's fashion. More to the point, I like it as a smart system of codes. I believe that, by refusing to learn these codes, a man denies himself an avenue of self-expression; in fact, he ends up using them anyway, only blindly, like the proverbial white tourist who doesn't know what her new Mandarin tattoo says. One of my most vivid, and livid, memories as a fresh arrival in the United States is my Cleveland classmates' laughing at my thrift-store T-shirt. At the moment, every Midwestern high schooler wore duvet-size white Ts influenced by gangsta rap; mine was a peach-colored

1970s ring-collar type that said REGGAE over the picture of a rainbow beaming out of a guitar. In about eight more years, this kind of thing would return on the backs of the Strokes et al., as an ironic affectation of poverty; my poverty in 1992, however, was quite real. This was a twenty-five-cent T-shirt from a twenty-five-cent bin at a Cleveland Goodwill. The fact that it had a guitar on it, as opposed to, say, a dried bloodstain, was already a tiny triumph.

"What, you like reggae? You listen to a lot of reggae in Russia?" someone scoffed. "It's just a T-shirt," I muttered, mortified. But it wasn't; it never is. It was a declaration of low social standing, of beta masculinity, and beyond all else of total incompatibility between my sense of humor and the interlocutor's, whose own T-shirt read BIG JOHNSON'S BAR: LIQUOR IN THE FRONT, POKER IN THE BACK.

Since then, I had tried on a few sartorial personas and eventually even developed a sort of personal style, best described as "bland plus one unexpected piece." In college, that piece more often than not was an Al Pacino–esque vintage leather coat; in New York, if and when I could afford it, something from Comme des Garçons and the like. In the late aughts, I hung a dandyish detour into Savile Row shirts and bespoke suits (always the sharp-shouldered British kind), precisely because I didn't *have* to wear a suit to work. At the time, I would chalk it up to "maturity." Ironically, it now strikes me as the most adolescent thing I ever did fashionwise—a painfully obvious bit of ostentation, kicking in just as my writing finally began to pay. Finally, as a synthesis, I had arrived at a kind of severe essentialism wherein I'd use name brands for the one item that made their name, no matter how high or low: Burberry=trench coat, Tod's=loafers, Ray-Ban=Wayfarers, Barbour=waxed jacket, Filson=shoulder bag, etc. For the basics, there was the omnipresent benevolent fascism of Uniqlo. My favorite overall maker of clothing, in the off chance anyone cares, was and remains Rag & Bone.

This, however, was not the view of fashion required of me now. I was expected to get more excited about expensive things than cheap ones, and the new more than the old. I would also have to forget my Anglophilia. Russia was all about Italy. In the early 1990s, as the Soviet Union fell, Versace and Dolce & Gabbana were the first two fashion houses to open boutiques in Moscow; their quick reflexes keep paying dividends to this day, since these two brands have basically shaped the Russian man's idea of looking good.* As a result, a country whose climate, not to mention burly physiques, might suggest looking to Berlin and Stockholm for fashion cues, ended up clumsily appropriating Milan's *sprezzatura*. Russia's Italophilia ran so deep that there existed several Italian, or "Italian," brands that catered exclusively to Russians, unknown back home. Bosco di Ciliegi, one of our two biggest advertisers, was a Russian firm that had translated its name ("Cherry Forest") to sound posher. It operated the grand GUM store on Red Square, itself a czarist-era copy of Milan's Galleria. Even its ultra-expensive Bosco Café, which juts out into Russia's central square for a direct view of Lenin's tomb, blithely served Italian food.

Most important, I was supposed to forswear my essentialism and embrace every brand's relentless, cynical diffusion into every trade under the sun. This meant enthusiastically championing things like Burberry perfumes, Brioni glasses, and Gucci watches. Watches in general were the bane of my existence; I simply didn't care about them enough one way or another. They were jewelry, with added geekspeak about movements and tourbillions to make it okay for straight dudes to covet. Admittedly, I also knew very little about them. On one of my first days at the magazine, I embarrassed

---

*Decades earlier, a similar process occurred in music, with Adriano Celentano and Toto Cutugno embraced by the same Soviet radio that wouldn't even conceive of playing, say, the Rolling Stones; one could argue that Italo disco remains Russian pop music's stylistic polestar to this day.

myself by pronouncing the first half of Jaeger-LeCoultre as "Jäger," not "Zhe-Zhe"; it was almost as bad as that famous bit in *Showgirls* where Elizabeth Berkley says, "Ver-sayss." This was a massive liability because, as I learned, the watches were incredibly important to the magazine's well-being—perhaps more so than anything else. Here's why: The American *GQ*'s advertisers had a target audience of, let's say, three hundred thousand men who might buy a three-thousand-dollar suit. The Russians were trying to reach the three thousand men around Rublevka who might buy a three-hundred-thousand-dollar timepiece.

So, this, in short, was my job: to figure out what Rublevka liked and to wrap it around a watch. And what Rublevka liked was Ksenia Sobchak, and her brand of mild dissent rolled into high-society gossip. Instead, I was giving them the Kermlins' scorched-earth satire, Ryvkin's Politblog, Volobuev's acidic essays, and an editor in chief in a ten-dollar Carhartt hat. At least, I told myself, the upcoming May issue might assuage some worries. Like many of my colleagues the world over, I was going all in on *Mad Men*.

The prestige-TV series about elegantly suffering ad executives was the perfect point where any magazine's materialistic and high-minded sides could meet. You could decode its John Cheever references on one page and analyze its characters' pocket squares on the next. "*Mad Men* is such an absolute brand fit for us," Dylan Jones, the kingpin of the British *GQ*, once marveled to a roomful of international editors. "We have to write about it. We can't not write about it. If it didn't exist, we would have to create it. Too bad we can't make people watch it!" Even *Mad Men*'s minuscule ratings, however, wouldn't stop us from cramming it down the world's throat. Luckily, it aired in Russia, too—on the Kremlin-controlled Channel One, to boot. So my next issue would have Jon Hamm on the cover and a rich *Mad Men* package to go with it: an essay by Volobuev, three exclusive interviews with cast members (procured via superhuman effort and old connections), a story about advertising, and finally an original comic by a *New Yorker* cartoonist. The latter used speech bubbles as a purely decorative element (one, for instance, just read, "blah blah blah"), which I figured I could run without translation.

The day was almost done. I looked over the *Mad Men* pages one more time, caught some typos, signed the proofs, and started putting on my coat to leave. The desk phone rang. It was the publisher again.

"Is everything okay?" I was half-expecting yet another advertiser emergency. Maybe Philipp Plein didn't feel admired enough. Turned out she was only asking me to translate all legible words in the comic into Russian; this didn't seem crucial. I felt some relief.

"Sure," I said. "I mean, I'd rather not, but if that's the rule . . ."

"It's not. But *you* have to watch out for this sort of thing," the publisher said. "As it is, we're already battling the perception that the Russian language is disappearing from *GQ*."

"We're battling *what*?"

"Go check Facebook."

For the past few months of my life, these words had meant nothing but trouble. It probably wasn't a cat video.

Seconds later, I was reading two public posts by one Eduard Dorozhkin, the deputy editor of *Tatler*. The *Tatler* people sat four floors down from us; the magazine they put out was an experiment in engaging the Rublevka crowd head-on. It was a gossip magazine for, about, and partly by Russian high society. Its popular last-page feature, called "A Million Dollar Baby," was a showcase for nubile heiresses, some as young as fourteen years old; *Tatler* also ran an annual debutante ball for them. Though our audiences overlapped, it read like a monthly dispatch from a wholly different solar system than *GQ* or even *Vogue*. Dorozhkin was, by all accounts, *Tatler*'s least dispensable employee: he wrote most of the magazine himself. He also had a lucrative sideline scalping tickets to the

Bolshoi via mass e-mail blasts, which was the only context in which I had heard his name. I must have met him in the Fur Fridge's stairwells and elevators, but I had no idea what he looked like. Conversely, Dorozhkin had devoted some amount of time and thought to my person, and had studied *GQ*'s April issue until he found a slightly misused word.

"Of course, people who were taught to speak on Brighton Beach don't understand such nuances," he wrote. "I expect Brighton to fully rear its head in the next issue." He then gave a few examples of the caricatured argot spoken by Russian Jewish émigrés in Brooklyn (and thus, supposedly, me). For the first few moments, my mind was too boggled by the pettiness. Then I realized something that should have been clear from the beginning: "Brighton Beach" was a code word for "Jewish." I hadn't given it a moment's consideration before, but I was, in fact, *GQ Russia*'s first Jewish editor.* Could *this* be rubbing Russians the wrong way? Even more than my being American?

Putin's Russia, for all its faults, was not an institutionally anti-Semitic state. This represented an epochal improvement over the U.S.S.R., whose university-admission quotas for Jews were no less real for being unwritten. If anything, Putin went out of his way to include the Jewish community leaders in as many photo ops as possible and personally attended the opening of Moscow's lavishly funded Jewish Museum. Like any number of political systems in the world, Russia's tolerated a certain share of people who preferred to blame their misfortunes on a mystical cabal of hook-nosed moneylenders, and, as in many countries—including the United States—its leaders were not above using their rage as political lighter fluid for their own ends. At the same time, many of these

---

*And the second, after Art Cooper, in the entire *GQ* universe, if I'm not mistaken—not that "Jewish Man Edits Magazine" is much of a historical milestone.

very people seriously considered Putin the evil Jews' protégé. Ironically, a more accurate picture of baseline Russian bigotry could be gotten from Alexei Navalny's brand of casual nationalism—where Muslims from the Caucasus elicited genuine prejudice (Navalny once retweeted a goat-sex meme), and the Jews merited merely a benevolent yet annoying hyperawareness: a Jew was seen as a peer but also kinda hilarious.

My Latvian childhood, on the other hand, had been filled with the kind of casual street harassment that the Soviet Jews learned, and taught their children, to just ignore. Once, as I've mentioned, three drunks attacked my father and myself around the corner from our house; only my father's brawling skills—he knocked down two men out of the three—saved me from serious trauma. Another nightmarish memory: a game arcade, an older teen (I am eleven or twelve) hissing, over and over, "Eww, a kike is here—now the room stinks like piss!" into my spit-flecked ear as I, mortified, try to concentrate on my *Street Fighter*. And then, of course, there were the subtler jabs—the jokes, the patronizing praise for the oh-so-smart *evreichik*, the weird instinctive lowering of the voice that many older Russians still employ when simply uttering the word *Jew*. And each and every time, I would just freeze up, do nothing, go home, and collapse into bed murmuring unsaid comebacks, dizzy with hate.

That's how I felt now. It wasn't just about Dorozhkin, of course. It was my helplessness in the face of everything: Ryvkin's beating, the fizzling protests, the idiocies of the job. A red rage-mist curtaining my field of vision, I found myself on the seventh floor, completely cognizant of the fact that I was there to break Dorozhkin's nose. Thankfully, he had gone home. Only his timing saved Moscow from having to wake up to "Editor of *GQ* Assaults Deputy Editor of *Tatler*" headlines.

Adrenaline-sick but now more or less in control of myself,

I went back upstairs and called in Roman Volobuev and Gosha Birger to ask their advice. The two proceeded to metaphorically perch on my left and right shoulders, with Volobuev exhorting me to kick Dorozhkin's ass and Birger insisting on a written complaint. In the middle of the agitated discussion, Birger absentmindedly picked up a new issue of *Vogue*, unglued a perfume sample strip, and smelled it, which for some reason made me collapse with laughter. The fugue was over. I decided to forgive and forget.

The next morning, the editor of *Tatler* e-mailed me. She had heard of my wild-eyed visit from the receptionist—I must have made quite an impression—and jokingly promised to censure Dorozhkin. Nothing happened; the posts stayed up. A few days later I ran into Dorozhkin himself, whom I'd now learned to recognize from Facebook, in the Fur Fridge lobby. He was a large, ruddy-faced fellow with small porcine eyes and a patchy red beard. His affect suggested open gayness, which made me want to resolve things peacefully even more; not only did I admire the Russians who had enough guts to be out in this cultural climate, but I also didn't want to counter his anti-Semitism with anything that might look on my part like homophobia.

"Hey," I said. "Next time you have something to say about me, do you want to just talk, maybe?" He stammered that he was merely protecting the purity of the Russian language.

His next post came from a business trip to New York. Dorozhkin found the city disgusting. After a few sentences about the subpar quality of its gay bathhouses, he arrived at the following kicker: "No wonder that certain Jew writers from the projects of Brighton Beach can't wait to leave [New York] for the glory and the titles of Moscow, specifically the titles of editors-in-chief at glossy magazines." Well, at least he couldn't claim he was protecting the language anymore.

I wrote to my bosses. No reaction. *Tatler*'s EIC joked her way out of it again. There was no way to make this stop. And, weirdest of all, "this" wasn't an anonymous web troll—it was a fellow Condé Nast editor, working four floors down, Jew-baiting me with complete impunity. Just like in my childhood, just like in that arcade, I did nothing. I'd whine to Lily. At work—where I now, naturally, kept bumping into Dorozhkin—I would look down or stare at my phone. On the way to and from the eleventh floor, I cringed every time the elevator stopped on the seventh. I concocted a feverish fantasy of going to *Tatler*'s ridiculous debutante ball and confronting him there, among the oil magnates and the daughters of the oil magnates, and the other oil magnates scoping them out for brides. That same day, however, my assistant, Masha, came to work with a swollen nose: she had gotten into a hack cab the previous night, and a man hiding in the backseat knocked her on the head and robbed her of an iPhone. I took this as a signal not to add to the violence of Moscow.

My pacifism lasted until *Swan Lake*. I am sadly indifferent to classical ballet, but Cartier sent us two free tickets (which normally ran to five hundred dollars each) and Lily had wanted to go to the Bolshoi for ages, and so we went. The great theater had just undergone a gut renovation that had lasted six years, cost more than a billion dollars, and left its insides looking like a banquet hall at a Ramada. Swans swanned, Nikolai Tsiskaridze as the Dark Prince pranced about like a circus devil, I drifted in and out of light sleep. And then, at coat check, I once again bumped into Dorozhkin. Of course he'd be there, too; his ticket scalping made the Bolshoi his second place of employment.

Once again I froze up and pretended not to see him, and once again I began whining to my wife about my inability to act, a schlumpy little stump speech I had delivered dozens of times before. My night already ruined, I knew I was now ruining hers, too, but I couldn't stop myself.

"You know what?" Lily cut in. "This is ridiculous. You've convinced me. Go hit him."

"Are you sure?"

"Just slap him. Don't cause any damage. Make it a gesture." Lily had gone to Columbia Law School.

Dorozhkin was standing about fifty feet away, on the theater's front steps, smoking with two theater ladies in evening dresses. I was wearing a suit jacket, a tie, and a formal coat. This was, indeed, ridiculous. I gave Lily my phone and walked over.

"Excuse me, I'll need to borrow him for a minute," I said to the women, taking Dorozhkin by the elbow and trying to lead him aside. "All right. Let's go sort this out."

"I know you're a boxer," he said out of the blue, his eyes darting side to side.

"What? I'm not a boxer."

"I'm not going anywhere."

"Should I fight you here, then?"

"I'm not going to fight you."

"Michael, this is ungentlemanly," said one of the women. They apparently knew me.

"Fine," I said, and opened my palm, slapped Dorozhkin across the cheek, and walked off. My mood improved at once.

"Ummm, I'm sort of proud of you?" said Lily tentatively, handing me back the phone.

Did this make me a hypocrite regarding the Ryvkin beating? Was my physical response to online abuse any more justifiable than Minaev and Bagirov's? I don't know. Maybe. Theirs involved two men laying a trap for one. Mine was a courtly slap in response to sustained viciousness. But I did come down to the level of Moscow. I allowed myself to be judged by the very set of *quién es más macho* criteria I claimed to ignore.

As expected, Dorozhkin took to Facebook at once—to rather

competently build an assault case against me. He described the incident, subtly tweaking the verbs so it sounded like I had hit him with my fist. He repeated the weird assertion that I was a pro boxer, which he seemed to genuinely believe, and claimed to be a survivor of four concussions, so any touch to his head was potentially fatal. He was going home to "try to live through this," he wrote, to the cops next, and to physical therapy after that. I was now officially a bully and a thug. Thankfully, on the steps of the Bolshoi on a *Swan Lake* night, there would be plenty of witnesses. The story ended as it began: as empty vitriol on a virtual page.

I had no desire to broadcast my side of it. What a strange, tiresome world have we built for ourselves: as people go from action to its description in near-real time, the action itself becomes just a news peg. Everyone is carrying their own spin room, at all times. After Dorozhkin's post, though, I figured I needed to say something.

"I'm not a boxer," I wrote after some deliberation. "I'm a Yorkie."

The next day, I ran into Karina Dobrotvorskaya at a restaurant. "Aah! Don't beat me!" the boss said, playfully throwing up her hands. So, I guess, I wasn't getting fired. No one got fired in Russia. Except, amazingly, Dorozhkin himself, whom Dobrotvorskaya proceeded to sack twenty-four hours later. Perhaps the portly Jewish girl with the last name Zaks was still in there somewhere. Or maybe it was her parting gift to me: Karina was leaving Moscow to become Condé Nast International's president of brand development, with over 120 magazines in her purview. *Tatler*, of course, immediately hired Dorozhkin back as a freelancer—someone had to write the magazine, after all.

The opposition was grappling with a related quandary to mine, writ much, much larger. With every new arrest, the state was testing the limits of its impunity; with every new gathering broken up, the protesters faced the same choice—go limp or punch back, amp up the anger or hope that the police somehow condemn themselves by overreaching (and creating an iconic protest visual in the process). On April 1, the white ribbons returned to Red Square. This time, only a couple of hundred protesters showed up, mostly hardcore *demshiza* types (a pejorative portmanteau of "democratic" and "schizophrenic," which even the Russian liberals themselves used to describe the permanently outraged yet somehow privileged demographic at the center of the movement). Sergei Parkhomenko, the bearded editor and publisher, appeared to be calling the shots. To me, the demonstration felt like a return to the failed "Strategy 31" days, when the demshiza would just show up on city squares on the thirty-first of every month that had thirty-one days, in order to call attention to the Constitution's Article 31 (freedom of assembly). It was like the Bolotnaya and Sakharov Square protests had never happened.

This time, however, the government had an entirely new response. It shut down Red Square, the country's main attraction, for the rest of the day. All of it. Several policemen hastily closed the Voskresenskie gates, pinching off the protest before it could reach the square, and locked them. Lenin, Stalin, Putin, and the macaque looked on, impassive.

The gap between the puny threat and the drastic response was jaw-dropping. Thousands of foreign and domestic tourists didn't get to shop at GUM or see Lenin's tomb. The financial cost (including to GUM's owners Bosco di Ciliegi, a private company) must have been massive. Disbelieving my eyes, I tried to approach from a side street and found two cops hastily blocking it off with metal barriers. Beyond them, the slightly concave expanse of the great square lay empty, wet cobblestone gleaming like caviar. "Sir, why is everything closed?" I asked, adopting my best version of fast-blinking provincial innocence. "For technical reasons," one of the cops mumbled. "And for how long?" "Until tomorrow." "But I'm flying back to Novosibirsk tomorrow!" "Can't help ya."

Shut out of the square, the demonstrators began to tie their white ribbons to the locked gates. Then, for whatever reason, the remaining hundred or so people decided to walk in a circle holding hands. For this crime, the cops arrested eighty-six of them, ripping them out of the circle one by one. The arrestees either complied, in a slightly somnambulant way, or went limp. Behind them, the human carousel linked back up, the circle growing smaller every time. When it was down to Parkhomenko and a few diehards, I turned around and went home, feeling uniformly disgusted with everything and everyone, including myself.

The next Sunday, April 8, the protesters came back for thirds, this time led again by the former deputy prime minister Boris Nemtsov. More arrests. Fewer attendees. Same white ribbons, same gray OMON buses. It was clear that things had arrived at some sort of impasse. The people had taken all the selfies, shouted all the slogans, and written all the clever placards they could. Now what? The demshiza members of the Orgkomitet kept trying to convince the realist faction, represented by Saprykin and other nonpoliticians, that the protests could at any moment crescendo into the Ukraine 2004 scenario—say, a permanent tent city on a central square. Never mind that the Ukrainians had a presidential candidate, Viktor Yushchenko, who'd had victory ripped away from him; all the Russians had was abstract principle and a swelling catalog of unlawful detentions to protest. "I have to confess a terrible sin," Saprykin mused in an April column. "I don't really believe in the escalation . . . the idea of 'fair elections,' in and of itself, isn't particularly inspiring.

"If the new leaders of the opposition," he went on, meaning Navalny and Udaltsov, "decide that the only way forward is to throw themselves on the bayonets, this will be a monstrous mistake. The problem is not that the protest in its peaceful and legal form just isn't threatening enough to the government. The problem is that its social base, after a few months' growth spurt, has hit the ceiling."

If the movement was choking in real life, you wouldn't be able to tell it from the Western magazines, which had finally caught up with it. The upheaval was certainly good to Moscow's chattering classes. I had never seen so many Russian bylines in the American press. Dmitry Golubovsky (the editor of Russian *Esquire*) in American *Esquire*, Masha Gessen in *Vanity Fair* and everywhere, Volobuev quoted in *The New York Times*, myself in *Time* bloviating about the already-irrelevant Prokhorov—this haul came from a single trip to an international magazine rack.

The U.S. media were buying the most romantic version of what we were selling. All of a sudden Moscow teemed with postgrad do-gooders, NGO lifers, think tankers, academic writers on fancy grants, each and every one in the twinkly-eyed "What do you need? How can we help?" mode, the mode that the rest of the world mistakes for malicious meddling and that in fact is a kind of adolescent excitability mixed in with unconscious condescension. A woman from *New England Review*, of all places, called me for Krasilshchik's and Faybisovich's phone numbers, though she was unable to pronounce either of their names and not particularly willing to try. "Don't worry, my husband and I are experts in revolutions," she said when I wavered. "We covered Hungary in the 1980s."

The possible apogee of this ridiculous phase was the dinner meeting between Garry Kasparov and a quartet of visiting American PEN Center officials. The powwow, which took place at a restaurant called the Sisters Grimm, was absurd from top to bottom—starting with PEN's evident impression that the former chess champion was anywhere close to a leadership role in this wave of the protests. I was told to come as well, at the last minute and for reasons unknown. The Sisters Grimm hid in a backyard less than a hundred meters from *GQ*'s offices, so I dashed right over.

The great master's features had softened since the time I, eight years old and as good a chess player as I'd ever be—which is to say, terrible—watched him eviscerate Anatoly Karpov.* His eyes, however, held the same coal-fire intensity. Around the champion sat four serious white men in button-down Oxfords, corduroy blazers, and whimsical sweaters. It became clear from the first few seconds of the conversation that I had been invited to this powwow as an "opposition"-affiliated editor. Something about this irked me. I would have been happy to see these very New York figures in any other context, but certainly not as a brave little Russian freedom warrior. Watching visiting Americans scramble to adjust the level on which to speak with me was quickly becoming one of my favorite pastimes; this time I managed to cram Farrar, Straus and Giroux, Binky Urban, *and* Christopher Hitchens into my opening sentence. All right? All right. Now we can talk.

Kasparov, however, was the one doing all the talking. And what he wanted to talk about was U.S. politics, on which he fancied himself an expert. A raging Republican, he despised Obama and was excitedly anticipating a Mitt Romney landslide come November. He also had some thoughts on Rick Santorum. The PEN people, obvious Democrats one and all, tried to steer the conversation back to the evils of Putin; Kasparov would have none of it. He was on a

---

*The epic 1984–85 duel, which stretched over two championships and during which Kasparov shrewdly tired his opponent out with an unprecedented series of forty draws, seemed like a metaphor for the perestroika itself: Karpov was dead-eyed and boring, Kasparov fiery and unpredictable. Needless to say, as Kasparov became one of Putin's harshest critics, Karpov remained firmly pro-Kremlin.

roll predicting which county in Florida was going to go which way and why. Most of what he said was dizzyingly detailed nonsense. Kasparov's bodyguard lounged a few feet away, reading a magazine. At some point, a female fan came to our table. "I admire you as a politician and a human being," she said. Then, with a sudden flourish, she thrust out her hand; in her palm was a chess piece, a black king. "This is for you," she said. "I was hoping to give this to you someday."

Kasparov thanked her, pocketed the king, and went back to discoursing on the electoral map of the United States until, rather abruptly, it was time for him to go. He had to fly to Capetown in the morning, he explained, and to Paris from there. Most of his days were spent on the international lecture circuit; he was also putting out a self-help book, aimed at executives, that would teach them to apply chess strategies in the boardroom. The moment Kasparov and his bodyguard stepped out, the button-down Oxfords looked at one another, dissolved into involuntary giggles, and spent the next hour mocking him like a gaggle of teenage girls. As we put on our coats, my eyes drifted to the restaurant's communal chess set, which was laid out near the entrance. Sure enough, it was missing a piece: the black king.

As April came into its own, the last patches of black ice melted into dirt, the boulevards ringed the center with green, and Moscow became its annual best self. Were it not for the tanks rehearsing the May 9 parade right outside my windows, life in the city's heart would be genuinely pleasant. Alas, there they rumbled, day and night, wrecking the asphalt and poisoning the air with diesel exhaust— just when the toxic sediment from the ice-melting chemicals had cleared and the smog hadn't yet set in. The Russians' unabating fixation on World War II, always encouraged from the top as one of the few things that could genuinely bring the nation together, had now acquired a more political aspect, too. The ribbon of St. George, a military symbol whose black and orange stripes originally symbolized gunpowder and fire, became the designated antithesis to the protesters' white ribbons: an all-purpose declaration of loyalty to the regime. The colors flew from the antennae and rearview mirrors of the same cars that had recently en masse begun to sport THANK GRANDPA FOR THE VICTORY window decals.* Youthful Nashi members passed them out in the streets by the handful. I even saw one on a Vespa. Next to our building, the city erected a cardboard cutout of a Soviet WWII-era machine gun, floating amid fluffy clouds in a wreath made of St. George's ribbons. You were supposed to pose for photos as if manning it, like an overarmed Cupid. Many did.

Before May 9, however, Moscow had another victory to celebrate: May 7 would see Vladimir Putin's third inauguration as president. The opposition prepared yet another protest for the eve of the event, the afternoon of May 6, dubbing it the March of Millions. At that point, I couldn't help rolling my eyes at the overconfidence. The wan weekly thing I watched on Red Square, combined and contrasted with the Western media's silly enthusiasm for the "revolution" (yes, it was now the time to throw scare quotes around the word), had left me depleted. Many felt the same. Saprykin, the novelist Boris Akunin, and other members of the original Orgkomitet decided to sit this one out; the march's official leader would

---

*It rhymes in the original. To wit, as Russia grew more belligerent, the tenor of the patriotic bumper sticker changed, too: in place of the thank-grandpa sentiment came TO BERLIN! (an allusion to a popular inscription on Soviet tanks, especially ironic when affixed to German-made cars), and an utterly bonkers cartoon of a stick figure with a hammer and sickle for a head sodomizing another stick figure with a swastika for a head. The inscription next to the figures read WE CAN DO IT AGAIN!

be Sergei Udaltsov, the nü-Communist who had taken his wedding photos in front of a Stalin portrait. When I woke up on May 6, I realized that this would be the first protest to which I couldn't be bothered to go.

It was Lily's late mother's birthday, so we went to visit her grave instead. Geralina Lyubarskaya, a famous Russian lawyer who had represented oligarchs and movie stars and, incidentally, Garry Kasparov, was buried at the Vostryakovskoe cemetery. The vast, tree-shaded necropolis used to be two separate cemeteries, one Orthodox Christian, one Jewish; there had been some mixing in the Soviet era, but the traditions still held. The two sides, no longer demarcated in any way, lay divided by a central alley. After the fall of the Soviet Union, the alley got narrowed down to make room for one more row on each side: the VIP graves.

Perhaps nowhere was the havoc that the post-Soviet history had wrought on Russia more evident than here. Marble monstrosities rose around us, three, four, five lots wide and up to two stories tall, some looking like a cross between Lenin's tomb and a Las Vegas gazebo. The giant slabs bore full engraved likenesses of the mostly Central Asian and Georgian men interred thereunder (even on the Jewish graves, despite the fact that Jewish law prohibits portraiture on them). All were men. Most died in their mid-thirties, and Russia's 1990s: risky business, whatever it was they were in. But it paid well, too, evidently. At least two of the men were depicted standing in the front room of a palatial mansion, with a checkered floor and a grand staircase. It was the same floor and the same staircase in both cases. I couldn't figure out whether they had come from the same household or the engraver just happened to offer a "mansion" option. The more modest graves behind them—Jewish surgeons and lawyers on the right, decorated Soviet Army officers on the left—were almost entirely obscured by these walls of gangster-chic marble, the way the formerly oceanfront

Art Deco buildings of Miami Beach's Collins Avenue are dwarfed by Trumpian skyscrapers.

Lily and I took the Metro home, only to find out that all four stops inside the Boulevard Ring—the ones from which we could conceivably walk home—were inexplicably functioning "for transfers only." *Ah, yes, of course, the March of Millions.* This, together with DDoS attacks on the opposition websites that would provide directions to or coverage of the march—including TV Rain and Echo of Moscow—was the authorities' unsubtle attempt to cut down attendance at the rally.* Within one month, the police had gone from shutting down Red Square to paralyzing the entire city center; if one were so inclined, one could read it as a sign of growing fear, but I was no longer so inclined. Lily and I got off the train miles away from home and, to kill time, went to see *The Avengers* movie, terribly dubbed into Russian.

We had no idea that, as a computer-generated Manhattan lay in ruins and superheroes traded wisecracks on the screen, a mile or so from the theater rocks flew and OMON helmets bobbed in the river, an indelible image of violent resistance. That day's altercation between the protesters and the troops would trigger a sustained, ferocious counterattack from the state that would make the words "May 6 prisoners" a key term of the next two years. The one rally I chose to miss would end up becoming the most important one of them all.

The accounts of what actually transpired on and near Bolotnaya Square diverge in all the obvious ways, and conspiracist

---

*Once again, as in the Red Square case, this tactic involved low-level public servants forced to mutter awkward lies. Lies have always been a hallmark of the Russian oppression apparatus, which, unlike its more flamboyant cousins, could never quite admit to its own evil. For example, when the Soviets blockaded West Berlin in 1948, they could have easily cited the duplicity of the capitalist allies, which had introduced a new currency in their sectors, as the reason for the asymmetrical response; instead, the roads and railways leading to Berlin were all suddenly closed for "repairs."

schmutz has coated every bit of solid information, including eye-witness reports. This skeletal account of the events is based solely on video evidence, most of it captured for Pavel Kostomarov, Alexander Rastorguev, and Alexey Pivovarov's fantastic vérité documentary called *Srok*, or *The Term*.

Like the February 4 protest, the March of Millions was designed (and approved by the mayor's office) in two parts: an actual march along a coordinated route and a rally at the destination. An outdoor stage festooned with the slogan "For Fair Government," somehow even less inspiring than the previous "For Fair Elections," awaited in the far end of Bolotnaya Square. When the marchers neared the square, however, they found that the OMON troops had cut off most access routes, leaving only a narrow bottleneck.

The crowd came to an awkward standstill. With some protesters getting impatient, Alexei Navalny, who marched near the front, suggested turning the situation into a peaceful sit-in, making himself comfortable in the middle of the road and directing the people around him to do the same. The problem was that Navalny—the protest's biggest name despite Udaltsov's status as its official leader—was so tightly encircled by the press that most of the marchers couldn't see enough to follow his example; people in the back kept pulling up, threatening to trample those who had sat down. The increasingly dense and nervous crowd kept pulsing against the largely arbitrary human border drawn by the OMON. After a few minutes, Navalny realized that a sit-in in these circumstances was a terrible idea, hastily exhorted his people to get back up, and took off toward the stage. Around the same time, someone breached the OMON barrier.

Within seconds, hundreds were getting pepper-sprayed, arrested, and beaten, including several of my reporter friends, and a few were fighting the troops. A pile of loose asphalt nearby provided the most aggressive protesters with projectiles. Later, one of the opposition's own conspiracy theories would posit that the asphalt had been strategically placed next to the bottleneck, in order to provoke the crowd into violence; this seems dubious for the simple reason that, in the constantly self-renovating Moscow, piles of loose asphalt lie absolutely everywhere.

All in all, the day's arrests would number between 400 and 650, depending on the source. Forty protesters and 29 OMON troops reported injuries; the only death was that of a photographer who fell from a balcony trying to get a better shot. The OMON quickly zeroed in on Navalny, who was still wearing a live mic for Kostomarov et al.'s documentary, and dragged him away; the tape preserved both his screams as the arresting officer applied an excruciating arm lock and his calm "I'll have you put in prison later," followed by more screams. Udaltsov, the protest's formal leader, made a run for the forgotten stage and attempted to make a speech—using, in a Monty Python–esque touch, three megaphones of varying sizes— when the OMON grabbed him, too.

The Kremlin proceeded to treat the riot as a crime of the century, dispatching 160 detectives to the case. Over the next months and years, thirty-two of the "May 6 prisoners" would be charged, names and faces plucked out of the crowd seemingly or genuinely at random, with the obvious message that even standing *near* a protest could get you imprisoned. The arrestees were old and young, nationalists and antifa, blue-collar and intelligentsia—a perfect cross-section of the protesting demographics. Their punishments were just as tactically randomized. Some of the thirty-two were sentenced to time served while awaiting trial, some were shipped to far-flung colonies, and some got away with surrendering their passports. The absence of any discernible pattern was part of the point.

The other part of the point was prolonging dread. If you had been out in the streets of Moscow on May 6, 2012—not even necessarily on Bolotnaya—you didn't know if and when the police would "find" you, or anyway a blurry face that sort of looked like you, on one of its tapes.* New "suspects" in the case were getting arrested as late as 2016. This way, participation in the protest could keep hanging over thousands indefinitely, as a kind of sweeping *kompromat* (blackmail fodder), even as the protest itself receded into what feels like the distant past. As of this writing, the investigation is still officially active, and some of the protesters are still serving time. Several got out in the amnesties of late 2013 and early 2014, when Russia was trying to put its best foot forward before the Sochi Olympics. The indisputably saddest story is that of a May 6 suspect named Alexander Dolmatov, who, fearing arrest, escaped through Ukraine to the Netherlands and asked for political asylum. His application rejected, Dolmatov ended up in a detention center for illegal immigrants, where he killed himself in January 2013.

A few prisoners successfully sued for damages through the European Court of Human Rights, which ruled in several separate cases that the arrests of the May 6 protesters violated their right to freedom of assembly, and their trials brimmed with irregularities; the Russian government, however, is not likely to come through with the actual payments anytime soon. Conversely, the six OMON fighters who testified for the prosecution about their injuries, which ranged from a sprained finger to a "reddening of the skin," received apartments in Moscow as a princely reward for their service.

May 6 was a fiasco for both sides. It was also the day that the Russian opposition, faced once again with the choice between words

---

*Our old buddy Sergei Minaev, who hasn't shown up in this story for a while (but will again!), was instrumental in helping the state conduct this slow-motion terror campaign; his pro-Kremlin online TV show *Minaev Live*, which miraculously *wasn't* hit by a DDoS attack that day, did a live broadcast from the rally, and happily handed five-plus hours' worth of video to the prosecution. The perfect placement of Minaev's cameras suggested coordination with OMON.

and fists, between going limp or punching back, made its first un-certain lunge for the latter option. With a few movements of a few people in a hot crowd, Russia changed yet again. The euphoric phase of "protestainment" was over. The Kremlin's flirtation with semi-controlled dissent was done. I had missed the exact moment it happened, but I'd have two years to face the consequences—starting the very next day.

Chapter Six

Anatomy
of the Protest

O n Monday, May 7, Vladimir Putin put his hand on the very Constitution his rule had helped undo and officially became the president of Russia for the third time. Old friends Gerhard Schroeder and Silvio Berlusconi looked on, as did a visibly miserable Lyudmila Putina, the wife he hadn't trotted out in public in years and would eventually divorce in 2014. But it was the run-up to the oath that proved more telling than the ceremony itself. To millions of viewers, Putin's re-re-ascension that day began with a televised spectacle so surreal that one might presume it to be a work of sabotage by a highly placed rogue—had all rogues not been swept out, and all television not stacked with loyalists, two presidential terms ago. Seven TV channels beamed out one image: Putin's motorcade cruising down a completely empty Moscow, cleared not only of potential protest but of all life.

As the presidential limousine and its escort—twelve motor-bikes and two Mercedes SUVs in a wedge formation—rolled down Novy Arbat Avenue, filmed from a hundred heroic angles, not a single unauthorized car or pedestrian tarnished the purity of the picture. It looked nothing like a celebration and a lot like a straight parable of tyranny, whose logical end result is a kingdom with no one to rule over. In this dead stillness, even the Cathedral of Christ the Savior, foregrounded in sweeping drone shots for some extra "God has willed this" symbolism, began to look like a computer graphic. The motorcade drove right into the Uncanny Valley.*

I spent the same morning calling up reporter friends detained in the Sunday protest—everyone had been safely released—and maniacally checking Twitter for updates. That perfect emptiness on the TV screens was hard-won—the OMON troops were on the loose throughout the city. In what had to be an act of symbolic in-timidation, they even raided Zhan-Zhak, space helmets and all, dragging customers out of liberal Moscow's ultimate safe space into the boulevard. Over at Alexei Navalny's house, a thirteen-hour-long police search had just wound up with a procession of black-masked men parading out all of his family's archives, computers, tablets, SIM cards, and mobile phones. Spontaneous protests were supposedly

---

*Within hours, footage of Putin's lonely ride would find its way online with added musi-cal commentary—"The Imperial March" from *Star Wars*, for instance, or Alice Cooper's "Last Man on Earth."

flaring up at Pushkin Square. Anonymous International, the hacker collective, meanwhile, retaliated for the previous day's DDoS attacks on opposition news portals by disrupting the government site Premier.gov.ru.

My apathy vanished without a trace, replaced by a touch of guilt. Pushkin Square was a few minutes from my house by foot. I walked there and immediately ran into my deputy, Roman Volobuev, who had the same slightly crazed look as, I assumed, I had.

"It's dead here," Roman said. "Just some Nashi bullshit."

Indeed, a few clean-scrubbed guys and girls of the Tomorrow Belongs to Me type trawled the square handing out St. George ribbons in honor of the inauguration. Back to the phones. Our heavily overlapping social-network feeds redirected us to Clear Ponds, a couple of Metro stops away: now something was brewing *there*.

The crowd at Clear Ponds, a rectangular park arranged around the titular pond, was smallish and very young; it mostly consisted of polite-looking students, with nary a familiar face present. This gathering, I realized with excitement, was the first truly leaderless protest I had seen in Moscow. It may have very well grown out of the natural park crowd. The sun was out. Birds chirped. The OMON were already here, picking people out of the crowd and throwing them into the nearby mobile jails.

At first, the pattern of the arrests seemed rather transactional and almost mutually courteous; the protesters had time to ask themselves whether they'd like to get arrested or not. Once that question was answered in the affirmative, one brandished a white ribbon or shouted out "Russia without Putin"—and, presto, she was hefted into an avtozak. A group of collegiate-looking young women sat down on the side of a fountain (behind them, a bronze heron statue had a white ribbon tied to its beak) and declared a sit-in, protesting the arrest of their friend. They then held an impromptu press conference: "This is our city, our park, and we're just going to stay here," declared the emerging leader, a full-figured girl in a white T-shirt.

If they were just left alone, the gathering would likely have dissipated within minutes—there was already a split between those who dug in and those who wanted to walk someplace else—but at that moment, the OMON had had enough and moved in en masse. The troops linked elbows, forming a kind of chorus line the width of the entire park. This riot-shielded corps de ballet then went through the grounds like a giant rake, dispassionately sifting out the protesters. When the OMON came across someone they deemed harmless—a dozing homeless man, two Azerbaijani elders playing chess on a bench—they rather gracefully parted just enough not to touch them, and went back to the business of compressing student flesh. It took them about ten minutes to push all of us to the west end of the park and out, toward the Metro station, where the protest disintegrated. I remember glimpsing a group of people dressed in full plushy gear as angry pigs and thinking I might be hallucinating. Nope, that was Nashi again, explained Volobuev, from some ridiculous astroturf thing called Piggies Against, originally created in 2010 to shame grocery-store owners for bad service (don't ask) but now repurposed, for an equally inexplicable reason, to harass protesters.

My next stop was Zhan-Zhak. That place's food was best described as French cuisine prepared for, and by, a cat; but I felt a need to publicly support them after the OMON raid earlier in the day. (As a reluctant B-list celebrity, I was finally beginning to find some uses for the fact that I was being photographed most places I went.) It seemed like the same thought had visited many people: the place was filled to the gills and buzzing with a doomed *A Feast in Time of Plague*–like intensity. All the regulars were here, sloshed and booming out apocalyptic predictions. Holding court at an iPhone-encrusted back table was the Hack Pack, a roving group of young Western reporters in Moscow.

Unlike the older, patrician *Times* and *Post* correspondents, whose jobs came with apartments, drivers, and interpreters (and who, like career diplomats, were rotated in and out before they could grow too attached to any one country), the Hack Pack were the new breed: they were often of Russian descent themselves, had little need for minders or handlers, knew the language well enough to get all the latest memes, and spent as much time hanging out with their Moscow peers as with one another. Though their appearance on the scene was a side effect of the industry's decline—news bureaus closed all over the world, leaving international reportage a younger, hungrier writer's game—their reporting on Russia was better and deeper than their ostensible superiors', and they scooped them constantly. (For one thing, they knew that the Russian opposition was no longer about Kasyanov, Kasparov, and human-rights advocacy long before their editors did.) My friend Julia Ioffe, who was writing up a storm for *The New Yorker*, *The New Republic*, *Foreign Policy*, and *Slate* all at once—while dating a prominent Russian opposition figure—was both the Pack's ringleader and its perfect representative. I wasn't, technically speaking, even a member: I admired the group and was friendly with most of the writers in it, but always felt a bit embarrassed around them, my Moscow job being almost impossibly cushy next to their unceasing hustle.

Around 9:00 p.m., a gangly Hack Packer named Olaf Koens—the joke about him was that no one had any idea whether he was any good, since he filed all his stories in Dutch—got tipped off via text message that Navalny was organizing his own sit-in at Kitai-Gorod, by the Heroes of Plevna monument. We tore out of Zhan-Zhak, hailed two separate rides (in those pre-Uber days you just raised your hand and a dozen beat-up Ladas would screech to a stop), packed ourselves in, and sped to Kitai-Gorod.

The Heroes of Plevna, a gilded rotunda—actually a small chapel—memorialized an 1877 Russo-Turkish War battle in which

General Mikhail Skobelev fought the Ottoman troops. On normal nights it was also, as I learned on the way over, Moscow's most notorious gay cruising spot. At first, the crowd around the monument numbered fewer than a hundred people. Navalny, fresh from his thirteen-hour search ordeal, sat on the steps of the monument giving an impromptu press conference to whoever cared to ask questions. "This is not a protest," he declared. "This is not a march." It was a gathering for gathering's sake. Everyone was encouraged to be on their best behavior. No demands, no slogans. None of us—including, I suspect, Navalny—had any idea what this was or where it was going. It felt light, safe, and a little sad, like a wake for a protest that could have been.

The square, meanwhile, filled up. Soon, about five hundred to seven hundred people were milling about singing songs by Kino and, oddly, the Rolling Stones' "(I Can't Get No) Satisfaction." Navalny took up a collection for foam butt cushions from the nearest twenty-four-hour sporting-goods store; within minutes, he had so much money that he had to beg people to stop giving him cash. Here and there I could see members of my team. The Kermlins arrived. Volobuev reappeared with two waifish girls (he had a talent for finding them everywhere). Half the crowd seemed to consist of reporters, but after May 6 it no longer mattered. The only difference between a reporter and an activist was that a press card got you out of jail faster. Ioffe was one of the few who bothered to fully stick to the impartial-observer protocol; when a protester handed her a bottle of water, she insisted on symbolically paying for it lest she could be accused of accepting gifts. Most of us, myself included, were increasingly relaxed about this stuff.

Perhaps because the protest had attracted a legion of Western correspondents, or perhaps because it wasn't technically a protest, the authorities evidently decided that a full-on OMON intervention like the one we'd escaped at Clear Ponds was a bad idea. Shortly after midnight, they finally came up with what they must have thought was an elegant solution: a city services truck with a water hose pulled up, because the rotunda apparently required an emergency cleaning. The truck made slow circles around the monument, pointlessly hosing down the asphalt; the protesters (who weren't protesters) ran from it laughing, and all but played in the water like Brooklyn kids in a fire-hydrant spray. The night scene acquired a sexy "May 1968 in Paris" feel, which was hardly the authorities' intention. When the OMON did finally arrive, another half hour later, the troops stood off to the side and watched with the kind of timidity that comes only from not having received clear instructions. In response, Navalny decided to take the non-protest mobile, again calling to mind the French Situationists with their concept of aimless ambulation as a form of protest. "We're just going for a walk," he declared, getting up. "We're! Just! Going for a walk!" the supporters began to chant at the OMON, cracking up as they did.

Thus began the strangest night and day of my life. Until 5:00 a.m. or so, we simply walked without stopping—a giggly, nervous, mostly quiet crowd that stretched out for several blocks—to Clear Ponds (the second time that day I ended up there), then winding back, in dark silent rivulets, through unlit side streets, one step ahead of the OMON all the while. They moved in, we moved. It was as simple as that. At some point, we found ourselves walking *with* the OMON, who no longer had any idea what to do. "How the fuck am I supposed to 'turn them away'?" a senior officer with a megaphone barked into his mobile phone within my earshot. "It's just me and five other guys here!"

At sunrise, the crowd silently dissipated so that everyone could catch some sleep—and then, amazingly, reassembled, like a bee colony, around Navalny. This was going to be the new kind of rally then: a rally in the authorities' eye only. The act of walking, or lazing about in a park, became a matter of perceived intent. The protesters would be doing the exact same things as loyal citizens—but they'd be doing them *in protest.*

By late afternoon, the movable non-protest crawled down Tverskoy Boulevard toward the TASS building, one of my favorite late-Soviet Brutalist slabs of concrete in the city. A rain began to fall, drenching the crowd, which at that point included Ksenia Sobchak—but not for long; I arrived just in time to see Sobchak detained and put into one avtozak, and Navalny into another. The instructions, apparently, had finally been received.

I dove into the crowd and saw Svetlana Reiter, a reporter for *Esquire*, being manhandled by the OMON amid a circle of people yelling at them to let her go. Finally, they did.

"By the way, your man Volobuev just got picked up," Reiter said nonchalantly, adjusting her clothes.

"What?!"

She shrugged. Apparently, Roman was filming Navalny's arrest on his iPhone and got arrested alongside him. There were now about six mobile jails parked around the TASS building; the OMON had let Volobuev keep his phone—he was tweeting away from the inside— but the windows were painted black and he couldn't tell me which of the buses he was in. I ran around in the rain asking the OMON to check for a detainee named Volobuev—which they did, with a degree of courtesy. Finally, Roman managed to orient himself by the diffuse glow of an electronic TASS billboard that seeped through the paint on one of the windows: his avtozak was the one parked across from the building's main entrance. I got in the face of the mustached colonel in charge and, doing my best to make it sound like a gruff boss-to-boss talk, managed to convince him that Volobuev was my employee on assignment (a white semi-lie). I decided that a good tack to take would be pretending to be angry at Volobuev and not the OMON—"I'll have a good talk with that fucker later," etc. While doing all this, I also held out my rain-soaked U.S.

passport for good measure. One of these factors, or their combination, worked. The colonel sent an underling in riot gear to the right bus, and Volobuev, to laughter and applause from his fellow twenty detainees, got out. The rest would be taken to the Solntsevo precinct for processing—a whopping sixteen miles away; all closer police stations were overflowing with the last three days' worth of detainees. We went to the nearby Mayak Café and had a few drinks to calm our nerves.

With Navalny in jail for fifteen days (and in danger of getting a two-year prison term for "inciting riots"), the roving non-protest was over, but it managed to toss out an unexpected offshoot. Some brave souls returned to Clear Ponds and set up camp beside a statue of an "unknown Kazakh," which Navalny had mentioned on Twitter during our night walk. The statue turned out to be a monument to a freedom-loving Kazakh poet, Abai Kunanbaev, and these people adopted him as a kind of mascot. On May 10, the #Occupy Abai hashtag was born.

By the eleventh, the scene at Clear Ponds had evolved into one similar to that at Zuccotti Park, with a dash of Burning Man. There were red-and-blue ABAI posters of the poet's face patterned after Shepard Fairey's HOPE poster, free sandwiches, campfire sing-alongs, lectures, and knitting lessons. A myriad of organizations, from the Left Front to the National Democrats to some poor saps repping Mikhail Prokhorov's postelection "youth movement" called New Time, milled about recruiting members. "Dear friends," shouted a hippie-looking guy from a "Horizontal Resistance Group," "everyone is invited to take part . . . in a self-organization and civil society betterment seminar . . . under that oak tree." Nearby, an elderly local resident was venting to a friendly police officer: "This isn't democracy. This doesn't look like people who want something. This is just a bum colony." The officer nodded at her and took eager notes. There was word that the city was preparing a noise-complaint case against the encampment—an unusually civilized way of dealing with this kind of thing—so the occupiers mobilized to keep the area pointedly clean and quiet. In fact, it was noticeably cleaner than the western part of the park, where the protesters *didn't* congregate.

The old-school opposition types, perhaps unnerved by their complete lack of authority with this crowd, disliked Occupy Abai's pacific silliness yet soon began to ape Navalny's roving protest idea. The novelists Dmitri Bykov and Boris Akunin, who had sat out on May 6 and 7, suddenly swung back into action, leading a so-called writers' walk down the boulevards. The action drew a completely different crowd, middle-aged and distinctly Soviet in clothing and style, leavened liberally with the two men's fan bases. Many people came clutching their books in search of autographs. Yuri Saprykin told me he hated the idea—he thought it elitist. There was, indeed, a fair bit of hero worship at work ("Dima, you're a genius!" someone kept yelling at the corpulent, pleased-looking Bykov, who drew the biggest scrum within the crowd). But it *was* massive—about twenty thousand strong—especially for a march organized without any permits or cooperation from the city. When I saw Sergei Parkhomenko in the crowd, he was ecstatic: "How are you liking our little walk, eh?" he said, beaming. He then added, to my surprise, "We'll show them Occupy Abai yet!"

This competition between two strains of protest was short-lived. On May 15, OMON and city bulldozers dispersed the tent city at Clear Ponds; the little republic of Occupy Abai ended up flourishing for all of five days. No Zuccotti Park for Moscow, then, no Christiania. Over the next two weeks, various activists, numbering fewer and fewer, continued the "walks" at Barrikadnaya, at the Okudzhava statue on Arbat, at Kudrin Square, etc., to rapidly diminishing returns. By June, you wouldn't be able to tell where and when the protests ended and the regular summery foot traffic began. All that was left to do was to study the passersby's faces for some hint of belonging to the same secret club as you. Dissent had returned to its historic place within the Russian society: the citizens' minds. The city swallowed the rest.

■

The Kremlin, meanwhile, didn't waste any time. A squeal of tightening screws rose over the State Duma building, next door to mine: the Parliament was passing new restrictive laws as fast as it could make them up—or, to be more precise, as fast as it could parse the president's wish list—often limiting floor deliberations to five or ten minutes.* On June 6, the Duma passed a law that banned most protest-related behavior, including the "walks," in an evident conflict with the Constitution that no court cared to examine. Fines for all unauthorized gatherings increased many times over. A punishment for libel was also back on the books after a brief Medvedev-era absence, with special added protections for state employees. The pathetic remnants of the parliamentary opposition tried to mount an extremely rare filibuster, to no avail. Under the guise of a law to "protect children from harmful information," a national online blacklist was created, and a formerly obscure state body called Roskomnadzor was empowered to block any website it didn't like.†

---

*That year's viral nickname for the Duma in the Russian media was "*vzbesivshiysya* printer," meaning "a printer gone berserk."
†The groundwork for this blacklist had been laid down by the businessman Konstantin Malofeev and an organization called the Safe Internet League, which he created to fight child pornography. Bizarrely enough, Arseny Bobrovsky, the creator of the satirical @KermlinRussia Twitter account, was Malofeev's publicist at the time and takes the credit/blame for the idea, which he says was a PR stunt. If the idea of a Twitter rebel cynically cooking up recipes for Internet censorship at his day job strikes you as odd, then you don't quite get Russia yet.

Grani.ru, the opposition portal, became the first such site. Navalny's blog followed soon enough.

Finally, the Duma wrenched open the definition of "state treason" to incorporate any assistance to any foreign entity in any activity "aimed against the security of the Russian Federation," with no further definition of "security." The latter tweak reflected the big-picture concept beamed down from the Kremlin: the spate of protests between December and May were the work of American meddlers in the State Department and the CIA, their fronts disguised as NGOs, and their local stooges.

Did Putin actually believe this? Hard to say. The idea—that no protest is genuine, that no political preference is based on moral principle, that the people are always somebody's pawns—is the cornerstone of the Putinist weltanschauung. It forms the putrid heart of the "post-truth" philosophy that Russia would soon perfect enough to begin successfully exporting westward—in the shape of its conspiracy-peddling news channel Russia Today, its "troll factories" fouling up social networks with canards and paid-up comments, its cynical support of the alt-right and the nihilist left, its probable collusion with WikiLeaks and a possible one with the forty-fifth president of the United States. But, again, did Vladimir Vladimirovich Putin, a breathing person, himself believe that Hillary Clinton, another breathing person, had distributed money and favors to an army of apostates to have him removed? He might; it dovetails, after all, with the worldview of a career KGB officer. Ultimately, however, it was irrelevant. As far as the Duma was concerned, this was the new gospel. The lawmakers were then invited to do their own interpretive dance around it, and responded with the typical showboating hysteria of underlings whose sole job is to beat one another at divining the boss's will.

The madness thus snowballed until, by the fall, no one was surprised to see Vladimir Zhirinovsky propose a ban on "foreign words that have Russian equivalents" or Alexander Sidyakin, a United Russia deputy, stomp his feet on a white ribbon while explaining that he wanted "to do to this ribbon what the people who financed these provocations wanted to do to our country." Human rights organizations and NGOs that received funding beyond Russia's borders were obliged to humiliatingly declare themselves "foreign agents." A proposed addendum to this law would include all foreign-owned media—such as, say, *GQ*—sending the Condé Nast brass into a brief panic, but it was abandoned along the way.

Yet another floated proposal, to ban foreigners from holding high-level media jobs, would have bounced me back to New York right there and then; that one, however, turned out to be only a tactical trial balloon with a curious backstory. The lawmakers had sent it out as a personalized message to Vladimir Pozner, a celebrated television personality with triple citizenship (Russia, France, and the United States). Pozner, who had evinced a mild distaste for the Duma's repressive tack, went so far as to call the body a *gosudarstvennaya dura*—a so-so pun that implied stupidity—on the air. Pozner promptly fell back in line and apologized, saving my job as an accidental side effect.

A much more palpable blow to the publishing house, and to all independent media, came in July in the form of a total ban on alcohol advertising. Liquor ads accounted for almost a quarter of *GQ*'s revenue. At the time, I assumed this was part and parcel of Russia's demonstrative return to virtue. In fact, the ban's real benefactors were not Orthodox values but domestic vodka producers, which had likely lobbied it into existence to begin with; research showed that, in the absence of ads aggressively exhorting him to drink foreign firewater such as cognac or whiskey, the Russian consumer quickly defaulted back to vodka.

As tends to happen in autocracies, not all repression needed to be spelled out in the language of law. The government simply set the tone, leaving the rest of the society to interpret it. And so it did. On June 7, the very next day after the Duma passed its anti-protest act, Filipp Dzyadko got removed from the helm of the ecstatically oppositional *Bolshoi Gorod* in favor of a more pliant editor, and Demyan Kudryavtsev was pushed out from the CEO seat at the authoritative *Kommersant*. Dzyadko's farewell Facebook post coined an instantly popular phrase, "links in a fucking chain," to describe these seemingly unrelated incidents; indeed, over the next year the fucking chain would keep lengthening, as the spooked oligarchs with interests in independent media had most of the New Decembrist–era editors replaced with loyalists or dopes.

Following her arrest alongside Navalny, Ksenia Sobchak, the inexhaustible multimedia dynamo, got fired from almost everywhere except TV Rain. Her steadiest paycheck had come from hosting a TNT mainstay called *Dom 2*, a reality show in the vein of *Big Brother*; this was now over. Muz-TV, a homegrown music-video channel, followed suit and booted her from a hosting gig at its annual awards show, whose posters (featuring Sobchak) were already plastered all over town. Like most of Russia's top TV personalities, Sobchak also used to moonlight as an emcee at oligarchs' weddings and birthdays, for up to one hundred thousand dollars a pop—that well had dried, too, since no oligarch in his right mind would hire her.

"Why is she doing this?!" a TV executive—at a channel where Sobchak, for a change, hadn't had a show—puzzled over dinner, his voice dipping to a whisper. "Does she really want all this? Does she want Putin out? But she's done so well under him! I don't get it." On his own network, a new reality series called *Escape from Gulag* had just gotten pulled from the schedule. "They're nervous up there. What they would dismiss as a joke last year, they'll take really personally this year." At this exact moment, a tabloid rang for a comment on Sobchak's last-minute removal from Muz-TV. The executive hung up: who knew what was safe to say in this new reality and what wasn't.

Sobchak's banishments came from the very top. Putin might or might not be her godfather, but he indisputably owed his career to the late Anatoly Sobchak and considered Ksenia part of the family. In his eyes, her "betrayal" was a deep personal affront. The inner circle, according to a friend of Dmitri Peskov's, Putin's press secretary, knew better than to even mention her name in front of the boss. In response, Sobchak doubled down in the classic rebellious-daughter fashion—by dating Ilya Yashin, a young, leather-jacket-wearing protest leader whose most resonant achievement of 2012 was hanging a giant banner next to the Kremlin that read PUTIN GO AWAY.

It was Sobchak's previous boyfriend, however, who at this moment suddenly became the new face of Moscow. His name was Sergei Kapkov.

Doughy, amiable, and looking fifty at thirty-five, as often happens with Russian bureaucrats, Kapkov had begun his career as a right-hand man to the oligarch Roman Abramovich in the latter's capacity as the governor of the Chukotka region. After a few uneventful years as a Duma deputy (representing, of course, the ruling United Russia party), he moved on to an even duller-sounding post as the director of Moscow's Gorky Park in March 2011. The appointment was likely engineered by Abramovich, whose girlfriend Dasha Zhukova had picked the park as the new location of her Garage Museum of Contemporary Art. And then something extraordinary happened: Kapkov took to his new job with a decidedly un-Russian—or at the very least un–United Russian—gusto.

Within months, the long-neglected park, known in the West

primarily as the setting for a dour 1981 thriller and to the Muscovites as the best place to pick a fight with a drunk soldier, turned into an urbanist paradise. Kapkov tossed out the cheesy fairground attractions, canceled the entry fee, hired progressive architects to spruce up the fixtures, strewed the lawns with beanbag chairs, and blanketed the area with free Wi-Fi. By August, the Moscow mayor Sergei Sobyanin had put Kapkov in charge of all of the city's parks and recreation areas. Another month later, in September 2011, Kapkov became the head of Moscow's Department of Culture, which put theaters, libraries, museums, and much more within his purview. His next job, everyone assumed, would be the minister of culture.

Against the dead-eyed gallery of United Russia officials—the only ones Muscovites had seen for a generation—Kapkov easily passed for hip. He spoke like a human being and kept the anodyne bureaucratese to the minimum, went to parties and movie premieres, and enthusiastically used Facebook (a sudden "like" from Kapkov, especially under a random Kremlin-bashing post, was a delight worthy of a screenshot). He had dated Sobchak, for God's sake. Unsurprisingly, a swath of the battered liberal elites pinned whatever was left of their hopes on him. For a certain kind of problem, usually involving the city's harassment of a small businessman or an artist, a "letter to Kapkov" became a legitimate shortcut to resolution. At the same time, Kapkov never pretended to be anything but a loyal Putinist—just with a twist of humanity. In one interview, for example, he blithely supported the arrests of people who wore white ribbons; instead, he invited protesters to "express themselves" in a fenced-in "free speech zone" inside, you guessed it, Gorky Park.

Over time, this turned out to be Kapkov's trademark move: as soon as the real estate prices, the corruption, or the newly reactionary realities of Moscow became too much to bear for this or that youthful enterprise, he would swoop in and offer to replant it in Gorky Park, like Mazay the peasant in the Nikolai Nekrasov poem saving hares from a spring flood in his little rowboat.* As a result, Gorky Park became almost parodically dense with hipster amusements. There were skateboard ramps, outdoor movies, beach volleyball on real sand, paddleboats, barbecue joints, bike rentals, dance lessons, site-specific art installations, a Chinese tearoom, a French café with a pétanque court, and a population of specially imported squirrels, because a park should have squirrels. It looked like something out of a Steven Millhauser book. My friend Alexei Kovalev, a journalist, acidly termed the result "Copenhagen in the middle of Karachi."

This metamorphosis wasn't, however, limited to Gorky Park. The fact could no longer be denied: the more politically suffocating Moscow grew, the tighter squeeze it put on civic life, the more comfortable, modern, and Westernized it became as a place to live. Mayor Sobyanin, who had replaced the flamboyantly corrupt and tasteless Yuri Luzhkov in 2010, put a premium on the flashy urbanist touches that had become a kind of international city currency, especially after Michael Bloomberg's exemplary spruce-up of New York: bicycle lanes, tiled sidewalks, new street furniture, cutesy municipal logos and tourist-board slogans by renowned marketing firms. One after another, Moscow's abandoned factory floors and industrial parks rebranded themselves as arty "clusters" with catchy names—Strelka, Vinzavod, Arma, Flacon, Artplay; in response, young people dove into retail with the same passion as they had into protest, opening everything from artisanal coffee roasters to white-collar boxing studios. The small-deeds theory was back with a vengeance. By the fall of 2012, however, Muscovites had coined a new term for this sort of thing. It was now called *Kapkovshchina*, or "Kapkovism."

---

*The simile won't be complete unless I mention that this grade-school staple, "Grandfather Mazay and the Hares," ends on a rather dark note: it turns out that Mazay is saving the hares now only to hunt them come winter.

Its ultimate symbol was a saccharine street sculpture, ten or so feet high, in the form of a white checkmark bearing the declaration "я ♡ москву": the millionth rip-off of Milton Glaser's iconic design and statement. Lily and I took to calling it "Mr. Mockby." Unveiled to great fanfare—where else—in Gorky Park, Mr. Mockby soon began appearing everywhere in Moscow that the urbanist hand had touched, in the margins of squares and greens, like a top grade the city gave to itself.

Kapkovshchina was at its heart a Potemkin village—a scale model of an idealized Western society plopped atop a rough city that still hadn't figured out rainwater drainage. But the model was a working one. As long as you picked your routes and stuck to them, you could build a daily routine genuinely indistinguishable from a New Yorker's—and, by God, I did. On any given morning, I might have a frittata at Oldich, a British-inspired café-cum-vintage-clothing store steps from the Fur Fridge; move on to the local outpost of Nobu, kitty-corner from there, for an expense-account lunch meeting; and end the night at Chainaya, a backyard basement speakeasy that routinely made the list of the world's top fifty cocktail bars. I got my haircuts at Chop-Chop, a Brooklyn-worshipping barbershop owned by the guys who used to run *GQ*'s website, and watched American movies at Pioner—one of the few theaters in the city progressive enough to show them subtitled and spare me the Russian dubbing, which made every woman sound like a grumpy waitress.

But whom did I really patronize with all these alternately precious and snobbish choices? Well, let's see: Oldich was the brainchild of a telecom tycoon's wife, who rented the ground-floor space from the offices of Russia's prosecutor general.* Moscow's Nobu belonged to the Agalarov family, the Azeri developers who palled around with Donald Trump (and would soon mount the infamous

---

*When the landlords pushed her out after two years, Kapkov swooped in with his Grandfather Mazay act yet again: Oldich spent its last summer as a pop-up in Gorky Park.

2013 Miss Universe pageant with him); Pioner was the property of Alexander Mamut, an oligarch who facilitated the silencing of independent voices at the online news portals Lenta.ru and Gazeta.ru; and much of Gorky Park's renovation, of course, was underwritten by Kapkov's old boss Abramovich. From every breakfast, the trail led right up to Putin's clique and the "administrative resource."

Therein lay, for many, an ethical dilemma. What Mamut, Sobyanin, Kapkov, et al. ultimately did was create safe playgrounds for the elite to mingle among themselves. (This argument rang a bell with me as a New Yorker, where the opening of the High Line park, with its sleek design and organic concessions, led to similar worries that a public space was subtly telling the poor to stay out.) Indeed, the "Kapkovized" parks and museums immediately took on a certain look and attracted a certain crowd; if anything, they separated the "protest electorate" from the people even further. Some of my friends decided that partaking in these luxuries meant indirectly legitimizing Putin. Alexei Kovalev, whose editorial job at the Russian Information Agency was wiped out in late 2012 by the presidential decree "on optimization of state media functions," went farther than most.* He loudly refused to set foot in Gorky Park, relentlessly mocked burgers and meatballs as a form of collaborationism, and devoted himself to hyperlocal NIMBY activities aimed against any urban improvements (jokingly labeling this type of resistance as "no brushing teeth, no washing ass"). It may have been a bit much, but the question of complicity was valid: weren't we all, in exchange for bike lanes and free Wi-Fi, willingly posing as extras in a giant tableau of docility and contentment created for Putin's eyes?

*The decree turned the RIA, a competent and objective news agency, into another zombie propaganda outlet. Kovalev later made his name as a one-man fact-checking operation, called the Noodle Remover, dedicated to debunking the Russian media's most outlandish lies.

A few months after my start at *GQ*, I got to visit Sergei Kapkov at his mansion in Skolkovo, an elite suburb of Moscow. The invitation was unexpected—I had barely spoken with him before—and very flattering until I realized I'd be there as part of an experiment. As one of his aides explained to me, Kapkov had never thrown a "real New York–style dinner party" before, and was anxious to get it just right. My presence would thus up the degree of true New Yorkiness. I didn't have it in me to tell Kapkov that no dinner party I had ever been to in Manhattan featured uniformed waiters and big bowls of beluga caviar. The host himself, however, looked great in a cardigan. I had a strong suspicion that his main sartorial reference for the event was *Frasier*.

As the feast went on, Kapkov spoke little but listened hungrily; he also kept fiddling with the living room lights, repeatedly told everyone he had a car on call in case anyone needed a ride home, and generally futzed about like a first-time dinner-party host, which he was. He had also strung up white balloons around the lobby, an addition so touchingly earnest it almost made me tear up; like a miniature version of his Gorky Park, the party was a collection of good things blindly thrown together in the hope that they'd add up to a great thing.

The guest list was just as eclectic. I had seen a mix of art-media and money-power types in one room before, but never this kind of dynamic between them. A glum, suited-up friend of Kapkov's, who worked for Abramovich, tried to show a young gallerist thumbnails of some photographs he had bought. "I don't know if they're good or bad," he said. "Well, why did you buy them?" she asked. "I liked them! But I don't know if they're good! So I need someone's opinion." The photos wouldn't load, which visibly upset him. I had never seen powerful Russians hunger for bohemian validation so nakedly. It was mesmerizing.

As I worked my way through a subcompact car's worth of caviar on my plate, another guest, a youngish Kremlin type, struck up a conversation. I had just learned to recognize these guys as *GQ* readers—the target audience, in fact—by their newly imbibed dress sense: sharp but just a bit too relentlessly high-end. And they had just learned to recognize me as the guy telling them to dress this way. Sure enough, he had some questions about the magazine, starting with the classic "Who's on the next cover?"

"Jeremy Renner."

"Don't know him. You working on anything big?"

"Big?"

"Big. Like what Sobchak used to do."

Son of a bitch. "Let's see," I said through the caviar. "A Vladimir Pozner interview . . . Confessions of an Oxford drug dealer . . . The profile of a guy suing the Eastern Orthodox Church."

"What?"

"Ah, it's a crazy case. This guy's a consumer advocate. He says the Cathedral of Christ the Savior is actually a for-profit business center."

The guest went silent for a while.

"Don't fuck with the Church," he finally said. "I know what I'm talking about."

"We're not, though. The guy is."

"Seriously. If you leave here with one piece of useful information, let it be this. They are like the fucking Mob. And they are going to be a very big deal now."

"What do you mean?"

"You'll see," he said.

The perfectly authentic, 100 percent New York dinner party continued.

The Cathedral of Christ the Savior, on the bank of the Moskva River, is the tallest Orthodox church in the world and the official seat of the Moscow Patriarchate. Beyond these two indisputable facts, its significance in Russian life is fantastically muddled. Few famous churches have made it to modernity intact—but the trans-figurations of Christ the Savior are unusual in their recency. The original nineteenth-century church was blown up on Stalin's orders in 1931 to make room for the proposed Palace of the Soviets, a monstrous ziggurat topped with a statue of Lenin. When first the groundwater and then the war scuttled that plan, the Soviets refitted the construction pit into the world's largest heated swimming pool. The symbolism of that act—turning a sacred object into a literal lack of one—was accidental but potent.

In the early 1990s, rebuilding the cathedral seemed like a natu-ral declaration of Russia's rebirth, and everyone from the poorest Muscovites to the newly minted oligarchs donated to the cause. Along the way, however, the construction once again took on extra symbolic ballast. Mayor Yuri Luzhkov had the original architect fired and replaced with his pet sculptor, Zurab Tsereteli, who slapped ahistorical bronze details all over it; the project then grew to include not just a replica of the original cathedral but also a vast complex that included completely unrelated pavilions, souvenir shops, ban-quet halls, galleries, underground parking lots, and even a car wash. Despite the cathedral receiving hundreds of millions of rubles from the city budget, all these facilities operated for profit—through a separate fund that belonged neither to the church nor the state; in the classic Russian fashion, the fund director's relatives controlled most of the businesses therein, as well as the two private security firms guarding the cathedral. Even the church itself was available for rent: a law firm took up an office right above the altar, and the opulent Hall of Councils hosted pop concerts. You could rent it for private events, too, for 450,000 rubles (about $7,750). "The Hall will impress you with its fittings and architecture," reads the artless ad copy on the cathedral's website. "You will remember this visit for a long time, as it is one of Moscow's most unusual and luxurious venues." In short, the new church *was* a symbol of the post-Soviet Russia—just not, perhaps, in the way the people who had donated their earnings to its reconstruction imagined. And so the Cathedral of Christ the Savior duly performed its main function—radiating grandeur—but remained unloved; when the Muscovites looked at it, they saw not the resurgent spirit of their country but another avatar of its government. Not God but Putin.

On the morning of February 21, 2012, this notion was front and center in the thoughts of the five young women in brightly colored tights and modest Orthodox headscarves as they entered the cathedral. In their backpacks hid microphones, video equipment, and a guitar. Under the babushkas were balaclavas.

■

Pussy Riot, the actionist collective whose masquerading as a "punk band" would soon make them the world's most recognizable Russians after Vladimir Putin, had been around for only three or four months. At the moment, Voina (War)—a radical art group from which Pussy Riot had sprung—was much better known, mostly for drawing a giant cock on the side of a St. Petersburg drawbridge that, when raised, faced the windows of the FSB.

Voina's Moscow offshoot originally consisted of two couples and had been active since 2008. That year, they got on the roof of Hotel Ukraine and projected a laser-beam Jolly Roger across the river, onto the façade of a government building; participated in a bizarre orgy in a natural science museum that seemed to obliquely critique Medvedev's election; and sabotaged a restaurant opened by the ultraconservative TV personality Mikhail Leontyev by speed-welding its front door shut. A later action involved the artists planting sudden kisses on policewomen in public spaces.

In the fall of 2011, Medvedev's de facto abdication and the prospect of Putin's return hit the group as hard as it did the conventional liberals. One of the two couples, Nadya Tolokonnikova and her husband, Peter Verzilov, felt the need to tweak their protest art to fit the looming us-versus-them era: to make it angrier, clearer, more accessible, more pop. Together with their friend Masha Alekhina and a few others, they conceived a masked all-female punk collective that would shout the simplest slogans possible in the loudest voice they could muster—as Tolokonnikova put it, "like we were sixteen-year-old girls who just discovered feminism yesterday." The members would be known only by prison-style handles like Tyurya, Garadzha, Fara, Kat, Serafima, and so on, and anyone could theoretically join. The name Pussy Riot was a blunt tip of the balaclava to the band Bikini Kill and the "riot grrrl" punk feminism of the 1990s; in the first of the group's several brilliant feats of branding, it was both immediately graspable in English and untranslatable into Russian, which simply lacks a word for female genitalia that's neither clinical nor a hard-core obscenity.

Pussy Riot's first concertlike interventions took place at Metro stations, on trolleybus roofs, and outside "glamorous" bars and clubs; as they sang and pretended to play guitars, they pelted the public with candy, detonated confetti petards, threw flour, and shook feathers out of pillows. At that point, very few people knew who stood behind the masked group (when I first arrived in Moscow, the erudite Tolokonnikova was suggested to me as a possible freelance author), and not many cared.

After the first mass protests, however, the pitch of the performances changed yet again. On December 14, 2011, Pussy Riot gave a "concert for political prisoners" on the roof of the precinct where the detainees from the Ruined Shoes Rally were held—including Peter Verzilov, who had been sentenced to fifteen days in jail alongside Navalny and Ilya Yashin.* The song they performed, "Freedom to Protest," was a simple call to occupy public spaces:

Fill up the city, all the squares and the avenues
There's plenty in Russia, put down your oysters
Open all doors, take off your shoulder boards†
Feel the air of freedom with us

On January 20, the emboldened collective took their act to Red Square for an instantly iconic performance at the Lobnoye Mesto, a sixteenth-century round brick platform from which Ivan the Terrible once addressed his subjects. This time, the song was a direct taunt in the opposite direction—from the people to the autocrat:

A rebel column is marching on the Kremlin
Windows blow out in the FSB offices
Behind the red wall, bitches shit a brick
Riot has come to abort the system

Riot in Russia—Putin is chickenshit

In retrospect, it is downright amazing—and indicative of how uncertain the government's hold was on the situation in those few winter weeks—that these two actions met little to no punishment. The policemen who watched the "concert for the political prisoners"

---

*At that point, the group downplayed Verzilov's role in its genesis, since it didn't quite fit the wrathful punk-feminist story line. His managerial presence came to light only after Alekhina and Tolokonnikova's release from prison in late 2013—to the extent where, in their *House of Cards* cameo, "Pussy Riot" were curiously presented to the public as the trio of Nadya, Masha, and Peter.

†Meaning those rectangles on military jackets that contain rank insignia. The Russian word for them, *pogony*, is part of everyday vocabulary, attesting perhaps to the overall militarization of the society.

simply went back into the precinct and shut the doors, letting the group finish the performance, get down via ladder, and leave unmolested. Pussy Riot's Red Square debut eventually resulted in a brief arrest for trespassing, but only after twenty-five minutes or so of uninterrupted action, and the entire group got off with a five-hundred-ruble (nine-dollar) fine. Meanwhile, among the hundreds of comments under the LiveJournal post where the collective published photo and video reports of the action, the calls to imprison, hang, rape, behead, etc., the unruly women were already proliferating. In this rare instance, the Russian police were more liberal than the Russian society. This would change soon enough.

At that point, Pussy Riot's performances were essentially video shoots: there was little in the way of actual singing or playing instruments, and the end goal of each intervention was a viral YouTube clip. This meant that their next project, a "punk prayer" at the Cathedral of Christ the Savior, would require careful pre-planning. For several weeks, the group rehearsed the integral parts of the act: getting through the metal detectors without alarming the church's private security; setting up the PA with the speed of a Formula One pit crew (they eventually decided not to plug in the guitar and just lip-sync to a recording). Last but not least, they got a legal consultation from Mark Feygin, a lawyer Tolokonnikova had recently befriended. Feygin concluded that the action was fairly safe—much safer than the Red Square stunt, in fact—and that they would probably end up paying a symbolic fine.

At 10:00 a.m., after the morning service let out, Pussy Riot entered the cathedral. From their practice runs they expected it to be nearly empty, and immediately noticed an unusual number of solitary men milling about: not the usual churchgoing demographic. They briefly debated turning around and postponing the performance, then decided to go through with it anyway. As soon as the women tossed off their winter coats and kerchiefs, pulled the bunched-up balaclavas down over their faces, and stepped into the chancel (a word that all secular Russia would soon learn, thanks to them), the men lunged.

In the ensuing forty-second chaos, Pussy Riot managed to commit to video about twenty seconds of wild pogoing, pretend-strumming, and lip-syncing. The backing track didn't even start—it would be added to the video later. It was a furious manifesto, destined to become that elusive thing of which I had dreamed all through college: a Russian rock song heard around the world.

> *Virgin Mother of God, drive Putin away*
> *Putin away, Putin away*
>
> *Black cassock, gold shoulder boards*
> *The congregation crawls and kneels*
> *The spirit of freedom lives in the skies*
> *Gay Pride is shackled and sent to Siberia*
> *The KGB head is their patron saint*
> *He herds the protesters as one into jail*
> *In order not to offend His Holiness*
> *Women must bear children and love*
>
> *Holy shit, holy shit, holy shit*
> *Holy shit, holy shit, holy shit*

Remarkably, after the cathedral's private security pushed the women away from the altar area, they were allowed to pick up their clothes and equipment and leave in peace. No one called the cops or filed an official report. As the group recongregated at the meeting point—a nearby Metro station—there was no sense that the stunt had sealed their fates. It just felt like a botched performance; Pussy Riot had had to abort missions before. There was one thing they, or the lawyers advising them, couldn't foresee: the massive backward shift in Russia's cultural politics that would arrive with Putin's reelection, at that point less than two weeks away.

The Kremlin's response to the protest wave would not be limited to blaming the usual bogeymen at the CIA and the State Department. Over the course of the winter and spring, it grew into all-out nativist paranoia. Unlike Soviet propaganda, which demonized capitalists but not the hardworking Americans and Europeans they oppressed, the new strain of anti-Western sentiment couldn't root itself in an ideological conflict: on paper, Russia was just as capitalist. This meant that the standoff would have to take the shape of a culture war. This time, the enemy had to be the West itself, with all of its supposed liberal values: rootlessness, atheism, feminism, homosexuality. The word *liberal* moved to the center of a semiotic cluster denoting all sorts of weakness and depravity. (The telling slur *liberast*, a portmanteau of *liberal* and *pederast*, came into vogue around the same time.) *Jewish* fluttered invisibly around, repped by the old standbys such as *globalist*, *international*, and *Soros*.

Standing up to defend Mother Russia against the scourge of Sorosian liberasty would be the equally commingled forces of nationalism, clericalism, patriarchy, and a somewhat authentically Russian notion of *gosudarstvennichestvo*, "statism," which basically erases any philosophical difference between a country and a government—so that the Czarist Russia, the Soviet Union, and Putin's hybrid regime begin to look like a smooth continuum and demand the same fealty. The Eastern Orthodox Church, never fully outlawed in the Soviet Union, was the obvious glue to hold this flimsy construction together.*

This was what the anonymous Kremlin insider warned me about at Kapkov's house. The church was about to be massively

---

*At the price of collaborating with, and allowing heavy infiltration by, the KGB—to which the "black cassock, gold shoulder boards" line in Pussy Riot's "Punk Prayer" directly alludes.

empowered. We were witnessing the beginning of the cynical "values" gambit that would soon make Vladimir Putin an icon of far-right movements everywhere, and Russia, with its sky-high divorce and HIV rates and a de facto sharia vassal state in Chechnya, into a conservative candyland. Punishing Pussy Riot—atheist, feminist, pro-gay, *and* anti-Putin—was a natural first move.

On March 3, the eve of Putin's reelection, Nadya Tolokonnikova, Masha Alekhina, and Katya Samutsevich—three members of the fivesome that staged the Cathedral of Christ the Savior stunt—were arrested and charged with "hooliganism motivated by religious hatred." Gone were the days of nine-dollar fines. The "religious hatred" caveat made all three eligible for up to seven years in prison. The other two women, to this date known only as Kot and Pokhlebka (Tomcat and Stew), managed to escape both the imprisonment and the subsequent fame.

With the help of Tolokonnikova's husband, Peter Verzilov, who remained unindicted and whose impeccable English was matched only by his almost alarming gift for persuasion, the case became a global cause célèbre. By April, Amnesty International named Pussy Riot "prisoners of conscience." The U.S. government "expressed concern." As the trial dragged on, dozens of Western stars—Madonna, Björk, even Danny DeVito—sang, spoke, wrote, and tweeted their support. A balaclava briefly became the new Guy Fawkes mask. Covers of "Punk Prayer" multiplied on YouTube. A chapter of Pussy Riot even opened in Olympia, Washington, the birthplace of Bikini Kill.

On a mid-August night, with the verdict in the case days away, I sat on the terrace at Strelka Bar, drinking a badly mixed fifteen-dollar daiquiri and writing a Pussy Riot op-ed for *The New York Times.* Nadya, Masha, and Katya meanwhile starved in the stifling cells of SIZO 6, the pre-trial detention center where the state had kept them since March. Glowing yellow at my twelve-o'clock across the river, on the far end of a garish footbridge, was the Cathedral of Christ the Savior. A couple of American tourists, a guy and a girl, leaned on the glass railing near my table to snap a better picture. They seemed very excited to see it.

The next thing I heard proved that, if nothing else, the forty-second action had simplified the manyfold significance of these golden domes once and for all.

"Excuse me," the girl said. "Is this the Pussy Riot Church?"

I stepped into my office and there it was, laid across the desk. The dreaded envelope with the circulation figures. Over my first spring and summer at *GQ*, a solid pattern had emerged: the prouder I was of an issue, the fewer copies it sold. My attempt to put a Russian on the cover—Denis Shirokov, a scandalous and handsome soccer player—ironically turned out to be a hopeless Americanism (the Russians preferred their sports stars to stay in the sports pages) and resulted in the worst-selling issue in the magazine's history. The Kermlins' political cartoon on the back page appeared to amuse primarily them and me. The *New Yorker*–style features in the middle section commanded abstract respect but little involvement. In my apathy toward Russia's ridiculous "high society," I had lost the Rublevka crowd but failed to bring in anyone to replace it; my only area of unqualified triumph was the website, whose audience I had grown tenfold and understood much better—but which accounted for about 4 percent of the magazine's revenue.

The big advertisers began to flee. Mercury pulled four pages from all three fall issues. Bosco threatened to pull out if we didn't offer them more "support"; they also disliked the magazine's direction, especially the long stories. Breguet pulled an ad because I was too sick to come to a concert they sponsored. Strangest of all, however, were the "negative comments" some sponsors apparently would make when I took Lily to society events as my date. This both infuriated and befuddled me—as much, apparently, as the idea of a wife as a friend and partner befuddled the Muscovites. The preferred states of being for a magazine editor were (a) married to a twenty-year-old bimbo, (b) gay, and closeted, of course, but just badly enough so everyone would have something to gossip about, or (c) having affairs all over the place.

Amid it all, Karina Dobrotvorskaya took me out to dinner to share advice (which boiled down to "be more like *Tatler*") and tell a story about a former deputy editor at one of the women's magazines who went crazy after several years of work. The editor ran around the Fur Fridge's front yard with a cross in her hand, damning everyone to hell and yelling "Condé Nast is evil!" until they took her to a psychiatric hospital. I wasn't sure whether this was intended as a pep talk.

Throughout the summer, the more room in my life this dismal nonsense took up, the more I fixated on the Pussy Riot trial, unfolding a couple of miles away at the Khamovniki District Court. Sometimes, in the absence of any major protests after May 6 and Occupy Abai, it seemed like the only significant instance of ongoing dialogue between the opposition and the state. The trial dominated the news feeds, creating new memes every day. The state, determined to treat it as a three-ring circus, tried to quote the Quinisext Council of A.D. 693 as a legal precedent, and rolled out a mad parade of witnesses, some unnecessarily doubling as "victims" to prove that the feelings of true believers had indeed been offended. One such witness admitted that he had only seen the group's performance on YouTube; his testimony included the instantly famous phrase "I assure you, hell is as real as the Moscow Metro." Two burly security guards claimed that the women's demonic dancing had distressed them so much that they were no longer capable of performing their duties. (Masha Alekhina tried in vain to direct the court's attention to the fact that the guards' testimony was identical to a word, including the errors.) The central-casting judge, Marina Syrova, had predictably infinite patience for the state's shenanigans. The three-lawyer defense, for its part, consisted mostly of showboating and histrionics, and spent precious cross-examination time on questions like "Doesn't Christ teach you forgiveness?" The only bulwarks of calm, reason, and common sense in the room were the three women on trial.

Like many people, I had started out dismissing Pussy Riot's early actions as juvenile fun, perhaps too openly optimized for Western press coverage; it almost felt like part and parcel of Kapkovshchina—now that Moscow has skate ramps, why not a radical feminist art group in the vein of the Guerrilla Girls! And, until I saw the primordial burn-the-witch anger it exposed, I didn't find the Christ the Savior stunt particularly clever, either. It was, in fact, the trial itself, specifically the three young women's behavior on the stand, that convinced me otherwise. As I watched them in that lurid glass cage, built a decade prior for the prosecution of Russia's political prisoner number one, Mikhail Khodorkovsky, and listened to their speeches—defiant but reasoned, brimming with biblical, classic, and modern quotes jotted down from memory (no Internet in SIZO 6)—I began to suspect I might be seeing something as historic as the trials of Solzhenitsyn and Joseph Brodsky. Indeed, *The New Yorker*'s David Remnick would soon call Pussy Riot's pointedly academic statements to the court "a kind of instant classic in the anthology of dissidence." The fact that two out of the three defendants already looked like movie versions of themselves—Tolokonnikova, an emaciated Angelina Jolie in her blue ¡NO PASARÁN! T-shirt, and beatific Alekhina with her Botticellian hair halo—was a weird, complicating element: it helped tease out the sexism in the band's detractors and in its supporters as well.

I was not exactly alone among the Russians in my growing admiration for the group, but the hometown opinion on Pussy Riot remained mixed at best. Even the liberal response involved language like "They should let those chicks go with a slap on the ass." Most of the debate about the trial was a roundelay of pointless syllogisms: What if it was your daughter up there? What if they tried doing this in a mosque? What if someone came into your house and defecated on the carpet? (The latter rhetorical device was, for some reason, very popular; one encountered it almost daily.) Navalny's few statements about Pussy Riot were full of caveats about how repulsive he found the performance in question. It was quite clear that, as much as they disliked the state and the state-coddled church, the mainstream of the Russian opposition remained even more uncomfortable with activist women.

This, in fact, was a feature of the protest movement I hadn't noticed in my initial excitement: for all its indignation about the "crooks and thieves" in the government, it pointedly didn't concern itself with any other kind of injustice. Even at the top of the opposition ladder, Putin-hatred easily coexisted with racist jokes and Neanderthal homophobia, just as the young Muscovites' newfound worship of New York's urbanist comforts didn't come with a side of New York values. Pride parades remained outlawed, and more homophobic legislation was on the way, but all of that lay outside the opposition's scope: it was assumed that no one except the gays would ever march for gay rights. Conversely, the "fair elections" rallies often featured columns with rainbow flags, while many Communists, anarchists, and others grumbled about having to march next to "faggots." The idea that liberalism partly meant upholding someone else's liberty—including their right to do something that's personally offensive to you—was still an alien notion.

Russia's music community wasn't much help, either. While Western rockers couldn't hand-draw FREE PUSSY RIOT T-shirts fast enough, Zemfira and Mumiy Troll, the biggest names in Russian rock, demurred from commenting when asked. Their reticence may have been partly rooted in the scene's forced political neutrality (when the best-paying gigs in town are private shows for Kremlin-friendly oligarchs, there's not much you can say without jeopardizing your bookings, à la Ksenia Sobchak). Mostly, however, it had to do with confusion about Pussy Riot's status. The international press mostly called them a "punk band," which was a bit reductive but made people from Madonna to the Red Hot Chili Peppers' frontman Anthony Kiedis feel like they were sticking up for their own; no stadium-playing Russian musician, on the other hand, would feel professional affinity with a group of masked activists running around quoting Julia Kristeva. If anything, they were confused by, and likely a little jealous of, all the global hoopla: "What's so great about Pussy Riot that all these international stars should support them?" wrote Valeria, a pop singer who had staged several failed attempts to break into the West herself. "They must be doing this because someone ordered them to." It goes without saying that, in the Russian mind, Anthony Kiedis takes direct dictation from Foggy Bottom.

On August 7, the eve of the closing statements in the Pussy Riot case, I opened Twitter and saw a long conversation between my deputy editor Volobuev and Navalny. "So if Pussy Riot go to prison," Volobuev asked, "and the May 6 protesters go to prison, what do we do next? More angry columns and Facebook posts? Another rally?"

"You tell me," Navalny tweeted back. "What's next? What's your ideal scenario?"

Fuck. The leader of the Russian opposition is asking my deputy what to do. FUCK.

"I keep waiting for a grown-up to come and tell us what the plan is," Volobuev wrote. "But it looks like we're the grown-ups. God help us all."

At that precise moment, my Twitter feed around their exchange exploded with photos of Madonna, who performed that night at the Olympic Stadium a few miles away. The Virgin Mary's self-assigned namesake—as close to an actual deity as the "Punk Prayer" could ever hope to reach—put on a balaclava. She then stripped to reveal the words "Pussy Riot" scrawled on her bare back, and launched into "Like a Virgin."

The stadium went nuts. Twitter went nuts. I even allowed myself a twinge of hope about the trial: Would Russia, with the eyes of the entire world on the case, really be dumb and cruel enough to send these women to prison? And if there's even a small chance that the answer is no, shouldn't I use my creaky pulpit of a slipping, institutionally sexist men's magazine to get even *more* eyes on it? As this tiny manic episode crested, I resolved to obtain and print an interview with Pussy Riot. I wasn't sure exactly how I'd do it, but I knew I would. What did I have to lose? Except more readers and perhaps my job?

The morning of the verdict, August 17, began with another handy caricature of useless privilege: I spent it at a tennis club near work. As I listlessly practiced my forehand, my coach—an Armenian-born Baptist—opined, like everyone in Moscow that day, about Pussy Riot. In his ideal society, based on "religious values," they would get death sentences. I tried asking leading questions ("And what would you do with gay people? What about drug addicts? Atheists?") to steer him to the realization that he'd be building a fascist dictatorship, but the punch line failed to land; turned out he didn't mind fascism. "All power is from God," he shrugged. Even Hitler? Even Hitler. I got out, stopped by work, tossed the racquet into my office, and went straight to the Khamovniki District Court.

The crowd in front of the courthouse radiated pregame jitters. OMON, priests, singing hippies, elderly crazies, activists in hand-knitted balaclavas—this scene could go any possible way at any possible moment. The people gathering outside ranged from Dmitri Bykov to the fanatic Orthodox provocateur Dmitry Enteo, whose own actions (like calling in bomb threats to rock concerts and tearing T-shirts off protesters) were, if anything, more radical than Pussy Riot's, though they naturally went unpunished. Yesterday's freak, Enteo was now the tip of the clericalist spear aimed at the Russian society.*

Inside the building, a sweaty crush of reporters, most Western, all hoping to get into the courtroom, took up several flights of stairs. The Hack Pack was out in full force: Ioffe and Koens; Miriam Elder, whom BuzzFeed had just hired away from *The Guardian*; and Shaun Walker, who had taken her place. A couple of bailiffs stood at the top picking out the winners more or less at random, provided that you begged. It was the usual Russian transaction between a person and the state: a unit of dignity for a unit of access. On one of the landings, a white-haired man in a tidy short-sleeved dress shirt—Masha Alekhina's father—sat alone on a little bench. Despair had become his resting face.

The moment I saw Nadya, Masha, and Katya, I felt something I hadn't yet felt once in Moscow, in a job that required me to deal with famous Russians almost daily: starstruck. Here, staring at three young women in a glass cage, I was finally in the presence of genuine celebrity. Here, finally, was a Russian band capable of taking over the world—a band with an edgy name, a catchy look, and a compelling story. Except it was not a band at all. And instead of a world tour, its members faced prison.

---

*In another illustration of how impossibly complicated the Russian life can get in comparison to the black-and-white story lines we keep imposing onto it, in 2017 Alekhina and Enteo would begin to date.

The sentence came. Two years. For forty seconds of dancing in a church. Eighteen days and nights per second. This was the humane option—the maximum punishment on the "hooliganism motivated by religious hatred" was seven years, the prosecution had asked for four; the fact that both Tolokonnikova and Alekhina had small children was considered a mitigating circumstance. Putin applauded the two-year sentence in his trademark manner, technically refusing to comment but at the same time describing the court's ruling with the slang term *zalepil im dvushechku* (slapped them with a deuce) that could mean only hearty approval. Katya Samutsevich would switch lawyers and get released on appeal in October; among the reasons for suspending her sentence the judge would cite her apologetic behavior. Alekhina and Tolokonnikova, who remained cool, smiling, and remote throughout the ordeal, would serve out most of their terms in two separate but similarly brutal and remote prison colonies, and not see freedom until December 2013.

In the 1960s, the trial of the future Nobel laureate Joseph Brodsky (which featured the iconic question "Who made you a poet?") accidentally made a star of the writer Frida Vigdorova, who kept surreptitious notes that became an underground Soviet classic. Pussy Riot might not match, or aim to match, Brodsky's talent for verse ("Putin is chickenshit" is not quite Nobel-literature material), but their trial created dozens of new Vigdorovas. The normally flippant and cynical Western correspondents were leaving the courtroom shaken and disgusted by the spectacle. At the same time, dozens of people were posting online a single word: *shameful*. (A few more went for an obscene two-word variation: *ebanyi styd*.) Outside the courthouse, the already-familiar scene of mass arrests had commenced. One balaclava-clad protester, Tatyana Romanova, spectacularly avoided capture by scaling the chain-link fence of the nearby Turkish embassy, where she proceeded to taunt the OMON from foreign territory. She eventually received a five-hundred-ruble fine—just like the one Pussy Riot had paid for their Red Square performance in what, as of this hour, felt like an entirely different era.

The next day, I contacted the group's three hapless defense lawyers, who could sneak my questions into their clients' cells and get handwritten answers back. The trio of lawyers shared one female assistant, who promptly replied: "It's such a pity that the lawyers themselves have not been profiled enough, don't you find?"

"Sure," I wrote back, "it's a terrible pity. Let me look for a writer to assign a profile of all three. In the meantime, may I submit my questions to Nadya, Katya, and Masha?" "When you have profiled the lawyers," she answered, "we can proceed with the questions for the girls." In other words, they were leveraging access to their clients for their own PR. Fine, two can play this game. Without alerting anyone at the magazine, I sent Lily to a lunch with one lawyer, Mark Feygin, and met with another, Nikolai Polozov, myself, with zero intention of running a story on either one. I got out of profiling Violetta Volkova, the third lawyer, by earnestly explaining to the assistant that we were a men's magazine, so she would have to pose for a sexy photo shoot.

The gambit worked, and the lawyers passed my questions along to Tolokonnikova, Alekhina, and Samutsevich. A few weeks later, Polozov handed me two thin stacks of loose, cross-lined paper. Tolokonnikova had written seven pages in tiny careful script, Alekhina five in strange vertical columns. Samutsevich's answers had been confiscated by the guards. Every answer was a full-fledged essay, well-considered and argued. I had no idea how they did this. The resulting interview came out in the U.S., British, Italian, Spanish, Portuguese, and Turkish editions of GQ. And, yes, in mine as well.

This exchange of letters began a kind of long-distance friendship that would lead me to hang out with Tolokonnikova and Alek-hina in Moscow and London, write the Russian dialogue for their *House of Cards* cameo, and even attempt to coauthor a book with them. Over time, many things would change. The anonymous Pussy Riot would formally kick out the unmasked duo for going too legit; Tolokonnikova and Alekhina would further split the brand into parallel solo projects, for rather banal *Behind the Music*-esque reasons; I would shift my opinion of their work back and forth a few more times—finding, for instance, the celebrity-assisted professionalization of their musical output ill-advised, their turn toward the U.S. issues clumsy, and their evident goal of joining the global-left iconostasis alongside Zizek, Chomsky, and Banksy a case of selling themselves too short. But for the honor and dignity alone with which they handled their arrest, trial, and prison, I never looked at Nadya or Masha with anything other than awe.

Several years later, perhaps in 2015, Alekhina took me to see a friend's band. It was a noise-rock outfit with minimal melodies and a very theatrical presentation. Not my cup of tea, but something about the singer's voice scratched at my brain. It felt . . . familiar. I listened on, occasionally sneaking glances at Alekhina, who smoked in the other end of the room, until it finally clicked. I froze in place, feeling a little like the protagonist of a latter-day William Gibson novel. Before me, in this dingy club, was the actual voice of "Punk Prayer." The vocalist was one of the anonymous women who had gotten away. I looked at the small crowd bobbing their heads to the distorted beat, wondering how many of them knew or cared. Then I stared at Alekhina again. After the prison and the fame, the hunger strikes and the state dinners, would she be happier now if she and that singer were to switch places? Would the singer? Ale-khina caught my quizzical look, pulled on her cigarette, returned her gaze to the woman on the stage, and smiled.

The night of Pussy Riot's sentencing, I joined the Hack Pack—Ioffe, Koens, Elder, et al.—and got uproariously drunk at Bontempi, arguing about the case through the bar's last call. I believed that the only correct response to a broken system was the Vaclav Havel strategy of proceeding as if it *weren't* broken. In my view, Pussy Riot's defense team had wasted a trial that should have revolved around a single legal question (Does a violation of church protocol rise to the level of religious hatred?) on populist posturing.* Even with the system stacked against them, they could have lost with dignity and prepared the grounds for an appeal, which might land in more reasonable people's hands. Instead, they fucked around in and out of court. One day before the sentencing, for instance, Mark Feygin decided to "address critics" on his blog by posting his work ID (to prove his professionalism) and his mother's birth certificate (to prove that he was not a Jew). Nikolai Polozov tweeted throughout the reading of the verdict; he would spend the next night, which fell on a Saturday, DJing at Zavtra (Tomorrow), a bar popular with both pro- and anti-Putin journalists, lifting his shirt up and spraying the sweaty crowd with bottled water while the clients whose case he had just lost prepared for a journey to far-flung prison colonies. I couldn't say much about this, though: in two weeks, I was scheduled to DJ at the same bar.

The opposite view—shared by most of the Hack Pack, especially Elder—was that, since the guilty verdict was preordained, making a mockery of the whole thing (tweeting, flaunting unpreparedness, trolling witnesses) was the most correct strategy. The lawyers simply mirrored the state's own approach to justice. The only way to

---

*Alekhina's and Tolokonnikova's own cross-examinations of prosecution witnesses, conducted out of their glass cage, were much better. They would, for example, ask the church's security guards how they would respond to a crime (call the police), then point out that they hadn't called the police on *them*; did this mean they had originally judged their actions harmless until ordered to think otherwise?

survive in a circus was to put on a clown suit—be it a balaclava or a rep tie. The moment for white-ribbon earnestness was brief, and now it had passed. The Russian penchant for turning everything into phantasmagoria, performance art, and postmodernist parody was taking over.

Two weeks later, from the DJ stand at Zavtra, I was blasting LCD Soundsystem and watching hipster protesters and hipster Putinists dance together like two senators' staffs bro-ing out at a D.C. bar. The difference was that, in this case, only one side had, and used, the power to send the other to prison. Yet, in a world of triumphing unreality, both existed in a symbiotic loop. I closed the set with Pussy Riot's latest, "Putin Lights the Fires of Revolution," and people in Putin T-shirts danced to it. Perhaps their T-shirts were ironic—or their dancing was, or they thought *I* was for putting it on. None of this made sense, or a difference, anymore. The protests were done. (In September, a widely announced "white ribbon" auto rally in Kaluga drew exactly one car.) Pussy Riot was done. Independent journalism was done. The only thing left to do was dance.

Chapter Seven

My Name Is
Matt Rushkin

O n December 14, 2012, President Barack Obama signed
the Magnitsky Act, a long-lobbied-for bill that had the
distinction of becoming the first concrete U.S. sanction
against post-Soviet Russia.* Sergei Magnitsky, an auditor at a law

---

*Interestingly, it came tied to the repeal of 1974's Jackson-Vanik Amendment, which
applied economic pressure on the Soviet Union to force it into allowing mass Jewish
emigration.

firm, had found evidence of a massive criminal scheme that involved Russian officials, police investigators, and the Mafia; all three worked in concert to gut one of his firm's client companies and steal $230 million it had paid in taxes through a fraudulent refund. Following the established Russian custom of vengeance through projection—accusing your enemy of your own sins—the same investigators whom Magnitsky had fingered then charged him with the very crime he had uncovered. They threw him in prison, where, possibly tortured, with untreated gallstones and pancreatitis, he died after eleven months without a trial. The stolen millions had gone into luxury real estate in Dubai and Manhattan.

The unusual driving force behind the new law was Bill Browder, Magnitsky's erstwhile client and, for a period, the biggest foreign investor in Russia. Having made a fortune in the wilds of the 1990s but then been barred from the country in 2006 as a "threat to national security," Browder threw his money and connections into lobbying for the act as if it were a personal vendetta against Putin, which it may well have been. He succeeded. The Magnitsky Act named the officials directly and indirectly responsible for the lawyer's death, froze their American assets, and barred them from entering the United States. More important, it created the framework for denying other high-level Russians similar spoils: from there on out, their names could simply be added to the list. More than any piece of high-flown rhetoric, the law recognized the damp, unimaginative greed underpinning the most baroque Russian villainy—that its end goal, more often than not, was not world domination but a Miami villa and a park-view classic eight.

Within two weeks, by December 28, Russia had responded with a law of its own: On Sanctions for Individuals Violating Fundamental Human Rights and Freedoms of the Citizens of the Russian Federation, a tit-for-tat retaliation against the United States. It was made toothless by the fact that hardly any Americans kept money in

Russian banks or fancied Russian real estate. (And, as much as the American liberals, myself included, wanted to see some legal repercussions for the likes of the torture-enabling G. W. Bush–era bureaucrat John Yoo, denying him *The Nutcracker* at the Bolshoi was not exactly what we had in mind.) What made the Russian law more than a symbolic exercise in reciprocity was one addendum. Effective January 1, 2013, it barred American citizens from adopting Russian children.

The adoption ban quickly overshadowed the rest of the bill, which was henceforth known as the Dima Yakovlev law. Dima Yakovlev, a Russian toddler adopted by a U.S. couple and renamed Chase Harrison, had died in a hot car in 2008, only three months after his arrival in the United States; the story made big news in Russia when a Virginia judge acquitted the adoptive father of involuntary manslaughter. The case was obviously tragic, but there was no pattern of disproportionate deaths or suffering among adopted Russian children in the United States. The government's newfound concern for their safety was pure opportunistic hypocrisy.* The Church unsurprisingly gave the law the same thumbs-up it gave Putin's every other initiative. Vsevolod Chaplin, the patriarchate's remarkably named and newly ubiquitous spokesperson, said that the orphans adopted by U.S. citizens wouldn't get "a truly Christian upbringing."

Within days, horrible stories poured in from the States: adoptions canceled at the last minute, couples showing off the rooms and clothes they had prepared for the children who would never arrive. If the idea was to land a blow, it landed. (In the State Department, Michael McFaul told me once, employees openly cried at their workstations when the news hit.) The reason Moscow decided

---

*On the very day of the law's signing, the Pskov governor Andrei Turchak suspended two officials who had signed off on Yakovlev's adoption. The last time Turchak was in the news was for ordering an attack on the journalist Oleg Kashin that left him in a coma.

to strike back in this particular way is still largely a mystery to even the most ardent Kremlinologists—What was the intended effect, and on which imagined audience? Did a freak faction in the Duma happen to have an adoption ban handy and see an opening? Regardless, it set up the blueprint for the Russian human-shield tactic of retaliating against all new sanctions by somehow hurting its own people in response; the tactic that became known, in online shorthand, as "bombing Voronezh."

In order to retroactively explain to ordinary Russians why their government had undertaken this feat of arbitrary barbarity, the Kremlin unleashed a news cycle dominated by a series of horror tales about the mistreatment of Russian children in the West, variations on the classic blood libel. In one insane instance, major state media gave a forum to a clearly disturbed woman who used to be married to a Norwegian man and now belonged to an astroturf organization called Russian Mothers. She claimed that the Norwegians dressed up her four-year-old son "in a Putin costume," whatever the hell that meant, and rented him out to be gang-raped by pedophiles.

This canard was only marginally more idiotic than the fake news items clogging up the Russian Internet: *the Swedes discontinued the use of "he" and "she," the French banned the words "father" and "mother," the Germans introduced mandatory masturbation lessons for eight-year-olds*, and so on and so forth ad nauseam. The state was crumpling up two carefully cultivated paranoias—xenophobia and homophobia—into one ball of hate, with kids as props. By June 2013, St. Petersburg's vile anti-gay law, which the opposition had mostly ignored in the excitement of early 2012 (and in its aforementioned apathy toward minority issues), went national. Called For the Purpose of Protecting Children from Information Advocating for a Denial of Traditional Family Values, it was another wild tilt at a nonexistent enemy, designed to stoke fears instead of allaying them. The law banned all speech that "create[d] false equivalence between traditional and non-traditional lifestyles"—this in a country whose pop stars' wardrobes suggested that Russia's biggest natural resource was rhinestones. Within weeks, I had to fight Condé Nast's in-house counsel for the right to publish a positive review of *Behind the Candelabra*, Steven Soderbergh's Liberace biopic. He objected to the use of the word *love* to describe a same-sex relationship (the logic: gay people can have sex all they want, but calling it *love* created the dreaded "false equivalence"). I threw a fit and threatened to quit on the spot. The review stayed. Somehow, the system weathered the blow.

As the second year of Putin's third term in power went on, a certain tinge of morbid farce began to color everything. The president himself gave off the impression of having checked out from this lowly plane and ascended to a higher one. Judging from the news, he spent most of his time communing with animals. He flew in a deltaplane leading a flock of cranes, rode horses, cradled tiger cubs, and once, in a video from a fishing expedition, planted a kiss on the head of a giant pike, which hopefully didn't create any false equivalences.

The Duma, where no one had previously been allowed to out-crazy Vladimir Zhirinovsky, now swarmed with freakish demagogues pulled from the margins and into the spotlight: Elena Mizulina, who wanted Eastern Orthodox Christianity written into the Constitution and thought the anti-gay law didn't go far enough (she wanted children forcibly removed from gay parents), was the new normal. The "crazies" provided a valuable service, since their initiatives could be used as deniable trial balloons. They also helped the Kremlin's general strategy, post-protests, of tarring everything Western, liberal, and democratic—including, to a large extent, the idea of a working parliament itself—as an unnatural foreign imposition on Russia. A buddy of Putin's nicknamed the Surgeon, a former dentist who formed his own right-wing motorcycle gang when Hells Angels wouldn't let him open their Russian chapter, became a political figure of some weight. The Surgeon showed up to Kremlin events in his custom Night Wolves uniform, which was meant to evoke a kind of leather armor but looked like unwashed fetish gear instead. On the street level, too, a whole class of *ryazhenye*—costumed pseudo-Cossacks and such—arose from the wilds of on-line forums and battle-reenactment camps, sensing, perhaps, their new franchise. The Union of Orthodox Gonfaloniers, who burned Madonna posters while chanting "Orthodoxy or death" and advocated for the canonization of pop singer Igor Talkov, was a fairly mundane example.

In his 1957 novel *Pnin*, Vladimir Nabokov draws, in a few precise strokes, a repulsive couple named the Komarovs, whose "ideal Russia consisted of the Red Army, the God's anointed Sovereign, kolkhozes, anthroposophy, the Orthodox Church, and hydropower stations." This was precisely the kind of dark dregs, postmodern yet backward, that swirled to the top now. It all reminded me of my childhood visits to Leningrad circa 1990, when on any given street corner you could see bearded monarchists wearing thrift-store medals, mystics hawking newspapers with blurry UFO photos, Tolkienists, Trotskyites, black-shirted fascists, and saffron-robed Hare Krishnas—with the difference that all were now working for the same side. It was a unified front of madness in the service of the status quo, repelling all protest by preventively parodying it.

The demoralized liberals, meanwhile, passed the time in an endless argument about who "sold out" the movement and at what point. Of course, a real answer to that question would have to recognize that these kinds of purity tests had helped doom the protest in the first place. The hubbub had risen to a point where someone in the current elite could have possibly harnessed it to unseat Putin, but it waned when no outreach was made by either side. Rather than reflect on their failures, it was much easier to keep pointing fingers instead.

More than a few of these fingers ended up pointing in my direction. As a willfully undefined figure whose whole shtick consisted of avoiding labels, I made an easy target; and, of course, my very coming to Moscow was, in the eyes of the self-hating Russian intelligentsia, an act of selling out. Now all my attempts at balance looked like equivocations. When I abstained from commenting on the latest outrage, I was hiding behind my American passport; when I went ahead and commented—as I did on the ludicrous Dima Yakovlev law—I was poking my nose into another country's affairs. If I did something off-brand for an editor of a glossy, like listen to Russian rap or ride the Metro, I was trying too hard to be cool; if I stayed on message, I was a privileged prick.

One of my last attempts to be useful to the opposition came during the so-called Arctic 30 affair. Greenpeace had staged a protest on a Russian drilling platform in international waters; in response, Russia seized its ship, *Arctic Sunrise*, detained the activists and the crew at gunpoint, and charged them all with piracy. Among the thirty was a photographer I knew, Denis Sinyakov, essentially imprisoned for doing his job. A friend and fellow photographer, Misha Friedman, came up with a plan to raise some money for Sinyakov's wife and small child: a fundraiser at a bar, perhaps with rum drinks as a nod to the "pirate" theme. The idea seemed like a no-brainer. I had worked as a bartender in the mid-aughts and could still mix a decent cocktail—and *GQ* had contacts at Bacardi, which, with Russia's new ban on liquor advertising, was happy to donate their product. The moment I announced the fundraiser, however, the broken telephone of Russian Facebook twisted it into a "pirate costume party," and met it with howls of derision. If I wanted to help, why wasn't I picketing at the Investigative Committee? Some liberal websites protested Sinyakov's detainment by going without photos for a day—why wasn't GQ.ru doing that? When I pointed out that I was trying to offer concrete aid to Sinyakov's family, and the no-photo protest actually took earnings away from his colleagues, a prominent journalist accused me of "measuring everything by money." The night, ignored and/or boycotted by the opposition establishment, ended up raising about a thousand dollars anyway. Remarkably, several of my Putin-supporting acquaintances showed up.

I understood the roots of such animosity, especially from former friends and self-described fans in the media. I was a tourist; they were stuck here. Most journalists were middle-class; I was, though not at all rich, conspicuously money-adjacent. One thing that kept puzzling me, however, was the discrepancy between this reception and the actual content of the magazine I put out, which was not only as liberal as *Afisha*'s (once you got past the clothes) but also written by many of the same authors.

The answer revealed itself early in 2013, at a relaunch party for Lenta.ru, at the time the main, and best, liberal news resource in the country. I felt emboldened enough to go by a couple of recent successes at *GQ*: the first-person essay, by an anonymous Russian student at Oxford, about dealing drugs to his posh schoolmates, which was a massive and controversial hit (and had even been approached for movie rights), and my own profile of the new leader of Georgia, which bet on his victory three months in advance and schooled the entire Russian press corps, most of whom sent their reporters into Tbilisi only on the week of the election. One of the few people I knew at the party was Daniil Dugaev, the editor of *Afisha*'s travel magazine, *Afisha MIR*. It quickly turned out that, while I obsessively studied all the magazines I considered my competition—that is, all lifestyle monthlies—Dugaev hadn't heard of either story and had no idea about anything I had been up to in over a year.

In the *Afisha* world, he explained to me, the glossies were considered to be the place where quality authors went to make a quick buck without their work ever being read back in the "scene." So, in their eyes, I had vanished. "All we see is your Instagram from, like, Milan Fashion Week," he shrugged, "and it's such a parallel universe."

"But it's not. It's the job. Am I supposed to only do half of it?" As ambivalent as I myself was at this point about the Fur Fridge, I wasn't about to let Dugaev disparage it.

"Ah, see, you take it too seriously. That's because, for you, Condé Nast is a real thing, a multinational company. And to us it's just this funny unpleasant building where people have to work long hours."

"Well, yes, I work for all of Condé Nast," I said. "I mean, Jonathan Newhouse hired me."

"I don't know who that is."

"Dude, that's just unprofessional."

"But I'm *not* a professional!" Dugaev gleefully agreed. "I'm a linguist!"

"Well," I said through my teeth, "as long as you know your place," and left the room seething. Within a few years of this conversation, both *Afisha* and *Afisha MIR* would no longer be in existence; Lenta.ru, whose new design the party celebrated, would be taken over by a team more loyal to the regime; and Dugaev would be living in Barcelona. Judging from his Instagram, he had taken up yachting.

This background hum of hostility was starting to take a serious toll on me. I was as depressed as I had ever been in my life, including my first lonely year in America. The Dorozhkin slap, and a combative TV interview a few weeks later that went viral on YouTube, cemented my reputation as a thin-skinned live wire. In a bit of self-fulfilling prophesy, I became exactly that. I began to stay away from liberal media events, where I was much more likely to be mocked to my face than at the various boutique-opening type deals; at least the kissy-kissy fashion crowd had the decency to wait until I was out of earshot. I became unpleasant to Lily for appearing miserable in her high-society arm-candy role, which made her more miserable, which made me more unpleasant. I struggled to complete tasks. When an opportunity opened up to write for *The New Yorker*, which only a few years before would have been the apex of my ambition, I couldn't rouse myself to do a half-decent job. I considered quitting—well ahead of the two years I had promised Dobrotvorskaya—but didn't want to give the snickering Russian onlookers the satisfaction of feeling that they had broken me; especially after LookAtMe.ru and *Bolshoi Gorod* had taken it upon themselves to compile all my "scandals" into comical year-end features, the image of a naive Westerner flailing against the Russian chaos being masochistically irresistible. My running back to New York would have only led them to luxuriate in their own weird self-hatred—*yes! We truly are the worst! Look at that weakling, unable to handle us, haha.* I needed an exit strategy, a move out that would look like a step up.

Meanwhile, with little to lose and sick of the "nothing is real in Russia" stance, I decided to lean into my reputation. I revamped the magazine, hiring younger writers and getting rid of the "legacy" columnists held over from the Uskov era: Dmitri Bykov, the mustachioed public intellectual, and Eduard Limonov, the superannuated radical whose writing (submitted in longhand and remunerated in cash) had gotten increasingly incoherent. I parted ways with the former for publishing his *GQ* columns in their entirety on his Facebook, from where they got picked up by other media without attribution, and the latter for slightly rearranging the words in one of his essays and reselling it to *Afisha*. I then had security *literally* toss out an ex-staffer who, at that point employed by my direct competition at *Snob*, had decided to drop by our offices (with future covers in full view) to visit a friend.

Roman Volobuev amicably quit to write and direct films, a move I envied with all my being. My new deputy editor, at Roman's own suggestion, was Elena "Lelya" Smolina of *Empire* magazine, lovely and smart and not-at-all-Russian in her affect, which was quickly becoming the highest praise I could muster. In her calm presence,

I could take a few deep breaths and wind down this brief reign of Yankee terror. Whereas I used to hand edit every article, headline, and caption in the magazine, I began to let go of the wheel a little. My principles were slackening in other areas as well. Since my refusal to accept flack gifts met zero recognition in and out of the office (and since the politically pure "opposition" editors happily broke this rule left and right), there was little impetus to keep it up. When Louboutin, a shoe brand whose bedazzled sneakers I had earlier sent back, presented Lily with free high-heel pumps, we broke down and accepted—though I did send them a three-hundred-dollar bottle of Dom Pérignon, which absolved me in my own eyes . . . though I had gotten the Dom Pérignon for free as well . . . though we were allowed to accept perishables. (Such was the accidental Communism of the glamorous set: everything you ate, drank, and wore was either a favor or a bribe or a direct-marketing freebie or a brand-ambassadorship obligation. Money barely entered into it at all.) The second time came easier. Soon enough, I was "test driving" a free Jaguar, just like Uskov had before me, though I did refuse to let it affect the coverage. With the flashy car came the traffic stops—and, before I knew it, I was counting off thousand-ruble bills to make a cop look past my expired New York license. It was easier than renewing one.

As my integrity dissolved in a swirl of equivocations, so did my archetypal East Coast do-gooder reflexes. I quit any feeble at-tempts at recycling. Waste-sorting bins occasionally appeared here and there in Moscow—but, naturally, no one trusted them ("It's a PR stunt to create a green image for the Moscow government," de-clared Greenpeace Russia in response to the latest campaign), and carefully sorted recyclables were generally assumed to end up in the same landfill as toxic waste. So why try?

In my new quest to stop worrying and learn to love—okay, to ignore—a dictatorship, I had no better role model than Condé Nast itself. In early 2013 I met with Darius Sanai, the elegant Iranian British publisher of *Baku*. Named after the capital of Azerbaijan, the magazine was "edited" by the Azerbaijani president Ilham Aliyev's daughter Leyla Aliyeva. The family paid Condé Nast's on-demand division to put it out.* The Newhouses' worry, Sanai told me, was that Azerbaijan would "turn into Libya" and Condé Nast would be stuck as the guys who published a propaganda magazine by a dictator's daughter. But for now, the Aliyevs were "on the acceptable side of unacceptable," as he smoothly put it.

Leyla aspired to turn Baku into a hip modern-art destination, art having become the ultimate legitimizing tool for the nouveau riche, and so her magazine ham-fistedly split international gallery and exhibit coverage with "Isn't Baku the greatest?" stories. Naturally, Aliyeva's own paintings were in there as well, alongside features on her parents and then-husband Emin Agalarov (crooner, developer, Nobu co-owner, and Trump's partner in 2013's Miss Universe pageant who went by just "Emin" in his musical endeavors). I suggested a couple of ways to make the magazine's striving less obvious—for instance, set interviews in Baku without making them *about* how much the interviewee loves Baku. Taking a page from *New York* magazine's playbook, I also recommended developing a "Baku point of view"—young and excitable, jumping on art trends all over the world without bothering to tie them back to Azerbaijan. (The implicit message being that Baku is the kind of place where cool people care about cool things.) By the end of the conversation, Sanai had invited me to come on board as a "consulting editor." I immediately accepted, quoting in my head the infamous Matt Damon monologue from *Syriana*: "You know what the business world thinks of you? They think a hundred years ago you were living in

---

*The Central Asian First Daughter market was a booming one. The same division used to put out a very similar vanity magazine called *K*—for Kazakhstan.

tents out here in the desert chopping each other's heads off and that's exactly where you'll be in another hundred years—so on behalf of my firm, yes, I accept your money." I was now an indirect employee of a South Caucasian strongman, and all without leaving Condé Nast!

Life untethered from opposition orthodoxy was immeasurably more fun. Somewhere between the Sobchak kiss and the Dorozhkin slap, something approaching actual fame began to congeal around me. I kept getting invited onto TV shows, including being offered a presenter spot at the Golden Gramophone, a music awards ceremony held inside the Kremlin (security puzzled over my U.S. passport for a week before clearing me for a pass). If I wanted to go to a sold-out movie or play, I just showed up, and the PR person at the theater let me in. When the likes of Scarlett Johansson or Adrien Brody came to town to promote something or other, I'd be the one plopped in front of them at dinner for awkward small talk. St. Petersburg's Buddha Bar flew in me, Lily, Vera, and Vera's nanny, all in business class, just so I could go to its opening. I began to recognize society photographers: the smiling young woman from *Spletnik*, the short Catalonian-looking brunette from *Buro 24/7*, the tall guy who always asked me to stand with my arms crossed. When I was at a party and no one photographed me, I would feel slightly unsettled.

I made new friends whose political views ranged from breezy uninvolvement with all things political to a kind of Kapkovian Putinism-lite to hard-core gosudarstvennichestvo. The brilliant rapper Oxxxymiron, né Miron Fyodorov, whose there-and-back-again biography mirrored mine, belonged in the first category. After repatriating to Russia from London, where he had spent some years steeping in the grime scene, Miron was clearly going through some of the same shit I was ("Should I lean in, carry on, be patient / or yield the field to my pale imitations?"), and his songs helped me survive Moscow by projecting my own arrogance and self-doubt on his furious verse.

The most colorful representatives of the third type—full-on Putin fandom—in my sight were the TV personality and PR maven Tina Kandelaki, a kind of Black Swan to her former bestie Ksenia Sobchak, and Kandelaki's boyfriend Vasily Brovko, whose Apostol Media agency was rumored to stand behind such things as the Chechen strongman Ramzan Kadyrov's Instagram, DDoS attacks on liberal media, and even the hounding of Ambassador McFaul. (Vasily denied all this.) I knew him mostly as a bespectacled dork tooling around Moscow in a Lamborghini.

Apart from Miron, who became a close confidant, more than a few of these were friendships of mutual convenience, goal-oriented and expirable, pop-up friendships; others, however, were rooted in the simple fact that these people were much nicer to me than the gang I had come here to join. None of these new acquaintances would prove to be as life changing, however, as an accidental introduction to a man named Fedor Bondarchuk.

None too unusually for Russia, Bondarchuk was a director, actor, producer, studio executive, TV host, entrepreneur, restaurateur, advertising spokesperson, style icon, and United Russia member. The only unusual part was the degree of success he enjoyed in all these disparate endeavors. As an actor, he was one of Russia's most recognizable and highest paid; as a director, he worked with the largest budgets in the Russian cinema; his flagship restaurant, Vanil, sat kitty-corner from the Cathedral of Christ the Savior since 2001. And, of course, his very public fealty to the regime had a little to do with all of the above.*

Our acquaintance began inauspiciously enough. In late 2012,

---

*This sort of thing evidently ran in the family. Fedor's father, Sergei Bondarchuk, directed the famous 1960s' *War and Peace* adaptation, for which the Soviet state provided a blank-check budget, *and* starred in it as Pierre Bezukhov. His follow-up, *Waterloo*, a coproduction with Dino De Laurentiis, employed more than fifteen thousand active-duty soldiers as free extras.

GQ had shot a fashion spread with a very young actor, Ivan Yankovsky. Using actors instead of models whenever possible was one of my pet causes at the magazine. The fashion team hated it, and now I began to understand why. Yankovsky was a third-generation heir to another grand Soviet acting dynasty; his family felt that he was sullying the name ("an Actor," as his agent put it in a letter to me, capitalization hers, "can't be seen modeling clothes") and demanded that we pull the story, which had already gone to print. This triggered some sort of crisis in poor Ivan, who proceeded to quit the movie in which he was about to star: a romantic comedy produced by, you guessed it, Fedor Bondarchuk. It now fell to me to smooth things over, lest *GQ* acquire Russia's most *GQ*-cover-worthy man for an enemy.

I gingerly reserved a private room at Nedalny Vostok, a seafood restaurant popular with Moscow's power brokers, and beefed up on all things Bondarchuk. The best description of him came from the screenwriter and director Dunya Smirnova, via Volobuev: "He's genuinely a good guy. He's the kind of guy who will sign off on our execution orders, then come in a private jet and rescue us. Because the former is a political act and the latter a personal one."

The first thing Bondarchuk did before sitting down was tuck in the tag on the back of our waitress's shirt; she all but had to be wheeled out of Nedalny Vostok on a stretcher. Bald-headed, goateed, and compact, with narrow darting eyes that widened every time he got excited about something, which was constantly, he turned out to be a manic Clintonian charmer. I didn't have to work him for a second—he was working *me*. Not because he needed anything, but because that was the way Bondarchuk interacted with people. The romantic comedy was swept off the table before the appetizers came: oh well, so he'd recast the main character, Ivan's loss. It was one of a dozen projects Bondarchuk was working on. Right now he was directing a big-budget movie about the Stalingrad battle, Russia's first ever in IMAX 3-D. Bondarchuk whipped out a model of an iPhone that he had apparently gotten before Tim Cook and showed me a few minutes of footage: soldiers on CGI fire, running in luxurious slo-mo. Yet another production of his was about to open next week; this was a big one, and he would really, *really* appreciate it if I came to the premiere.

"No problem," I said, thoroughly entranced. "What's the title?"

"*Soulless.*"

"Like the—"

"Yeah, the book. What?"

"Nothing. Cool." *Soulless* was the bestseller by Sergei Minaev. Of *course* Bondarchuk would be producing its adaptation. It took me a few seconds to realize I had just stepped into an episode of *Curb Your Enthusiasm*: in order to patch things up between the magazine and Bondarchuk, I would need to essentially endorse the guy who had beaten up my friend.

After putting in a call to Andrew Ryvkin, who gave me his formal blessing, I went to the premiere. *Soulless* the movie, shot in beautiful steel tones by Fedor Lyass, was vastly preferable to the book. Where Minaev's nameless banker of a protagonist just fucked around and pontificated, the screenwriter Denis Rodimin gave him a love interest from the wrong side of the tracks—and I mean *wrong*: a brittle activist clearly, and fearlessly, based on Nadya Tolokonnikova of Pussy Riot (though her on-screen art collective, Free Radicals, seemed inspired more by the early actions of Voina). The movie's climax depicted, in a not wholly unsympathetic way, a violent nighttime protest steps from the Fur Fridge, complete with burning barricades and images of the OMON beating up students. *Soulless* would go on to become a huge hit—in part for daring to address, however superficially, the chaotic and broken essence of 2012. Bondarchuk, then, was not as simple as he seemed. A Putin-era creature par excellence, he had perfected the art of being everything to everyone, but his definition of "everyone" was secretly wider than Putin's.

As for the business of patching things up, it worked *too* well: before I knew it, I had a cameo in the same romantic comedy Yankovsky had abandoned.

The movie—called *Odnoklassniki.ru*, after the eponymous Russian clone of Classmates.com—was no *Citizen Kane*, or even *Soulless*. Its plot involved an aspiring copywriter who receives a magic laptop that makes every status update on his Odnoklassniki .ru profile immediately come true. Let's say he uploads a picture of a new Lamborghini with the caption "my new car," and there it is. This, of course, leads him to become conceited and start playing God, and then learn a valuable lesson. The script, I was told, took several years to get right.

The movie's director, Pavel "Hoody" Hoodyakov, and his wife, Korneliya Polyak (who produced and played the female lead), had come to filmmaking through hip-hop videos, both Russian and American—so the movie also costarred Snoop Dogg as a computer repairman, because why the hell not. Pavel and Korneliya were a lot of fun in a kind of night-clubby, cocaine-y way, although they lived pointedly clean. They were two of the only three people I knew who actually owned and used Vertu phones; the third was the CEO of Vertu. Their political views, which slipped out in bits and pieces, were an interesting localization of the hip-hop penchant for respecting success *qua* success, which made Putin the ultimate hustler.

My role, if you could call it that, was a belligerent, drunk American film director on the set of a Russian TV commercial, and consisted entirely of yelling variations on "I can't work like this." (In a sense, this was remarkably on point.) Since dialogue in a foreign language didn't affect the movie's rating, I took the chance to rewrite my lines as an endless stream of obscenities; the Hoodyakovs seemed fine with me working blue. For inspiration, I studied

J. K. Simmons's amazing monologue in the "Taylor Stiltskin Sweet Sixteen" episode of *Party Down*: "I will rip off your dick and fuck your dog with it. (*pause*) To death."

The day's filming took place in a large white-walled soundstage, already familiar to me from *GQ* photo shoots. After Yankovsky's exit, the lead was now played by Petr Fedorov, an intense dramatic actor fresh off Bondarchuk's *Stalingrad*. In "my" scene, Fedorov's copywriter character, high on his superpowers, takes over the set of a lame bottled-water commercial, kicking out the director (me). The commercial-within-the-movie consists of four bikini girls dousing themselves with the water in front of a white Rolls-Royce. The lead self-douser, the whispers on the set went, was a "bought" role—the girl's sugar daddy had paid to cast her. Sure enough, she botched her one and only line, which was "My talents bring luck," take after take, while the cream of the Russian cinema patiently waited on both sides of the camera.

Also in the scene was the Hoodyakovs' best friend, Timati, Russia's most commercially successful rapper. (The white Rolls-Royce behind the writhing women was his; its well-being concerned him greatly throughout the shoot.) Unlike the abrasive and virtuosic Oxxxymiron, Timati was as cuddly as a tattooed teddy bear, a so-so rhymer, and a devoted fan of the Putin administration, a fact that popped up in his lyrics with increasing urgency. Born into brand-new money as Timur Yunusov, Timati was part Jewish, part Tatar. In Russia, this combination was enough to make him "black," a self-chosen designation he made the centerpiece of his Black Star empire, which has at various points encompassed a record label, a line of impressively derivative clothes, a barbershop, a burger franchise, an online gaming company, a soccer team, and a mobile carrier service. His biggest claim to fame outside Russia was a European dance hit called "Welcome to St. Tropez," a greeting Timati was fully authorized to dispense: his father had a villa there.

In the interminable waiting periods that account for 95 percent of every film shoot, Timati and I made small talk, most of which he insisted on keeping in English, and exchanged phone numbers. Then it was my turn to go before the camera and spew profanity, and amid my jitters I all but forgot about this encounter. A couple of weeks later, my phone rang in the middle of an editors' meeting. It was Timati. He phoned to say that he had written a song called "*GQ*."

At first, I thought this was a prank. It wasn't. Jay-Z's "Tom Ford" had just come out, ushering in a very brief era of "brand rap." In his search for a brand that would denote the same kind of sophistication to the Russian ear, Timati explained, he hit upon the title of my magazine. Now he wanted my opinion on the song. My opinion, at the moment, was roughly along the lines of *Holy shit.*

That night, Andrew Ryvkin and I went to Timati's studio on Leninsky Prospect to preview the track. We anticipated clouds of pot smoke, someone asleep in a corner, buxom women lolling about—you know, a rap studio. Timati's lair turned out to be nothing of the sort. If not for a couple of massive security guys out front, it would have looked like a dentist's office. Timati, like the Hoodyakovs, was drug- and alcohol-free and demanded the same from his colleagues and hangers-on.

Andrew and I sank into a leather couch and listened to a rough mix of the song. It was a brass-driven stomp, catchy as all hell. Each hook had twelve iterations of the title *GQ*. In fact, the title *was* the hook.

Real gentlemen always fresh
GQ, GQ, GQ
Intellect attracts cash
GQ, GQ, GQ
The aroma makes the girls moan
GQ, GQ, GQ
Gonna make it all the way on my own
GQ, GQ, GQ

I composed myself and took the news back to Condé Nast. Now the company had to choose one of the three possible reactions: we could haughtily ignore the song; actively fight its release on trademark grounds; or just ride this tiger, see where it takes us, and pretend this was the plan all along. I lobbied hard for option number three. Didn't we want a new audience for the magazine? Well, there it was, on a platter. An admittedly weird platter, but still.

Another week later, I was swinging a golf club at the camera for the song's video, directed by—who else—Pavel Hoodyakov. Around me, dancing and vamping in black tie in front of the giant black letters G and Q, was a who's who of the Putinist elite: the megarestaurateur Arkady Novikov, the TV host Garik Martirosyan, the developer and crooner Emin Agalarov, the stand-up comedian Vladimir Vinokur ("he has Putin on speed dial!" Hoody admiringly whispered into my ear), the media magnate Sergei Kozhevnikov, and, of course, Fedor Bondarchuk.

Emin Agalarov, his Italianite handsomeness rendered non-threatening by modest height, was easily the most enigmatic character in that crowd. As the vice president of Crocus Group, established in 1989 by his father Aras Agalarov, the "Donald Trump of Russia," he was the rare musician with the distinction of regularly playing lavish shows at the venue he also owned. The Agalarov family did indeed share some similarities with the Trumps: their holdings included golf resorts, convention centers, hotels, malls, restaurants, and even a luxury watch brand, U-Boat. Despite this, he was unerringly nice; I recall him being very polite in our few brief conversations, and—unlike Timati, or for that matter Donald Trump, Jr.—downright shy, which seemed at odds with his line of work. For the "GQ" video, while everyone else, myself included, mercilessly mugged for the camera, he played the grand piano.

The shoot went on. Women in Gatsby-style flapper costumes

licked pieces of ice shaped like the letters *GQ*. Confetti rained. Timati did doughnuts on a tiny red motorbike. There was a pony. It had taken me less than two years to get here from Sakharov Square.

Even the screenwriters of *Odnoklassniki.ru* couldn't have come up with a more obvious moment for the protagonist to look back and realize "this wasn't me anymore"—except, of course, it was. It was all me. Thus, the only way to stay sane was to farm this part of me out. To put it on autopilot, dim the lights, turn up the music, and exit from the back intact. What I needed most was a new self that could sit around in peace and make merciless fun of the other one. The theater of the absurd needed an absurd reflection. Suddenly, I knew what the next step would be. I called the wittiest person I had met in Russia.

"Can you take the next train to Moscow?" I asked. "I need your help on something."

"Sure," said Andrew Ryvkin somewhere in St. Petersburg. "What's up?"

"We're writing a sitcom about me."

INT. MOSCOW BOOKSTORE—DAY

RUSHKIN looks over his audience—all of seven or eight people. One is a mildly attractive woman; the rest are men. Most look like they have wandered into the bookstore for warmth. LENA, seated next to Rushkin on the dais, stares daggers at the woman, sensing competition.

    RUSHKIN
    Uh, good evening. My name is Matt Rushkin.

Silence. One man abruptly stands up and leaves.

RUSHKIN (CONT'D)

I hope everyone's read the book. So, why don't we go straight to the Q&A?

READER 1

How would you describe your stylistic influences?

RUSHKIN

Great question! I consider myself a kind of critical humanist, in the David Foster Wallace vein.

READER 1

I meant your clothes. Would you say they're more trad or preppy?

WOMAN

How did you decide to become a writer?

LENA

(under her breath)

Whore.

Recounting the plot of *Rushkin* would essentially mean recapping this book with a few extra flourishes. The title character, Matthew (né Dmitry) Rushkin, is a New York writer with one successful novel under his belt and half-forgotten Russian roots upon which his agent pushes him, blocked and broke, to capitalize. Upon Rushkin's arrival in Moscow for a book tour, his "cult following" turns out to consist of one ultra-devoted fan, Lena; while there, however, Rushkin reconnects with his childhood friend Roman Terekhov, who has grown up to be a hard-living celebrity photographer, and meets Anton Belokochanov, a flamboyant and manipulative oligarch. Rushkin's spiraling descent into the absurd heart of Moscow, with Roman and Anton as his deviant tour guides, forms the rest of the show.

Rushkin is haughty, hypochondriac, confused, ultimately kind but weak; a love child of Alvy Singer and Niles Crane. The driving force of the entire series is the battle between his ethics (long abandoned by everyone around him) and his desire to be rich, famous, and loved. In almost every episode, Moscow throws Rushkin a new temptation—a free car in exchange for "five positive and seven neutral" mentions of its make in his next novel; a sham engagement to a starlet looking to polish her intellectual bona fides ("So you want me to be an Arthur Miller to your Marilyn Monroe?" "A what to your who?"); and, of course, a constant barrage of attention from Moscow's most beautiful women while the Brooklyn girlfriend Heather stays confined to a laptop screen, unable to offer anything more than Skype sex on a bad dial-up connection. Of course, Rushkin succumbs to each and every one of these enticements. And, of course, every time he does, it ends in disaster.

Every emotion I had experienced in Moscow I now poured into *Rushkin*. Everyone I had met became grist for the mill. Timati turned into Dvizhzh, a "patriotic" rapper dying to break into the U.S. market. Kandelaki and Brovko's Apostol Media became the evil "Archangel PR." The Terry Richardson–like photographer Roman Terekhov was a purely comic invention, his penchant for getting into trouble and his appetite for every illegal substance known to man making him a cross between Tracy Jordan of *30 Rock* and Ray of *Bored to Death*. On the other hand, oligarch Anton, who mocks and mentors Rushkin in equal measure, was based almost entirely on Fedor Bondarchuk, down to the speech patterns.

The plot of the pilot episode is a Lynchian dream-logic refraction of the Dorozhkin incident. Promoting his book at a TV round table, Rushkin gets casually Jew-baited by Anton, who's there to talk up a publishing house he just bought. In response, Rushkin freezes up live on air. He and Roman spend most of the episode crafting the appropriate response, until finally, drunk and high, they head over to the offender's club to beat him up. Instead, Anton asks Rushkin to run the publishing house for forty thousand dollars a month ("I know, not much. But enough to keep you in those knit ties of yours"). Rushkin sells out on the spot—but as he exits the club, the bottled-up rage takes over, and he gets into a physical fight with the coat-check lady. Roman takes a photo of the skirmish, and the meek New York intellectual Rushkin wakes up next morning a rich and controversial Russian celebrity.

I hadn't written for the screen since college, and never comedy. Luckily, I had Andrew Ryvkin for a partner. Andrew and I had similar comedic sensibilities—we both worshipped *30 Rock* and *Louie*—and even some previous joke-writing experience. Back in September 2012, I got my hands on the script for the upcoming GQ Man of the Year ceremony, my first as the magazine's editor, and shuddered at the quality of the jokes in it. A representative one went "The Man of the Year awards are such a glamorous and exclusive affair that after each one a few coat-check workers become professional fashion critics." I called Andrew, we pulled a pot-and-pizza-fueled all-nighter, and came up with a few replacements. It was fairly innocuous stuff, Conan O'Brien–style. The coat-check joke, for example, retained the same set-up: "The Man of the Year awards are notorious for their strict dress code. This year alone, they had to beg Ksenia Sobchak to take off her balaclava . . . while [very tall] Mikhail Prokhorov was finally revealed to be three schoolboys in a trench coat." Ivan Urgant, the ceremony's once and future emcee, would use none of it (he largely improvised his whole bit anyway). But we knew we could work together.

Rushkin's pilot script took about two weeks to write; two more, and we had a rough outline of the season. It was a strange beast, edgy in form without being all that political in substance. Most of the humor came at the expense of the oblivious Gorky Park hipster crowd, whose hypocrisy annoyed Andrew and myself more than the genuine Putinist fervor did. My favorite recurring character was Edik Nemezidov, an ultracool "disruptor" of a bullshit artist constantly milking Anton for venture money, who becomes Rushkin's nemesis (his last name literally meant "nemesis," with the added bonus of also containing "Idov").

NEMEZIDOV
(sneering)
Oh, what do you know, you early twenty-first-century relic. You probably still listen to "Kanye West" and order your plane tickets "online."

RUSHKIN
Where else would I order them?!

NEMEZIDOV
Please. Everyone's using Bombr. It's an app that lets amateur pilots underbid each other to fly you places.

Whenever we could tweak the corrupt "patriots," we did. One minor character, bestselling author Arthur Shein, was a goof on the anti-Semitic, anti-liberal novelist Zakhar Prilepin, and quickly revealed to be Jewish (the last name Shein sounds Russian with a long "i" and Jewish with a short one) as well as gay. Most of the jokes, however, were just dumb fun at the expense of the dying publishing industry.

JUNIOR EDITOR
. . . and downstairs is the book warehouse, but

it's a bit crazy there right now. February is when
our "Rabid Rats" come out.

RUSHKIN

Ooh, "Rabid Rats," that's a good title.

JUNIOR EDITOR

Yes . . . a title . . .

Rushkin may have been a bit of a therapy session for me, but it certainly wasn't a j'accuse. At its heart lay an earnest love letter to Moscow's craziness. To get to that love, however, you first had to make your way past wall-to-wall profanity, drug use, masturbation, gay jokes, Jewish jokes, Nazi jokes, and, finally, the title.

The word *Rashka*, a bastardized English "Russia," was an immigrant's snarky way of referring to the abandoned motherland: derogation through diminution. By coincidence, it was also a legitimate Ashkenazi Jewish last name. There was even a Valery Rashkin (pronounced the same) in the State Duma. Still, naming your show and the title character after, essentially, an anti-Russian slur could only be sending one message. That message was "We're never getting on television."

■

If your idea of Russian TV is still the "Worker and Parasite Show" from *The Simpsons*, or those North Korean newscasts whose quavering anchors look like there's a gun trained on each of them from above the teleprompter, you'd be as disappointed as I was to see the real thing circa 2013. Like most Russian mainstream entertainment, it was bright, proficient, loud, sentimental, and second-rate without becoming entertainingly third-rate; most of it looked of a piece with its counterparts throughout Continental Europe. Even when the main thrust of its propaganda became the supposed contrast between the wholesome Russia and the decadent West, this message was somewhat self-defeatingly delivered via very Western-looking graphics and chyrons, by spry anchors wearing Brioni and Gucci.

As early as 2004, Putin had consolidated control over all television news, instituting a system wherein the main talking points would float down from the Kremlin itself. Network heads would take weekly instruction from Putin's chief ideologue Vladislav Surkov, and later from his replacement Vyacheslav Volodin, and their surrogates would be inserted into the news organizations' management. (Incidentally, the most corrosive legacy of Putinism might be the Russian media professionals' firm belief that the U.S. media are run the same way.) But the regime left show business more or less alone. Oddly enough, for the first twenty or so years of its post-Soviet existence, Russia all but disregarded fictional entertainment as a way to promote new values.* The only true peculiarity of the Russian TV drama and comedy was this: it was watched by people who hated the people who made it, and made by people who hated the people who watched it.

The reason for the near-total disharmony between these two groups was relatively mundane. The Russian TV market was vast but cheap. Even in 2013, before the fall of the ruble and the loss of Ukraine as a sales market, its per capita ad revenue was one-sixth of Germany's and one-tenth of America's. Russian production budgets were comparable to those in, say, Brazil. The viewing public thus split into two categories. One was the mostly middle-aged, mostly female audience that had acclimated to simple sitcom, soap-opera,

---

*The idea is less exotic than one may think. The BBC, for instance, has used a long-running soap opera to help instill new civic culture in Kazakhstan and is now doing the same in Ukraine.

and competition-show fare, whom content producers detested for supposedly not giving them the berth to try better things. The other was the younger, more sophisticated audience exposed to U.S. and British premium-cable content, which often ran on Russia's Channel One, and later Netflix and its local equivalent Amediateka (not to mention pirated copies streaming through VKontakte); they, in turn, ended up hating domestic broadcast productions for not measuring up to, say, *Game of Thrones*.

The producers couldn't help it if they tried: the average cost of making an hour-long broadcast drama in Russia was about three hundred thousand dollars per episode, as opposed to three million dollars in Hollywood. If you were an actor, a director, or a screenwriter living in Moscow—in 2013 still one of the most expensive cities in the world—the solution to this discrepancy was to take on ten times more work and do it ten times faster: first drafts heading straight into production, actors learning their lines on set, crews shooting twelve to fifteen pages of script a day. Ultimately, the logic went, who cares if the smart ones won't watch and the dumb ones won't get the difference.

That cynicism, and not the low budgets, ironically made the real difference. After all, the Danes and the Israelis were able to turn the limitations of their national TV industries into formulas for global hits. The Russians, on the other hand, simply didn't feel that their television—and pop culture in general—was a part of any global process. "The Russian viewer," went the deadening saw, "watches TV with her back while slicing salami." On Channel Two, the corporate lingo referred to the audience as *zritelnitsy*, "vieweresses." Even as the coming era of Netflix, and America's growing comfort with subtitles, meant that almost any country could break through if the idea was cool enough, Russia seemed content to stay a country of "analogs"—a local term for both licensed adaptations of Western hits and the shameless rip-offs.

Still, in the sea of pap, islands of fine content proliferated. At Channel One, as long as its news division stayed in line with the latest twists in the Kremlin policy, the eccentric visionary Konstantin Ernst did pretty much whatever the hell he wanted, from running *Mad Men* to handing prime time over to Valeria Gai Germanika, the closest equivalent of which would be entrusting ABC to Abel Ferrara. Channel Two, whose shows catered mostly to the vieweresses of a certain age, occasionally put on a lush miniseries, often a literary adaptation (*Life and Fate, Quiet Flows the Don*). And STS and TNT, which wisely refrained from news content altogether and thus eluded Kremlin control, successfully mixed lowbrow comedies with increasingly ambitious original dramas.

Whatever censorship existed there was mostly self-administered, and a matter of individual daring. On *The Kitchen*, a long-running original sitcom on STS, one of the main characters was gay, and while the humor his sexuality occasioned was roughly on the *Police Academy* level, it was not, per se, anti-LGBT. You might even say it implied the dreaded "equivalence between traditional and non-traditional lifestyles" by presenting both as equally silly. *The Gym Teacher*, an edgier TNT sitcom, commented freely on right-wing nationalism and corrupt politicians.

In the Russian feature-film industry, which subsisted on a cocktail of federal and semi-private funding, things were more depressing. Out of more than a thousand Russian films released between 1992 and 2013, only seventy or so had been profitable at home. At the same time, the number of screens exploded, and film revenues grew at a compounded 27 percent a year: in other words, the Russians watched more and more movies, just not their own. By 2010, Hollywood films were outgrossing them five to one. By 2013 or so, Hollywood was marketing to Moscow directly: the number of Russian actors and locations in American films hadn't quite reached the level of sycophancy shown the Chinese, but it was getting close.

Domestic cinema was thus a budget line item—yet not a fully developed propaganda weapon, either. Through the 1990s and the aughts, almost all of Russia's "patriotic" movies were bottom-up attempts to curry political favor (Yuri Grymov's *Strangers*, a 2008 anti-American screed, was financed by a second-tier political party), self-aggrandizing ego trips (like 1998's *The Barber of Siberia*, Nikita Mikhalkov's Oscar bid *and* an oblique exploration of his presidential ambitions), or simply ways to painlessly embezzle some federal funds.

This all changed on May 21, 2012, with the arrival of the current minister of culture, Vladimir Medinsky. His appointment was yet another facet of the across-the-board screw-tightening in response to the May 6 protest. Just a year earlier Medinsky, a prolific writer and World War II enthusiast given to anti-Western conspirology, had been a fringe figure; now he was a top enforcer of Putin's third-term agenda. He wasted no time before starting to directly dictate his preferred topics to the filmmakers who took federal funding: space exploration, sports achievements, that sort of thing. He also took steps to load the dice toward domestic product, by pressing theater chains to adopt a minimal quota on Russian films (20 percent) and to move big Hollywood premieres up or down lest they coincide with big Russian releases, market be damned. Neither measure seemed to help. As more and more state money flowed to "socially significant" films about the various glories of Russia, more viewers stayed home or opted for the latest *Pirates of the Caribbean*. Out of the movies that received state financing in the Medinsky era, Russia's biggest hit in terms of profitability was *Kiss Them All!*, a wedding comedy.

This, in short, was no country for *Rushkin*. I figured I would show the script around just for the hell of it—and then, perhaps, produce the pilot myself for ten thousand to fifteen thousand dollars, shoot it on the streets with photo cameras and available light, put it online, and try to make some money back with alcohol product placement. God knows the characters drank enough. The reaction of the first executive to read it was something out of *Barton Fink*, and roughly what I had expected: "When you're ready to make some real money," he said, "bring me something about a cop." The second, however, was Slava Murugov, the head of STS, who had by that point greenlighted a number of ambitious series, like *Quest* and the zombie drama *Day After*, and was looking to do something with an international angle. Murugov couldn't help noticing that his viewers, conditioned by golden-age Western TV, demanded something more than local adaptations of *Everybody Loves Raymond*. Murugov was intrigued enough to show it to a friend: Fedor Bondarchuk.

Before I knew it, I was sitting at a table in Vanil, with an equally direct view of the Pussy Riot Church and Bondarchuk's shiny shaved dome, and awaiting the verdict—from, essentially, one of the show's main characters. Bondarchuk was finishing up a conversation with Sergei Kapkov. Finally, the men got up and did the half-hug, half-handshake thing, and then Bondarchuk slid over to my table.

"Okay, look," Bondarchuk said. "I'm not sure this will ever get past the pilot."

"Fair enough," I said.

He held a masterly pause. "Wanna shoot it and find out?"

"*Hell* yes." I hesitated, then decided to go all in. "Also, in that case, would you, uh, potentially be open to . . ."

"Playing Anton? I was going to ask *you*."

From that moment, things moved extremely fast. We found a great young director, Eugene Nikitin, and auditioned a dozen Rushkins until we hit upon the perfect one: Simon Steinberg, a theater actor who looked like a young Jeff Goldblum, with both the nerdiness and the strange animal magnetism that entailed. Meanwhile, surreally, the *Rushkin* script—which, after all, was only a half-hour sitcom pilot—led to two more commissions in two vastly different genres. (I had the presence of mind to realize that this had more to do with the paucity of fresh talent on the Russian market than with our unbridled brilliance.)

One was an invitation, also from Murugov, to develop a series about the Russians in London. The genre and the tone were up to us. The idea of a show that would by necessity be half in English, with British actors, was almost too good to be true—and certainly unlike anything else on Russian TV. But what would it be about—runaway oligarchs? The Litvinenko poisoning? After a few days of brainstorming, Ryvkin came up with the answer: "Let's do Oxxxymiron."

My friend Miron Fyodorov, the British Russian rapper, with whom Andrew had also gotten close, once made a living by working for a Russian consulting agency in London; the outfit's services ranged from Oxford test prep for oligarch kids to getting a Savile Row tailor shop to open in the middle of the night. Within hours, Ryvkin and I came up with the basic idea for *Londongrad*, a fast-paced picaresque—half comedy, half thriller—that would allow us to both engage all the stereotypes of the Russian London and keep an ironic distance from them. The main character, Misha, a brilliant if anarchic Oxford dropout, ran a one-man "fixer" business catering to the rich Russians' whims while mercilessly mocking them privately; his sidekick and love interest, Alisa, was a rich, spoiled Moscow girl hiding out from her politician father. The latter allowed us to sneak in some social commentary, though the only truly radical thing about *Londongrad* was its complete refusal to address nostalgia. In the Russian culture, life abroad had always been depicted as a tragic exile. Ryvkin and I, wandering Jews both, instead offered a vision of fully integrated young Russians for whom London was just another city, not a backdrop to an existential crisis. Mostly, however, *Londongrad* was about the sheer screenwriting pleasure of spinning twisty five-act stories set in a slightly heightened, *Ocean's Eleven*–esque world.

The other offer, which came from Bondarchuk, was to write a sequel to Russia's top-grossing domestic film of 2012: *Soulless*. Once again, our paths intersected with Sergei Minaev's, but this time in the most satisfying way possible. A year before, he had beat Ryvkin in the street—now Ryvkin and I were handed his most prized possession. Like Matt Rushkin, we couldn't say no to an offer like this.

As 2013 neared the end, my head swam with possibilities. On November 25, *Londongrad* began shooting in London. I was going to take Lily to Copenhagen for her birthday weekend but changed tickets so the Danish trip became just a dinner at Noma, and we hopped over to London for the shoot. One of the goofier touches of the show was the idea that one of the supporting characters, the plainspoken Stepan, would be driving a Soviet Lada sedan with a right-side steering column; when I approached the set and saw the actual car, summoned to life by a few throwaway lines in the script, my feeling of having crashed into some sort of parallel wish-fulfillment universe was complete.

Timati's song "*GQ*," and the peacocking video for it, had meanwhile become one of the year's biggest hits. The torrent of contempt it unleashed from my former liberal cohorts was spectacular. Everyone hated it. Everyone assumed it was a paid advertisement for *GQ* that I had somehow put together. And everyone couldn't stop hate-watching it, or hate-quoting the line "intellect attracts cash." The song's success bound me to spend some evenings with Timati and his friends, including Emin Agalarov, who lived in a kind of self-contained Elysium of neon lighting, low-slung cars, booming beats, silicon, San Tropez, shimmery mini-dresses, and food on sticks. I had never been a part of anything like this.

On one of these evenings, Lily and I found ourselves at Nobu (synergy!) for a welcome party of the Miss Universe 2013, a Trump-Agalarov joint. Crocus Group wanted *GQ* to cover the pageant; I had always found these things to be beneath any kind of coverage, and going to the Agalarovs' events was a way of politely declining it without pissing off the hosts. (At the party, I passed the time making notes for *Rushkin*: "*Matt Rushkin among the beauty queens. Miss Turks and Caicos is conjoined twins.*") Two years into my Russian life, I was still a New Yorker, and Donald Trump was a New York joke, one I couldn't believe had chased me all the way here to Moscow. Then again, it made perfect sense. I left early, bumping into Steven Tyler of Aerosmith on my way to the elevators.

Next day came the big dinner at Crocus City, the Agalarovs' giant mall on the outskirts of Moscow. All eighty-seven pageant contestants mingled in full evening dress and sashes; guests were treated to a synchronized swimming routine in an indoor fountain, which I later found out was a regular feature at this mall. At the dinner itself, I got seated at a table with Miss Latvia, which I appreciated, but still skipped out before dessert. If Trump was ever there, I missed him—and with him my chance to claim an eyewitness angle on the weirdest Russian-American story of my lifetime.

This world may have held a touristy allure for me, but Emin Agalarov was fully of it, and so were the Trumps. It made absolute sense to me that, when Emin's publicist Rob Goldstone would approach Donald Trump, Jr., to offer dirt on Hillary Clinton on the Russians' behalf, Don, Jr., wouldn't even perceive this offer as issuing from a foreign, let alone hostile, actor. The Trumps can't see these types of Russians as foreigners because they belong to the same global class, that of the second-rate nightclubby strivers; they are all compatriots in a supranational state of *poshlust*. If there is no sense that they belong to different cultures, it's because they genuinely don't.

Three years later, on November 9, 2016, when Trump won (and Lily and I swigged rum and held back tears in our Berlin apartment), that entire crowd would be ecstatic. Hoody would Instagram himself hoisting up a silver-and-gold Beluga vodka bottle in front of a TV screen that showed Trump's acceptance speech. The caption said, "Congratulations Mr President!!! Start celebrating @realdonaldtrump #USA #RUSSIA," followed by the two countries' emoji flags. Timati, for his part, would later publish a photo of himself at the Statue of Liberty sporting a Putin T-shirt. That was the sick joke of it all. While disadvantaged, embittered, and riled-up voters in the United States felt that by electing a lewd outsider they had finally delivered a blow to the global elite, the heiresses and coked-up club kids all over St. Tropez were the ones popping the corks. *Their* guys won, too.

For the moment, however, in 2013, I felt almost at ease in this crowd. Politically, Russia seemed to be normalizing after a brief fit of overreaction. Alexei Navalny had been allowed to run for mayor of Moscow and received over 20 percent of the vote. On December 19, with the Sochi Olympics approaching, the Duma rolled out an amnesty for political prisoners that seemed to herald a new thaw. By Christmas Eve, Alekhina and Tolokonnikova of Pussy Riot were back in Moscow; I met them in person for the first time without a glass cage to separate us. Denis Sinyakov, the Greenpeace photographer whose family I had tried to help with my ill-fated cocktail night, and the rest of the Arctic 30 were released as well.

Most important, Russia's political prisoner number one, Mikhail Khodorkovsky, was free after ten years in prison. This could have been a momentous turn for the opposition—martyrdom had erased all his shortcomings; Khodorkovsky wielded Mandela-level political capital. He chose not to use it. In what was without a doubt his end of a bargain with the Kremlin, he flew straight to Berlin, where he ensconced himself at the Adlon Kempinski and made an anodyne statement. Khodorkovsky would eventually move to London and run a rather ineffective organization from there, devoted to supporting opposition candidates for the Duma.

The Hoodyakovs' movie, *Odnoklassniki.ru*, premiered on December 5, with Snoop Dogg in attendance. After the screening, Pavel reported that Snoop, who had been dozing for most of the film, laughed at my cameo; I could check "make Snoop Dogg laugh" off whatever bizarro bucket list would include this line item.

The production on the pilot for *Rushkin* began five days later, on December 10. Simon Steinberg's very Jewish appearance was giving the network some jitters, but otherwise we were good to go. With Ryvkin off to take the lead on *Soulless 2*, I ran around doing everything from finalizing the costumes to composing a chalkboard menu for a Brooklyn café where one flashback was set (*Amy's Nostrand Ave. Backyard Chicken: $14 half / $25 whole / $40 live to adopt*). I spent my free time, of which there wasn't much, on the margins of Fedor Bondarchuk's inner circle, which was equal parts cinema luminaries and political movers, including Surkov.

Perhaps the "bloody regime" was all in the opposition's heads. Sure, Russia was a mild autocracy. So? So was Singapore. And who really hates Singapore? In the grand scheme of things, it was still in the period of the post-Soviet transition, and the people were living better than ever in its tortured history. Russia was on the acceptable side of unacceptable.

My TV projects met no censorship or resistance. The abstract anti-Western sentiment emanating from the Ostankino TV tower didn't seem to touch me. Quite the opposite: both *Londongrad* and *Rushkin*—one about the Russians in the West, the other about a Westerner in Russia—were going to series. One got the green light for a whopping forty episodes, the other for twenty. To cap it all off, Lelya Smolina and I sold a movie treatment to the famed producer Alexander Rodnyansky. It was a kind of Cyrano-meets-*Sabrina* romantic comedy, again half in English, set in the world of Ukrainian bridal agencies in a quirky, charming Odessa.

After two years of failing to please anyone with my vision of how American journalism could be transplanted to the Russian soil, and driving myself to near-clinical depression over it, I had stumbled upon a vocation at which I was demonstrably, measurably *good*: American television transplanted to Russian soil. The relief I felt surprised even me, in part by retroactively illuminating the misery that preceded it. I informed Condé Nast that I would be leaving *GQ* as soon as they found my replacement.

For the February 2014 issue, one of my last, I wrote the editor's letter (I had even made peace with that hated genre) about the upcoming Sochi Olympics. It was easily the most optimistic piece of writing about Russia I had ever committed to paper, titled "Olympian Calm." Here is the gist of it.

We have blamed the advent of the Olympics for the last two years' steady tightening of the screws and their consequent loosening, with Pussy Riot as Exhibit A in both cases. But everything I've read—and, frankly, written— about the Games has failed to mention the most important thing. The point of an Olympiad is simultaneous imitation of and substitution for war. In 1896, when the modern Games began, there was little in the way of international tourism; the only context in which regular citizens of one country saw citizens of another, especially in uniform, involved bloodshed. Before globalization, the very sight of a column of foreigners marching under their colors *not* to kill you, was a shocking and heartening rarity. The Olympics existed for the same purpose as the World Fairs, the kind that allowed an idealized mini-USSR, with its marble worker statues and an exact copy of the Mayakovskaya Metro station, to set up shop in Queens. It's not a coincidence that the second and third Games—Paris 1900 and Saint Louis 1904—took place at the respective World Fairs.

A part of that spirit lives on today, in the age of EasyJet and Google Translate. The erratic behavior of the host country before the Olympics is first and foremost a panic before important guests show up: I've got nothing to wear, no one's going to come, nothing's ready. You start moving the furniture, get carried away, paint the ceiling. You call a decorator, yell at the decorator, apologize to the decorator. The guests are almost here and the damn suitcase is still out.*

Here's the thing: this panicked state is useful. Every country, including the superpowers, should experience it every once in a while. It is this panic that gave us the liberalization of South Korea, the direct train from Beijing to Tibet (albeit temporarily), the long-overdue equal rights for Australian Aborigines, and those little orange TetraPaks of cream still fondly remembered by everyone who's been a kid in Moscow in 1980. Sochi is bound to leave behind the same kind of legacy. Exactly what it will be, we'll find out only after the fact. Which is soon enough.

And we did, and it was. In two short months, Russia was at war with Ukraine.

---

*A reference to Louis Vuitton's ill-fated December 2013 promo campaign that centered on a pop-up building decorated to look like a thirty-foot-high steamship trunk in the middle of Red Square. The fashion house clearly didn't realize that the image of a giant suitcase called to the Russian mind only fear, chaos, flight, emigration, and the camps— and looked like a twisted parody of Lenin's tomb to boot.

Chapter Eight

Zavtra

U kraine was exactly like Russia, except it wasn't. Even the word *Ukraine* meant "heartland" in its own language or "outskirts" in Russian, the two interpretations uncannily reflecting the two vantage points. Ever since the breakup of the U.S.S.R., the largest of the former Soviet republics occupied a strange place in the Russian psyche. Ukraine was a cautionary tale and an aspirational one, a provincial backwater that also happened to be more confidently European. While Russia spent centuries flailing around in search of its identity, Ukraine's was self-evident, grounded in its own rich soil. Its language, to the Muscovite ear, sounded like a parody of Russian but underpinned a robust and independent pop culture that often left Moscow behind, especially when it came to music. Similarly, the political Kiev often seemed like a joke—fisticuffs in the Parliament, a merry-go-round of shifting alliances at the top—but at least it was *alive*; the chaos was the best proof that things weren't stage-managed by a (or even the) Surkov, or if they were, then so poorly that it didn't make a difference.

The capital, Kiev, was a largely Russian-speaking city; Ukrainian editions of international magazines came out in Russian as a matter of course. But the westernmost parts of the country felt impenetrably foreign to a Russian, closer in look and temperament to Poland and Austria. Odessa was the historical nerve center of Russian Jewry and conducted its affairs with the panache of a free Mediterranean port. And Crimea—well, Crimea was a special case altogether. In 1954, when the newly installed Nikita Khrushchev moved the peninsula from the purview of the Russian Soviet Federative Socialist Republic into that of the Ukrainian Soviet Socialist Republic, the re-designation was as arbitrary as it was inconsequential. After the empire split at the seams, however, many Russians felt accidentally robbed—and the Crimeans who identified as Russian felt, if not abandoned, then somewhat unmoored. That said, with no visas required to travel either way, there was little organic support for reunification on either side of the border. In the 2010 local elections, Crimea's Russian Unity party got 4 percent of the vote.

Ukraine's Westward drift was meanwhile becoming more pronounced. In 2012, official work began on an "association agreement" with the European Union, which many saw as a step toward

E.U. membership. In November 2013, however, president Viktor Yanukovych abruptly stopped the process—after a series of visits with Putin—and got a massive sweetheart loan from Russia instead. The loan's interest rate was to be renegotiated every three months, which, taken together with the Kremlin's hand on the gas valve, guaranteed Ukraine would stay within Moscow's orbit or face instant economic crisis. It was a remarkably shitty deal. The people poured into the streets, many flying the E.U. colors as the movement's symbol.*

A tent city, much like the one at Occupy Abai but far more populous, sprang up in Kiev's Independence Square, known simply as the Maidan. Initially, the protesters were mostly students, and their grievances were limited to the broken promise of the E.U. association agreement. The more violently the authorities cleared the square, the broader the crowd became—and the broader its demands. On February 18, 2014, after intensifying skirmishes with the police and *titushki* (street provocateurs alternately fighting and impersonating protesters), the encampment was attacked in earnest, and the clashes escalated into urban warfare. By February 21, dozens had been killed on both sides—marking perhaps the first time anyone perished in battle under the flag of the E.U.—and a gaggle of European negotiators and foreign ministers helped hammer out a deal to stanch the bloodshed. Yanukovych fled for Russia. The Maidan was victorious.

This kind of scenario must have occurred to some of the Bolotnaya Square protesters two years before. In reality, the Russians had neither the numbers (one hundred thousand at the peak of the protests against Kiev's estimated four hundred thousand to eight

---

*Unlike the Russians, the Ukrainians had a fairly recent taste of successful protest—2004's Orange Revolution, also against Yanukovych; the pro-Russian president, however, rode the wave of ensuing chaos back to power in 2010.

hundred thousand) nor the unique motivation of a binary choice between East and West. Now, and far more important, the same scenario must have occurred to Vladimir Putin. The image of curious Ukrainians taking selfies on the grounds of Yanukovych's hastily abandoned residence must have resonated with the Russian president even more. There but for the grace of God and the timidity of Moscow's middle class went he.

An obvious requirement for a street revolution is having on one's side, however temporarily, brawlers prepared to hurt and be hurt; those are usually found on the right or the left side of the Overton window. The genteel Russian opposition of 2011–2012 didn't reach this far in either direction. The Ukrainian did; out tumbled the Right Sector, a paramilitary group spontaneously formed from soccer hooligans and fringe ultranationalists. The Right Sector were admirers of Stepan Bandera, a Ukrainian leader who, thinking he could triangulate between Hitler and Stalin, forever marred himself by entering World War II on the Nazi side. Their involvement in the Maidan, while more logistically than politically significant, gave Russia a plausible opening to dub the entire revolution as "fascist." The victorious Ukrainians then made a number of unforced errors to bolster that fiction—abruptly canceling a law that would recognize Russian as the country's second official language, banning Russian books and films, and generally behaving as if they were fighting Russianness itself and not the insidious influence of the Kremlin.

The two countries' cultures disengaged in a flurry of tit-for-tat sanctions and mutual banishments. Okean Elzy, a top Ukrainian band that had supported the revolution, had to cancel their show in St. Petersburg because no venue would let them in. Ukraine rolled out its own blacklist that included, among others, Timati. Every Russian public figure who showed sympathy for Kiev, every musician who agreed to perform there, was lambasted at home as "pro-fascist," including the mild elder-statesmen rock stars An-drei Makarevich and Boris Grebenshikov.

The likelihood of Putin really believing that power in Ukraine had been usurped by neo-Nazis is close to zero. The "fascist" scare was little more than an easy way of selling Russia's subsequent actions to a populace still obsessed with World War II. By mid-2014, the Kremlin propaganda had stripped the word *fascist* of any remnants of meaning; many Russians combined their "anti-fascism" with the fervent belief in a Jewish conspiracy, coming up with the slur *zhidobanderovtsy* (kike-Banderites) in a stab at a grand unified theory of the goings-on in Kiev.

Putin may, however, have genuinely credited the revolution in Kiev, just as he had the 2011–2012 protests in Moscow, to the United States and its meddling Gosdep.* It bears mentioning again and again that Putin's philosophy, mirroring both the KGB's institu-tional mind-set and Surkov's cynical postmodernism, precluded belief in any genuine protest, or democracy as anything other than a device for making the masses believe they have agency. In this worldview, Russia and the United States still jostled for spheres of influence, and the United States had just grabbed itself a new piece. The only logical response was to grab back. On the night of Febru-ary 22, while discussing the logistics of Yanukovych's exfiltration with his security advisers, Putin already broached the topic of tak-ing back Crimea.

The next day, the Sochi Olympics closed with a lush, pacific, and pointedly European ceremony that featured an elaborate trib-ute to Russian literature, the Bolshoi and Mariinsky ballets, and tableaux inspired by Chagall and Malevich. At the exact same time,

---

*It didn't help that the likes of John McCain took it upon themselves to visit Kiev at the height of the protests and to extol the "revolution," lending even more credence to the Kremlin's view of the Maidan as a U.S. creation.

as if on command (though "as if" might be superfluous here), pro-Russian rallies began in the Crimean city of Sevastopol. By February 27, the "green men"—Russian soldiers without insignia—took over the key buildings there. The whole Anschluss took three weeks from idea to execution. On March 16, in a referendum held under the plausibly deniable Russian gun, Crimea voted to separate itself from Ukraine, and two days later signed a treaty admitting it into the Russian Federation.

At the same time, Moscow was jump-starting separatist movements all over Ukraine's Russian-speaking east, which looked similarly grabbable. The initial rebellions in the Donetsk and Luhansk regions may have been organic, but their swift transformation into "people's republics" was heavily aided by Russian paramilitaries. (In Donetsk, the mercenary Igor Girkin, under the nom de guerre Strelkov, or "Rifleman," swiftly declared himself warlord, made his troops sign oaths of allegiance to him, and ordered executions for petty theft.) The Russian media began to refer to the entire area as Novorossiya (New Russia), a forgotten czarist-era term, blithely reasserting Russia's imperial birthright. Unlike in Crimea, however, the Ukrainian government sent in the army, ushering in an all-out war.

Once again, despite the easily provable fact that the first generation of rebel leaders consisted largely of Russian operatives, Moscow denied all involvement; the soldiers captured by the Ukrainians or arriving home in coffins were said to have fought in Ukraine as volunteers in their free time. For the Kremlin, the "green men" lie was the first one of a new kind: a power lie whose obviousness was part of its message. Putin knew that everyone knew he was lying; this turned the lie into more of a brash invitation to the West to do something about it or shut up. Merely pointing out the falsity came across as weak. Its real power, though, lay in the fact that the Russians knew Putin was lying, too—and approved.

This was a new dynamic. The public and the president were in on the same joke.

The fervor and scope of celebration boggled the mind. Crimea's return wasn't just the world's largest landmass adding a little more landmass. It was payback for all the humiliations of the 1990s, vengeance for Russia's perceived diminution at the hands of the United States, a de facto return to the imperial Soviet glory, the ultimate comeback. Western scorn was not a side effect—it was the point: the real Russians would bear it with pride and circle the wagons around their leader. All others were free to go have sex with goats in Amsterdam or whatever. The great post-Soviet Russian dream, it turned out, was this: to do something that America would really, really disapprove of, and to get away with it.

Putin's approval ratings, always high but never as stratospheric as one might think, hit a historic peak of 86 percent. The preceding fourteen years had all led up to this. The quiet functionary had become the new coming of Ivan III, a "gatherer of the Russian lands." Who needed the candy-ass Olympics when there was *this*?

As for those few within Russia's borders who didn't see any cause for celebration, they had never felt less at home in their own country. The victory cry *Krym nash* (Crimea is ours) became Russia's theme song, catchphrase, and watchword. It separated the 86 percent of the "patriots" from the "national traitors"—a term uncorked by Putin himself in his triumphant March 2014 speech—once and for all. Unlike with other divisive issues of the era, there was very little room in the middle. You were either ecstatic about Russia's newfound might or horrified at its unilateral upending of the postwar European order. For instance, Eduard Limonov, the former opposition icon and too-prolific columnist whom I had serendipitously fired from *GQ* just before, was downright jubilant. Crimea so exhilarated Limonov—who in his National Bolshevik days once personally tried to invade Kazakhstan—that all of his opposition to Putin, predicated in part by the leader's failure to protect Russia's "historic interests," ended right there and then. Soon, he moved his "edgy" column to the Putinist tabloid *Izvestia*.

Shockingly for the already-battered opposition, however, a number of its own unexpectedly joined the triumphant camp. "Oh shit, she's gone all *Krymnash*" was a popular refrain that spring, the two words now jumbled into a single slur. Maria Baronova, an activist and recently released May 6 prisoner, supported the Anschluss. So did opposition reporter Oleg Kashin—and, one suspects, Navalny, whose answers on the topic have been understandably evasive (lest he praise Putin) but whose nationalist views meshed well with the Crimean adventure. With little to say to their former allies, many liberals opted for mass banning sprees, scrubbing their social-network feeds of any Krymnash sentiment and locking themselves even tighter in the bubble.

The arguable apex of the madness came in the form of a nationally televised motorcycle show called *The Return*, put on by the ludicrous biker Surgeon and his leather buddies the Night Wolves. An annual celebration of what can only be described as Russia's answer to redneck culture, the show took place in the newly Russianized Sevastopol. The boxing champion Dmitri Chudinov administered a beating to the dark-skinned French boxer Mehdi Bouadla, knocking him out in the third round; Steven Seagal played the blues for an hour and a half; the main attraction, however, was the theatrical show itself, which purported to tell the story of Crimea's unification with Russia.

Surgeon's spectacle, financed by a fifteen-million-ruble grant from the Ministry of Culture and broadcast live all over the nation by the TV channel Rossiya 2, looked like an infernal parody of the

Sochi Olympics' opening ceremony. It began with a staged tableau of happy life—women cradling babies, a girl on a pony. Then, an air-raid siren sounded. The lights turned red.

"Victory. Fiery, sacred, divine," Surgeon intoned from a platform. "My motherland has dealt Stalin's ten blows to the hairy trunk of fascism." (I am translating this faithfully.) "We rose from the ashes, rebuilt our cities, and thought that this flowering would last forever. But the enemies who hate our country bought up the Soviet Union, took its territory and its army, devastated its great factories, slashed our land into pieces, and left the stumps of the United Russian State bleeding and radiating intolerable pain.

"But the healing is upon us," he continued. "And it's coming from the Russian Sevastopol. The poisonous dough of fascism overflowed the kneading trough of Kiev and began spreading all over Ukraine. The new battle with fascism is inevitable. Stalin's eleventh blow is inevitable!"

At this moment, the music turned to the kind of symphonic metal that connotes evil, and a sound clip of Barack Obama's speech played—oddly enough, from his keynote address at the 2004 Democratic National Convention: "I stand here knowing that my story is a part of the larger American story." A pyramid with the all-seeing eye appeared onstage, festooned with a dollar sign. Dozens of people writhed under a white tarp, literalizing the "fascist dough" rising at the U.S.-Masonic command. Snippets of revolutionary chants from Kiev intermingled with Hitler's speeches. The "fascists" breached through the tarp and goose-stepped into a large human swastika. At that moment, in the show's pièce de résistance, two hydraulically operated, fifteen-foot puppeteer's hands appeared above the arena, a ring with the Great Seal of the United States on one of the bony fingers. A suspended globe, already stabbed with the Ukrainian trident symbol and bleeding, burst into flames. "Tell me, Ukraine, for how many thousand euros did you sell the Kievan Rus to Europe?" sang a band called Thirteenth Constellation, one member of which wore an Armani Exchange logo T-shirt. Then it was biker gangs to the rescue. The action awkwardly switched to a regular shit-kicking stunt show, with some of the stunts performed to two different instrumental renditions of "Smells Like Teen Spirit."

For the big finish, the Surgeon read some verse about the awakening of the Eurasian superpower, and a woman cooed downright erotically about "the Russian sword," which "has the strength of strengths and the power of powers / It's the visible part of the spirit." The show ended with the raising of a giant heraldic sign that combined the Soviet state emblem with the two-headed imperial eagle. The image was astute. It no longer mattered which regime was which. In place of any coherent ideology came the new fascistic cult of Russia's "strength." The entirety of Russian history since Ivan the Terrible could now be re-sorted according to it: Alexander III was strong, Nicholas II weak, Stalin strong, Gorbachev weak, Yeltsin weak, Putin strong.

Despite the unprecedented national glee, however, even the defeated and disjunct opposition must have seemed to Putin like an active threat. Behind the smoke of the fireworks, the Kremlin was furiously working to make sure that nothing like what happened in Kiev would ever have a chance of happening in Moscow. The State Duma's "berserk printer" was back in action. Not a week seemed to pass without another new law designed to curb free speech or civil liberties. Impugning the U.S.S.R.'s conduct in World War II was now illegal. So was disrespecting Russia's "territorial integrity." (In theory, this meant that going on Facebook and typing *Krym ne nash*, "Crimea isn't ours," was a felony.) Any mention of ISIS, by law, had to be accompanied by the pointless parenthetical "terrorist organization outlawed in Russia." Mentioning drugs or suicide in a way that could be construed as "instructional," which meant at all, was illegal.

Since 2012, Russian independent journalism had already learned to live with shoddily framed hate-speech legislation and a censorship body—Roskomnadzor—poised to shut down any website for so much as an unruly user comment. This, however, was different. The new regulations weren't there just to sow the usual paralyzing confusion about what was allowed and what wasn't. They were vigorously applied, with the express purpose of snuffing out the remnants of the free press.

The editor in chief of Lenta.ru, Galina Timchenko, was fired for publishing a story that linked to an interview with the Right Sector leader Dmitry Yarosh. The entire staff walked out with her, and were replaced with more pliable employees. TV Rain lost its advertisers and its lease after running an admittedly silly online poll that asked viewers whether suffering through the deadly Leningrad blockade was more justified than ceding the city to the Nazis. At least Mediazona, a website focusing on justice and prisons and financed by the members of Pussy Riot, found some ways to have fun with the new reality. It started using the word *Roskomnadzor* as a synonym for suicide, as in "An eighteen-year-old student Roskomnadzored herself."

As I was rummaging through my office in search of an auction lot I could donate to a last-ditch TV Rain fundraiser, a boss informed me that London wanted a story removed from my last issue of *GQ*: the Kermlins' interview with the TV anchor Yevgeny Kiselev. The interview had been done before the war, and Kiselev, a careful man, had said nothing controversial, but the very word *Ukraine* was now a red flag. "I know the law is on your side and common sense is on your side," the note said, "but the people who destroyed Lenta weren't guided by law or common sense. As a private citizen, I am on your side too. But I am a hired employee of an American company . . ." There was no need to read on. If anything, this only made me happier to be leaving the magazine, the profession, and, at least temporarily, the country.

My last day at *GQ* was April 25, 2014. I handed things over to the amiably bearded Kim Belov, who used to be Uskov's second in command and whose selection was meant to signal the magazine's return to apolitical congeniality. The art department presented me with the farewell gift of a framed mock cover, as required by the local tradition, with the cover line I rather liked ("American Idov"); Roman Volobuev stopped by with his two-week-old daughter in a sling; a female staffer whose name I strained to remember suddenly professed long-held feelings; everyone got drunk. Early the next morning, I got out of Russia for several months—traveling first to Italy, where Lily and Vera already were, and then to Berlin, which we liked so much that our summer stay there quietly mutated into an apartment search.

Volobuev and I weren't alone in having exchanged magazines for movies. All around me, the young and/or the ambitious were leaving the napalmed husk of Russian journalism for the marginally greener pastures of screenwriting, or combining the two. Ironically, reporters, with their capacity for structured storytelling, made far better screenwriters than the graduates of Moscow's vaunted Gerasimov Institute of Cinematography—which mostly dedicated itself to pumping out little Tarkovskys whose megalomania preceded their first student short.

The Ukrainian-set rom-com that Lelya Smolina and I had the uncanny timing to sell in December 2013 was dead for the most obvious reason, but I was happy to work with her on several episodes of *Londongrad*. Another refugee from journalism to join the

Londongrad team was Lena Vanina, formerly of *Afisha*. An intuitive and quirky writer, Vanina was cursed with the looks of a French film star (naturally, she was Volobuev's ex) and a glowing core of Obama-esque human decency as rare around these parts as plutonium. She soon became one of Lily's and my closest friends, as well as a collaborator on almost everything we write in Russian.

As it happened, Vanina had also cowritten Volobuev's directing debut: a wholly remarkable twenty-five-minute TV pilot called *Zavtra* (Tomorrow). Where *Rushkin* or *Londongrad* were unusual for Russian TV, *Zavtra* was unimaginable. Set two years ahead, in 2016, it depicted the aftermath of a presidential election—after a dark-horse win by an opposition candidate.

The initial idea belonged to Natalia Sindeeva, the founder and CEO of TV Rain. She imagined the series as an earnest, semi-documentary exercise in visualizing the opposition's goals: if a group of young, attractive people gathered around a desk and discussed Russia's problems as if they were running it already, then perhaps one day they could—or at least the notion wouldn't seem so outlandish. Instead, Volobuev managed to talk Sindeeva into letting him make *Zavtra* into the news channel's first scripted series, and to write it as a dark, dry, British-style comedy.

In the pilot episode's teaser, a female Russian American reporter, based on our mutual friend Julia Ioffe, accosts the future president's campaign manager in the men's room as the first polls begin to close and the opposition hunkers down for the usual humiliating loss: "What if you actually win?" she asks. "We've got some ideas," he deadpans, blinking back a tiny flicker of panic. The show then skips forward to the new administration's first day. On the surface, it's part straight-up liberal wish-fulfillment porn, part parody of Bolotnaya Square's wildest dreams: the Kremlin staff hug the ill-lit hallway walls as a cadre of hipster girls in little black dresses strut by in wedge formation to replace them; a slightly dopey dreamboat who looks like Ilya Krasilshchik is settling in as the new president's spokesperson; TV Rain appears to be the country's only functioning channel (Yuri Saprykin stops by for a cameo); in Vladislav Surkov's office—meticulously re-created from photographs, down to the poster of Surkov as Che Guevara—wired idealists on their third sleepless night mull over cabinet appointments.

It takes only a few minutes to see how hopelessly out of its depth the new administration is. They can't fill basic posts. Their cobbled-together center-left coalition has weeks to live. They make a wan overture to the powerful governor of a Far East region that's clearly two or three episodes away from seceding. Meanwhile, someone has hacked the former president's phone and is tweeting obscenities from it (one character, hazarding a password guess: "Did you try 'GlorytoRussia'?"), and no one can figure out how to pay Moscow's electric bill. In the last scene, the city goes dark.

TV Rain was at a similar loss about *Zavtra* itself. Instead of pro-democracy agitprop, what they had on their hands was more of a nuanced satire. Its only aspirational quality, ironically, was the authors' presumption of an audience mature enough for something like this. Instead, Sindeeva thought of nothing better than to screen the pilot for the stars of the real-life opposition, who, including Navalny's people, unanimously decried it as unhelpful and mean. I, for one, found its tough-love approach brilliant.

Far more important, however, was the pilot's very existence; you can watch it on YouTube and TV Rain's site to this day. That's what made our new occupation especially satisfying in comparison with the old one—no matter how naive or quixotic our attempts to nudge Russian TV toward the West, they resulted in actual completed works.

For my part, I spent the summer juggling two writers' rooms, for *Londongrad* and *Rushkin*, in Moscow and Berlin. Sitting in an outdoor café on Schiffbauerdamm and coming up with plot twists in the company of friends from Moscow and London—Owen Matthews, of Oxford and *Newsweek*, had joined the team as a British slang consultant and stayed on as a writer—was not a bad way to live.

Rushkin was harder to crack, as comedy often is. Two episodes into the season, Andrew Ryvkin quit, complaining that the show and its protagonist too closely hewed to my life. "Even though I think the pilot script is great," he wrote, "I can't go expanding on a humorous version [of] your autobiography—you can do that better than anyone out there, me included. For me, it's my autobiography that I have to work on." I dug in and wrote one episode myself, but it felt all wrong. The jokes begged to be tested aloud, batted back and forth, stretched to the logical dead end (which in my and Ryvkin's case invariably involved Nazi humor) and snapped back. Lily, who had gradually gone from sounding board to editor to full-blown coauthor, was busy on *Londongrad*. I gave the call to the *next* two wittiest people I knew: Arseny Bobrovsky and Katya Romanovskaya, the Kermlins. After they said yes, almost the entirety of my *GQ* team had officially been reinvented as a screenwriting collective.

Just as the Kermlins and I finished riffing our way through *Rushkin*, the first sixteen-episode season of *Londongrad* began shooting in mid-August. I came to the set armed with a U.S. notion of the head screenwriter as a showrunner, to quickly learn that no one expected me there at all: Russian TV was still largely a producer's medium, and writers were seen as cheap hired labor who moved on to the next gig as soon as the current one paid up. I resolved to change this. Frankly, I had little choice: a Russian crew shooting a half-English show in London was constantly getting mired in the intricacies of the setting. Things like why an aristocrat would wear a battered Barbour jacket, or why the sign on the wall of a psychiatric clinic wouldn't say "Insane Asylum," all had to be explained, sometimes at a high volume.

The biggest enemy, however, was not ineptitude but apathy. During one of my first days on the set, I was shocked to find out that the sound engineer was allowing for lightly botched or noisy dialogue takes whenever the actors spoke English.

"Who cares?" he shrugged when I confronted him. "No one's going to hear it under the Russian voiceover."

"Did it ever occur to you," I yelled, "that someone might want to watch this show *outside* Russia?!"

The engineer looked genuinely perplexed. "Like who?"

Thankfully, as the shoot went on, I encountered this attitude less and less. It seemed that having even a couple of non-cynics on hand slowly but surely made everyone else perk up, too. By the time Lily, Lena, and I were done shaking the life into the crew, *Londongrad* looked—well, not exactly authentic, but more like an American series set in London and inexplicably filmed in Russian.

As for censorship, I kept expecting it and not finding it. Perhaps TV drama's low status, as something people watched with their backs while slicing salami, made it into the kind of safe haven that glossy magazines used to be before 2012. The few restrictions I did encounter concerned the typical network-TV aversion to vice (swearing, smoking, alcohol) rather than, say, social satire—of which we snuck in plenty. Even a grim riff on the ex-FSB spy Alexander Litvinenko's radiation poisoning somehow sailed through. So did the overall portrayal of Moscow as a kind of glam Mordor to which the characters get *threatened* with returning. For the few scenes set there, my request to the season's three rotating directors was "shoot it like you've never been to Russia before."

The one peculiarity of Russian television that did bug me was its near-total ban on real-life brands in the shot, stemming from a somewhat psychotic fear of "hidden advertising." As the local saw went, "American TV blurs the face of the crash victim, Russian TV blurs the logo on the car." We managed to squeeze some enjoyment from this, however, by coming up with fake Italian luxury brands (Fergutti), pub drinks (Foofaraw Summer Shandy), and finally wine labels that contained plot spoilers in French.

All this cosmopolitan fun began to feel a little surreal as soon as I flew back from London, or stepped outside the giant Moscow soundstage where we filmed our interiors, and confronted the day's news. The relations between Russia and the West hadn't been worse since the Cold War. The United States and the European Union hit the Russian elites with several rounds of economic sanctions, targeting banks, energy firms, defense contractors, and individual businessmen and officials, who joined the vastly expanded version of the Magnitsky list. Even Yuri Kovalchuk—the majority shareholder of STS, the channel that was going to air *Londongrad* and *Rushkin*—was under sanctions, though the network itself was not.

If the initial hope was that Russia would respond to the pressure by getting out of Crimea, or at least ending its adventure in eastern Ukraine, it was naive to say the least. Not even the tragic destruction of a Malaysia Airlines passenger plane that July, which the Donetsk rebels accidentally downed with a Russian-supplied missile, and which we briefly hoped would end the war through its sheer awfulness, dissuaded Moscow from digging in. Instead, it just brought out more lies, more obfuscation, more coordinated trolling, more Photoshop, more fake tapes of "CIA operatives" conspiring in Russian-accented English.

A month later, in August, Russia struck back at the West with a bizarre counter-sanction—a total ban on agricultural imports from the United States, the European Union, Australia, Canada, and Norway. The move, another sterling example of "bombing Voronezh," deprived regular Russians of not just food but certain medicines. It also functioned as an accidental admission that the only Russian product worth withholding from the world, the only Russian export anyone truly wanted, was money.

Ironically, most Russians mistook Putin's counter-sanction— felt within days, as grocery stores' cheese aisles turned into cabinets of curd curiosities—for the effect of the Western sanctions, which didn't target consumers. Even I made this mistake every once in a while. The link "European sanctions=no more European products" just made too much sense. The idea that Russia was somehow sticking it to the French by not eating Camembert was harder to follow.

Naturally, the Russians were told to wear these deprivations as a badge of honor. The Internal Affairs Ministry banned all international travel for its employees—including regular beat cops—affecting more than a million people. Who needed Egypt or Turkey if Crimea was now "theirs"? Aeroflot, a genuinely well-meaning company caught between its business goals and its Kremlin masters, was ordered to offer cheap subsidized flights to Crimea. (E.U. sanctions immediately made mincemeat of its long-planned low-cost daughter airline, Dobrolet.) Grocery store shelves groaned under newly arrived, and largely terrible Crimean wine.

A whole cottage industry of boorish defiance sprung up. T-shirts bore slogans like DON'T MAKE MY ISKANDERS LAUGH (an Iskander is a ballistic missile) and THE TOPOL'S NOT AFRAID OF YOUR SANCTIONS (so is the Topol); ubiquitous portraits of Putin as a sunglasses-wearing badass in a camo parka, sometimes accompanied by the inscription THE WORLD'S MOST POLITE MAN; racist invective against Obama; sexist putdowns of Hillary Clinton (out of office by then) and Angela Merkel. For two weeks in September 2014, someone ran free street kiosks where Muscovites could exchange any T-shirt with a foreign inscription or logo for a "patriotic" one. Official Russian Army clothing boutiques proliferated in the center of Moscow, selling more of this stuff. Sheremetyevo airport essentially turned into a giant fuck-you merch booth with a sideline in aviation. An idiotic vogue for "banning" Obama and other world leaders gripped provincial businesses. During a trip to Vladivostok, I saw no fewer than five of these signs in three days. One, professionally manufactured and backlit, adorned the wall of the city airport's duty-free shop. It denied service to Obama, Merkel, François Hollande, Shinzo Abe, David Cameron, and several Ukrainian officials.

This tawdry, insecurity-masking swagger found its fullest expression in Sanctions Bar, a new nightclub steps away from the FSB headquarters and just under a mile from Red Square. The space used to house a restaurant named Raikhona, whose house copy promised "a golden palette, combined with the color of clear sky and calm sea, creating a heavenly glow filled with warmth and softness." Now its logo was Barack Obama's caricatured face inside a Ghostbusters-style "stop" sign, and in its window glowed a rhyming neon slogan: "The sanctions can't bruise us / They only amuse us." The owners were the same as before.

After the first Iraq War, Saddam Hussein had a mosaic of G.H.W. Bush's face installed on the lobby floor of the Royal Tulip Al Rasheed hotel so that international guests would be forced to trample it. The Sanctions Bar merely made the visitor drink under dozens of world-leader caricatures lining its walls. Most were simple and crude. In one, Putin courteously shook hands with Merkel while their shadows on the wall revealed him sodomizing her. In another, titled OBAMA SURFACE TO AIR, Putin dispatched Obama skyward with a soccer kick. Then, however, there were the next-level meta-posters, which showed the supposedly shocking effect Putin's awesomeness was having on the West. In one, a terrified Obama, staring at photos of Putin at his most heroic, prays, via thought bubble, "PLEASE BE PHOTOSHOP!!!"—which not only plumbed new levels of irony but accidentally illustrated the Kremlin's true M.O.: Russia's newfound greatness was not just an illusion designed to cow the West. It was an illusion *of* cowing the West *with* this illusion, designed to be sold back home.

The new face that Russia actually turned to the outside world was a kind of Mos Eisley for angry white people, a haven for everyone at odds with the globalist liberal order. It held out treats for the tinfoil-hat left and the thuggish right. The broadcasting of its English-language propaganda arm, RT, added up to something like a unified manifesto of paranoid illiberalism. In this version of the big tent, Alex Jones and Julian Assange were equally welcome. In France, it cultivated both Marine Le Pen and the left-wing environmentalists arguing against fracking in Poland, which would have disrupted Russia's gas exports. Some of this maneuvering had a specific purpose: to feel out the weaker E.U. members, like Alexis Tsipras's Greece, which might split the E.U. vote on further sanctions. And some was just contrarianism for its own sake, claiming a "unique way" where there wasn't anything resembling one.

The veneer of cultural conservatism that Russia had acquired after the anti-gay law and the Pussy Riot trial was a good example of the latter. It was a total sham, hilariously at odds with Russia's own libertine, high-AIDS-rate, high-divorce-rate reality, but some poor Western souls bought into it. In one case, a German family who wanted to shield their ten children from sex education went so far as to move to the Novosibirsk region, where they meant to start a farm; they lasted two months before going back. It was hard to laugh at these people, though. They were no more or less naive than liberals like me, drawn just two years earlier to a very different but equally nebulous vision of Russia as a wish-fulfillment theme park.

I met one of these disillusioned seekers myself during a family visit to the U.S. embassy. My daughter, Vera, had grown enough to need a new passport—the picture in her first one was taken when she was two months old. Besides Lily, Vera, and me, there was an-other family in the room: a squat, affable-looking bearded man and his three moptop sons, ages ten, eight, and six. As Lily and I filled out the form, we briefly forgot Vera's height and began to argue about it. "Three feet," the bearded man shouted, with a Texas twang I hadn't heard in years, from the far end of the room.

"That's a useful skill," I said.

"Military." We began to chat. The man—I'll call him Bob—said he had been living nomadically in Europe, came to Russia in search of a purer life, and got into unspecified trouble with the Moscow cops on day one; he was now waiting to be sent back to the States, where he hadn't been for many years. The prospect worried him. "Is it true that things are pretty scary in the States right now?" he asked.

"What do you mean?"

"You know. Immigrants comin' over."

"Yup," I said. "Just like for the last hundred and twenty years or so."

We fell silent for a bit. Vera, meanwhile, happily played with Bob's kids.

"Can't live in Europe anymore," Bob said abruptly. "It's done. It's . . . They teach masturbation there. To eight-year-olds. Fucking disgusting." He sighed, shook his head and went out.

"Daddy takes us to the shooting range to shoot guns!" the el-dest kid blurted out, unprompted. This was clearly something he was not supposed to say within Bob's earshot, but dying to.

"And he *makes* guns, too!" added the eight-year-old.

"That's, uh . . . cool?"

Bob came back with a cup of water. "But Daddy," said the youn-gest kid, his eyes wide with surprise, "that's *government water*."

"It's okay," said Bob.

"There's no vaccine in it?"

"Vaccines have fat from dead old people in them," the ten-year-old interjected, as an aside for my benefit.

"Wrong," said Bob. *Well, small mercies*, I thought. "It's DNA from aborted fetuses."

Vera's passport was ready, her second, at the age of three. I took it from a red-haired clerk in the window (who looked at Bob and gave me a quick "*this fucking guy . . .* " side nod–eye roll combo), signed for it, glanced at the official portraits of Obama and Hillary Clinton on the wall—it was a rare sight in 2014 Moscow, an undefaced Obama portrait—and we left. As I write this two years later, I can't help thinking that Bob might like America a little better in its present state. Whatever it was he searched for in Russia, a part of it ended up coming home with him.

One might think Russia's aggressive backward turn, just as some of my biggest dreams had started to come true, would make me want to Roskomnadzor myself. In fact, it was quite the opposite. I felt light-headed with relief. At last, after twenty-odd years of shuffling about the stage, the players were on their marks. I remembered arguing with Julia Ioffe when she wrote that everything that happened in and to Russia since 1991 was one single period of "post-Soviet transition," only we were just too close to it to realize it; now I thought she was right—and that this period had just ended before my eyes. Things were somehow crisper, simpler, in sharper focus. Domestically, Russia had had something like a therapy breakthrough: it admitted to itself that it didn't know how to be a *country*. Shepherding the surrounding nations was the only thing that gave its vastness a point and its citizens an identity. And internationally, it was the bad guy again, which made a certain kind of sense. It was the perceived villainy of its authorities that lent timelessness to its uneven literature, relevance to its crappy pop music, and big shiny halos to its dissidents, most of whom were otherwise too complicated or flawed to fully embrace. Now, and only now, could we finally move on to the next great Russian story.

On a more egotistical note, I wasn't sure what this meant for my work. I had no way of predicting how this new Russia would handle *Rushkin*, or whether I could, in good conscience, continue writing it at all. Its humor was, after all, predicated on the idea of Russia as a crazy but somewhat lovable place. I didn't even know how the relatively apolitical *Londongrad*, with its vision of fully Westernized, free Russians moving breezily between Moscow and London, would fit into the picture. It was quite possible that none of this stuff would see the light of day. Yet I worked harder on these scripts than I had ever worked on anything, and, especially once we settled into Berlin, I finally felt more or less myself again. My Moscow celebrity receded from me like a bad chemical, washed out by meaningful work and *trocken* Riesling. The cycles of vanity search, followed by depression about the results, followed by another vanity search, subsided. I barely followed the news.

In October, I received an invitation to the St. Petersburg International Media Forum, a film market and festival that, for the first time, would include special screenings of several TV pilots. I looked at the program of the latter and gasped. It consisted of *Londongrad*, Volobuev's *Zavtra*, the indie director Boris Khlebnikov's comedy *Hot and Bothered* (in which Volobuev had a recurring part as an actor), our mutual friend Alexei Agranovich's semi-scripted miniseries *Glavkniga*, and *Rushkin*.

It looked like we didn't realize the extent of our own infiltration of the formerly impenetrable Russian TV industry. As Volobuev, Lena Vanina, Ryvkin, Lily, and I careened around St. Petersburg, drunk on praise and attention as well as just plain drunk, darting from screening to screening in a slight daze—most of us were seeing each other's finished work for the first time—it began to dawn on us that we might have accidentally stumbled into creating some sort of movement. All of our shows (except *Londongrad*, which was a sleek-looking beast) shared a certain shaggy sensibility; all were shot by people who took their cues from both modern American comedy and European art-house cinema, and hardly any from Russian TV. In fact, our evident M.O. was to half-consciously pretend that the latter never existed at all before we showed up. Overnight, Volobuev and I became poster kids of the new hipster television.

This lovely delusion held for about two more months. In December 2014, the ruble collapsed to historic lows, instantly paralyzing the dollar-dependent worlds of Russian TV and film. The crash mostly had to do with oil prices, which had halved over the fall, but was sold to the public (in both Russia and the United States, it needs to be noted) as a direct result of the sanctions. Russia's last enticement, easy money, was gone. With the ad revenues vanishing, programmers turned back to tried-and-true formats like multi-camera family comedies, tossing out everything that smacked of risk.

Of the shows that premiered to such fanfare at the St. Petersburg International Media Forum, only two would make it to air: *Hot and Bothered*, which the TNT channel decided to market as a traditional sitcom, and *Londongrad*.

Rushkin, with its Jewish American protagonist and absurd humor, was unsurprisingly gone, with only the pilot and a heap of scripts left to commemorate our efforts. *Zavtra*, too, was no more. TV Rain threw together a half-assed fundraising campaign for it, but the channel itself—banished from most cable packages and having switched to an all-subscription online model—needed the money more. This was not a great time for subtle musings on the opposition's readiness to govern.

Indeed, nothing short of a liberal exodus was under way. The economic downturn accomplished what Putin's demonization and bullying of the protesting demographic couldn't: people were leaving in droves. Even those of my friends who stayed put were exploring various plans B. Everyone with so much as a drop of Jewish blood applied for Israeli citizenship. The line at the consulate, Smolina said, "felt like 1992." This wave of emigration, however, wasn't like the one my parents caught. No one was saying tearful farewells. No one was preparing to start life over as a dishwasher or cab driver. There weren't even that many goodbye parties. People were simply electing to sit a few things out.

Ilya Krasilshchik of *Afisha* and Galina Timchenko of *Lenta* cofounded Meduza, an independent news site, in the safety of my native Latvia. As one of the few quality Russian news media left standing, it quickly began siphoning off other *Afisha* and *Lenta* veterans until an entire mini-community of exiled Russian journalists formed around it. Those who had the means bought apartments in Riga: spending more than 250,000 euros made you eligible for E.U. residence.

Eugenia Kuyda, another former editor from *Afisha*, moved to Silicon Valley and made a name for herself on a "memorial chatbot"—an app that imitated the speech patterns of her dead friend after analyzing thousands of his text messages. The *Afisha* and Strelka Institute cofounder Ilya Oskolkov-Tsentsiper spent most of his time in London. So did Alexei Zimin, the bearded restaurateur and former editor of *GQ*, whose culinary career had begun with an ambitious bid to replicate Jamie Oliver's empire in Russia—magazine, TV show, and all; he now ran a vodka bar in SoHo. Vladimir Sorokin, Russia's preeminent novelist, whose 2011 *Day of the Oprichnik* had foretold the country's rightward turn, moved to Berlin. Kirill Serebrennikov, the brilliant theater and film director, stayed at the helm of the progressive Gogol

Center but now lived within a twenty minutes' walk from me in Prenzlauer Berg.

Many of the people I knew were settling in my *other* hometown—New York. The LookAtMe founder, Vasily Esmanov, he of the small-deeds manifesto, moved to Brooklyn and started an English version of one of his websites, Hopes and Fears, which lasted for about a year. Tikhon Dzyadko, the youngest of the three Dzyadko brothers, began to work at RTVI, an independent Russian-language TV network headquartered there. Alexei Navalny's abrasive press secretary, Anna Veduta, moved to New York as well. Andrew Ryvkin went to Los Angeles to try his luck in Hollywood.

The formerly inseparable Kermlins broke up. With our collaboration on *Rushkin* over, both began to work for different parts of Mikhail Khodorkovsky's London-based Open Russia foundation, presumably avoiding each other in the hallways. Pussy Riot traveled the world, turning more and more into traditional opposition celebrities in the Garry Kasparov vein. I met up with Tolokonnikova, Alekhina, and Peter Verzilov in London that November. I was in the U.K. for yet another *Londongrad* episode (this one set, and shot, at Oxford, which had miraculously let us use its buildings). They had come to visit the British Parliament, speak at the Henry Jackson Society, address the Cambridge Union Society, and so on. It was after eleven at night and pouring—what the Brits call "a little freshness in the air"—so we went to the seemingly only open place in Chelsea, a terrible chain steak house. Pussy Riot were a big operation now, overgrown with barnacles of volunteer staff, which included a somewhat baleful-looking woman named Inge. Their plan for the next morning was to meet with the exiled Russian oligarch Yevgeny Chichvarkin and to visit Julian Assange at his Ecuadorian embassy hidey-hole. I had zero desire to meet Assange, but tagged along for the former.

Chichvarkin met us at the Bulgari Hotel wearing fuchsia jeans, boots with pink paint splashes, and a T-shirt that said WAITING FOR A REVOLUTION above a picture of a duck. He was a raging libertarian of the let-the-losers-die-out persuasion, so I was curious to observe how the dialogue between the anti-Putin left and the anti-Putin right would proceed. Alas, very little of any dialogue happened at the table. The oligarch was quite hungover and, for the first forty minutes or so, stayed largely silent. Everyone ended up agreeing that the bloody Putin regime had to go, Chichvarkin paid for our forty-pound breakfasts, and we went our separate ways.

In a few more months, Tolokonnikova and Alekhina barely would be on speaking terms with each other as well. Alekhina worked with Belarus Free Theatre, an underground theater group; Tolokonnikova's solo output gradually turned to expensive-looking, mostly English-language music videos criticizing racism, sexism, corruption, and Trump.

■

On March 5, 2015, while *Londongrad* was filming, *Soulless 2* came out in theaters. Ryvkin and I had refashioned it into a corporate thriller in the vein of *The Firm*, with the banker protagonist dragged out of a cozy exile on Bali and forced to infiltrate a corrupt state corporation. The prosecutors doing the forcing were then revealed as equally corrupt, with the scheme going all the way up to the Kremlin. I had no idea whether any of this would work at the box office: there had never been a Russian corporate thriller before, much less one in which the role of the evil corporation is played by the state. In the last scene, the main character, à la Alexei Navalny, was seen leading a massive street rally, like the ones that had attracted me to Russia in 2011. Reflecting the ambiguity of our own feelings, the scene's meaning was willfully muddled: Was it a street protest or a sanctioned election rally? Was the hero an opposition leader, a new establishment fixture, or a double agent once again? More important, who was *I* in this equation? By getting a film about Kremlin-level corruption into Russian theaters, was I doing something cool or just helping the system perpetuate the notion that Russia has free speech? By building this movie out of a Sergei Minaev franchise (with whom I had never met while writing the script and who, by the time of the premiere, had bullied his way into the credits as one of the screenwriters, despite having little to do with the film), was I showing him up on his own turf or ultimately adding to his glory?

For once, life held less ambiguity than the movies. On the day of the red-carpet premiere, Boris Nemtsov was being buried. A real-life opposition leader, the former deputy minister and an outspoken critic of Putin, a member of the protests' Orgkomitet, he had been gunned down steps from Red Square on February 27. At the time of his death he was working on a report detailing the degree of Russia's involvement in eastern Ukraine. The image of Nemtsov's prone body with the Kremlin stars glowing in the background would be too outlandish for any thriller. In one of the versions of the *Soulless 2* script, the street rally scene—and the film—ended with a shot of the protagonist in a sniper's crosshairs. Thinking about that now made me queasy.

Putin, in a dry statement, called the murder "extremely provocative," a deliberate choice of words that hinted (deniably, as always) at a false-flag operation. The Kremlin's army of online trolls immediately ran with this, declaring Nemtsov the opposition's "sacrificial lamb"—slaughtered to reinvigorate support for the cause. At the same time, marginally more respectable sources were busy pinning the death on the entanglements of Nemtsov's love life. Just as they did after Anna Politkovskaya's 2006 assassination, the investigators quickly found the triggermen—five Chechens with a direct connection to Ramzan Kadyrov's security services—and then went no further, or higher.

"It says something about Russia's messy, fitful return to dictatorship," wrote Boris Kachka in *Vulture*, "that, in the week after the murder of Nemtsov, the best performing movie in the country, beating out *Focus* and *Cinderella* this past weekend, was a thriller whose villain works deep within the Russian government." Indeed, *Soulless 2* ended up as the highest-grossing domestic release of the year. I doubt that politics held the key to its popularity, though. I think we simply made a decent genre movie in a genre no one in Russia had tried before.

Londongrad, which debuted on STS on September 27, 2015, was a trickier proposition for the new reality. Here, as I had worried, was a show featuring cosmopolitan characters moving freely within London's proverbial "layer cake," right when the Russians were told once again that the West was the enemy. *Londongrad*'s ads, which were originally to feature Union Jacks, focused on something less offensive—a double-decker bus. "You have no idea how wound up people in the provinces are," one of the network's affiliates said after a presentation. "A guy walking down the street in our city wearing a Union Jack T-shirt will get beaten down." To make it seem like the show was about the Russians *triumphing* over the West, as opposed to integrating into it, the channel added to its title the boastful slogan *Znai Nashih!*, which translates loosely as "That's How Our Guys Do It!"

My own biggest fear about *Londongrad*, however, wasn't that it was too elitist or too Western. With all the propaganda Russian TV had spewed at them, many Westernized Russians—the ones I imagined would enjoy *Londongrad* the most—simply refused to watch a series because it was Russian. The first Twitter reactions to *Londongrad* sounded the same note over and over: "It's watchable, probably because it wasn't filmed in Russia." "As much as I hate everything Russian, I might give this one a try." "God help me, I can't believe I am watching a Russian TV series." "I might watch it later. I'm in no mood to see my compatriots."

My fears were allayed when the show opened to an unexpectedly huge 20.5 audience share. I found it especially heartening to see *Londongrad*'s instant popularity with teens. They didn't even care about the foreign setting; they just wanted the two leads to kiss. On one site devoted to romantic fan fiction, one author expressed her shock after conflating the characters' names into one, after the 'shipper fashion (Misha + Alisa = Milisa). It was the first time in her memory that the names were Russian; I was particularly proud of this achievement.

Season two was a given: STS had greenlighted it before the first one even ran. The newly impotent ruble, however, meant that filming a Russian show in the U.K. was now an almost impossible proposition. The production house, Sputnik Vostok, had spent so much of its rapidly devaluating budget that it could barely afford the show's star, Nikita Efremov. And so they asked Lily, Lena, and me to write the second season in a way that would reduce his shooting days by 50 percent; we promptly had him kidnapped for a few episodes and represented by a GPS tracking dot on a computer monitor. Next went the London street scenes. Much of the action now had to take place on a soundstage or around the few Moscow buildings that could sort of pass for London. Finally, Sputnik Vostok ran out of the means to keep me and my team. With the scripts still in first draft, the studio fired all of us on a flimsy pretext. A shadow crew of much cheaper screenwriters, it turned out, had already been hired behind our backs a month before and given our "beat sheets" (scene-by-scene episode synopses) to work from.

It was only several months later that I found out who one of these screenwriters was: Katya "Kermlin" Romanovskaya, my former star reporter at *GQ*, whose only previous experience writing for the screen was *Rushkin*, and whom the entire team considered a close friend. My incredulous reaction was best summed up by Roman Volobuev, who wrote: "And these people have something against Putin?" Friendships ended; the show went on, sort of. *Londongrad*'s second season ended up looking like a community-theater production of the first one, and its ratings quickly put an end to the series.

As for *Rushkin*, the doomed autobiographical sitcom that started the whole adventure, its life and death had a curious postscript. A year later, a brand-new sitcom appeared on STS, titled *How I Became Russian*. The main character was a New York writer in horn-rimmed glasses who got stuck in Moscow after befriending a bald-headed oligarch and a trickster named Roman. In other words, it borrowed *Rushkin*'s entire plot. The jokes, though, were different. Reflecting the spirit of the new time, they skewed broad and cheap, revolving around the Yank's naïveté, hypocrisy, political correctness, and inability to grok the great truths self-evident to any Russian. At the end of each episode, the hero Alex Wilson, played by a Polish actor, sat at his computer like Doogie Howser and tapped out the valuable lesson he had learned about Russia, narrating platitudes in a comical mushmouth accent:

> So! What is Russia? Russia is a country with no dividing line between outsize hospitality and indefatigable drunkenness. A country with the world's longest roads that host the world's largest traffic jams. A country where excessive egotism stands next to total altruism. And it's the only place on this planet that can fit the vastness of the big Russian soul.

At first I could do little but scoff. Yet, as I masochistically watched *How I Became Russian*, I began to see something else in it as well. Beyond the ostensible humor lay self-flattery, of course, but beyond the self-flattery glimmered a kind of resignation. It was as though the Russians, having despaired of impressing America and then to intimidate it, just made up an American who'd love them, and articulated through him their own dream of who they'd be if things hadn't gone so wrong: goofy, sentimental, hard-drinking folk, not too far removed from the soil, happiest at the holiday table. It was the *knowledge* of that dream's unreachability that, in turn, formed the bedrock of the Russian character. Neither Putin's "gathering of the lands" nor Surgeon's dank fantasies about the might of the Russian sword brought that dream any closer to reality. Only an outsider's approving eye could do that. And if the outsider wasn't there, they'd just have to imagine him.

The show ran for one season to dismal numbers, then got canceled. The producers currently claim that it has become wildly popular in China, where, according to a Russian newspaper, "its public rating on one film website has almost equaled that of *Game of Thrones*."

My Moscow story is done. My best friends and collaborators are there; my most interesting projects are there; I even keep a small apartment on Begovaya, piled high with the detritus of my *GQ*-era life that I can't bring myself to either throw away or move to Berlin. But I'm no longer *of* Moscow, if I ever was.

I am no longer fully of New York, either. Moscow couldn't make me fall in love with itself but, curiously, it made me adore New York a little less. Before Moscow, I was a stereotypical adherent of the people-living-anywhere-else-must-be-kidding cult, a cult that my writing for *New York* magazine enthusiastically helped perpetuate. It took some time and perspective to start discerning the provinciality in some of our obsessions; and it took seeing the Moscow-hipster adulation of New York in its full Gorky Park bloom to realize that a lot of things we take as the quintessence of the city are just haute-bourgeois creature comforts dressed up in a bit of local color. As of this writing, Lily and I are Berliners as much as anything else—an easy transformation, because Berlin feels a lot like the best parts of New York and Moscow jammed together. My German is nonexistent—but then again, after a childhood in Latvia, living in a place where I can't read half the street signage comes naturally to me. Slight alienation amid Gothic spires and cobblestone is, ironically, my comfort zone.

Ever since November 2016, however, this hardly matters. I am no more or less alienated than the dreamers who filled the Russian streets and squares in December 2011, or my New York friends, or liberal Democrats anywhere from London to Athens. All of us are now denizens of a new world: this much we know, and little more. This world doesn't have its orthodoxy down yet, and things can turn on a dime at any moment. In this sense, it feels a lot like Russia.

It is also a world where Russia looms impossibly large. The Kremlin, after years and millions wasted on pointless chest-beating, after countless PR campaigns to "improve Russia's image abroad," suddenly got what it wanted: Putin's face on every magazine cover, Putin's name in every politician's speech. The fear and the grudging respect. The West is finally as obsessed with Russia as Russia has always imagined it was. My e-mail is filled with Western offers to write a TV series about Russian hackers, Russian spies, Russian assassins, shadowy Russian puppet masters controlling the White House. Advanced Persistent Threats. Active Measures. The Russophobia in some of these ideas borders on racism.

My actual thoughts on the matter wouldn't make for a good TV show. I don't know what difference it makes whether the current government of the United States has been compromised by Russia or not, because to be compromised by Russia simply means to be compromised by greed and insecurity—which the Trump administration demonstrably is. I should know. I have allowed myself a light version of this compromise, and observed more serious cases up close. The Russian compromise means nothing more exotic than resigning yourself to be a hack (as opposed to a hacker) because you don't trust your employer, your peers, or your audience. It means coating self-interest in righteous blather. It means the timid focus on the bare minimum. It means copying what works. It means a calming illusion of irreality—the idea that consequences and reputations don't really exist and that no institution is bigger than the avarice of the person in charge of it. This cynicism, coupled with endless conspiracy theories about everything, is at its core defensive (it's hard to be disappointed if you expect the worst), but it amounts to defeatism. And that, in turn, means that whoever manages to resist this illusion will eventually win, because corruption makes for lazier enemies. You might be dead by the time you win, like Sergei Magnitsky, but you will win.

Meanwhile, in the supposedly triumphant Russia, things continue to deteriorate. Boris Nemtsov's murder is no closer to being truly solved; the opposition's attempts to put as much as a plaque on the bridge where he—a former deputy prime minister—was gunned down have been fruitless.

The attack on the already-defeated press does not let up. In 2015, Russia adopted sixteen new laws and orders constricting its freedom; ninety-seven more came down the pike in 2016. Mostly, however, the press is being done in by the terrible economy. *Kommersant*'s well-respected weekly magazines, *Power* and *Money*, are gone (bringing to mind the old Soviet joke set at a newspaper kiosk: "There is no *Truth*—*Russia* is sold out. The only thing left is *Labor* for three kopecks"). In 2017, Condé Nast killed two of its seven Russian titles.

The government's assault on free expression in the arts has meanwhile both intensified and grown incoherent, as various unleashed gonzos of the late Putin era—from Cossacks to a small sect that deifies Nicholas II—bump chaotically against the Kremlin's own culture-war machine, sometimes aligning and sometimes, as with the furore over the film *Matilda* (about the young Czar's affair with a ballerina) coming in conflict. The most prominent victim of this newly unnavigable reality turned out to be very close to us.

In late 2016, Lily and I got a rare chance to write a script for Kirill Serebrennikov, one of Russia's greatest and most provocative directors; even better, it would be about the Soviet underground rock scene of the early 1980s—there were few topics closer to my heart than that. In May 2017, with our film, titled *Summer*, in pre-production, Serebrennikov found his theater and Moscow apartment raided by the OMON on absurd embezzlement charges. Despite him being a mere witness in the case, the detectives confiscated his passport, locking him in Russia. Yevgeny Mironov, one of Russia's premier actors and a Putin loyalist, handed the president a letter from the cream of the nation's artistic community vouching for Serebrennikov; in response, Putin was overheard to murmur "fools," which was, at the time, taken as a condemnation of the police overreach. The director proceeded with the film—as well as an opera he was mounting in Stuttgart and an adaptation of Pushkin's *Little Tragedies* at his own Gogol Center.

On August 20, Lily and I visited the set of *Summer* in St. Petersburg, and were blown away by the sheer energy and beauty of Serebrennikov's vision. It was all we could talk about on the way back. By the time we got to Berlin, the news had broken: the state had arrested Serebrennikov, no longer a witness but a suspect, at his hotel less than a day after our visit. In a superfluously cruel flourish, the detectives had driven him from St. Petersburg to Moscow in the dead of night, in a rickety van; there, a court remanded him to house arrest. (A few hundred Muscovites came out to protest, a few thousand signed petitions.) As this book goes to print, Serebrennikov, banned from using phones or computers and allowed outside the house for two hours a day, awaits trial. *Summer* is frozen until his return.

Putin's "fools" remark may have been meant not for the overzealous detectives but for the intelligentsia who thought they could change things with a letter. One of the very few ways to make sense of Serebrennikov's shocking persecution is to see it as the unofficial start of Putin's fourth presidential campaign: a signal for the opposition to keep even quieter than usual. In any case, Russia's leader, now ruling longer than Brezhnev and closing in on Stalin's numbers, is headed for another easy win against his usual cast of designated losers. In October 2017, one new name has appeared in the coveted spot of the "manageable opposition" candidate in the race. That name is Ksenia Sobchak.

Alexei Navalny, the only semi-plausible threat to Putin in 2018 and beyond, has been in and out of courts on an array of ridiculous pretexts. At the same time, his YouTube video investigations of high-level graft, which widened to include allegations against prime minister Medvedev, have effectively made him the opposition's sole leader. A new wave of youthful protests, which picked up in March 2017, double as Navalny's campaign events. The New Decembrists' fitful attempts at "horizontality" are gone. Navalny issues the calls for the rallies, coordinates logistics, negotiates for the permits, and, in the case of a protest on June 12, 2017, redirects the crowd at the last minute to a new location. That day, denied a stage and a sound system at the agreed-upon place (Sakharov Square, again), the protesters were told to "join" an official Russia Day street celebration unfolding on Tverskaya instead, leading to skirmishes with OMON and a record seventeen hundred arrests.

Before the protesters showed up, the festival had consisted of elaborate, costumed outdoor re-creations of Russia's historical milestones (which led to some unforgettable visuals, such as wooden-shielded medieval warriors protecting schoolkids from OMON troops). Every single one of the tableaux involved war. The cult of military prowess as Russia's defining virtue continues to claim the people's minds. In the fall of 2017, the government unveiled a garish monument to Mikhail Kalashnikov, the inventor of the AK-47 (shown cradling his deadly brainchild), in the middle of Moscow's Garden Ring. *Crimea*, a big-budget cinematic saga about "true love and friendship against the backdrop of true events of 2014," financed in part by the government, opened at the same time. The same year, according to a Levada poll, the Russians named annexation of Crimea as the proudest moment in their history, second only to the victory in World War II. A petty land grab beat out Sputnik and Yuri Gagarin's space flights, "the achievements of Russian science," and "great Russian literature."

Our house in Berlin, on a quiet cobblestone block in the former Soviet sector, stands a few hundred yards from the Wall memorial at Bernauer Strasse, where, on August 13, 1961, people were throwing themselves off roofs and out windows in the hopes of landing on the Western side of the street. Narrow paths bisect the lawn, marking onetime secret tunnel routes. The memorial's heart is a quiet park fringed by hundreds of iron posts, spaced just widely enough that you can walk between any two—once a lethal transgression, now a single step. Every time I fling myself between the posts to catch the M10 tram, I try to imagine what a Moscow that fully owned up to its brutal pasts, instead of repackaging them as facets of national greatness, would look like. Perhaps something like this.

The one question my three years in Moscow have resoundingly failed to answer is the biggest one I had heading in: the degree of my own Russianness. No such issue, surprisingly, exists for my daughter. In the most tangible and lasting result of this adventure, it has become apparent that Vera's native language is Russian, which means I'll be able to embarrass her by blasting Russian rock and hip-hop for as long as I live. I have successfully kicked the identity can down the road to the next generation. With any luck, that generation will get a better world, and a better Russia.

Acknowledgments

My love and gratitude, first and foremost and always, to Lily. Thanks to all my friends in New York, Berlin, and Moscow for helping me survive these chaotic years; most of you are already in the book. Thanks to my parents and their preternatural patience with my choices. I owe a debt to Karina Dobrotvorskaya for taking a chance on me and patiently guiding me through strange terrain; all my failings as an editor of a glossy magazine are my own. Special thanks to Sarah Condon and Slava Murugov, without whom I might still be writing scripts "into the desk," per the Russian expression. Thanks to every editor who's made me better, including many whose work has directly affected parts of this book—Mike Benoist, Jon Gluck, Courtney Hodell, Adam Moss, Jim Nelson, Choire Sicha, Ben Wassterstein, and others; the incomparable agent Binky Urban and everyone at ICM on both coasts; and to every Berlin coffeehouse with electric outlets and Wi-Fi, the ideal places to write (until about 8 p.m.). This book was written to the soundtrack of Luke Haines, Kaleida, Mogwai, the New Pornographers, OQJAV, Oxxxymiron, Pantha du Prince, Petlya Pristrastiya, Run the Jewels, and the title theme from *BoJack Horseman*.

Index

Printed in the USA
CPSIA information can be obtained
at www.ICGtesting.com
LVHW091139150724
785511LV00005B/412

9 780374 538163